GREAT VERSES from the psalms

CHARLES H. SPURGEON

GREAT VERSES from the Psalms

CHARLES H. SPURGEON

Selections from
The Treasury of David

Edited by Norman Hillyer

ZONDERVAN PUBLISHING HOUSE
OF THE ZONDERVAN CORPORATION
GRAND RAPIDS, MICHIGAN 49506

GREAT VERSES FROM THE PSALMS
Copyright © 1976 by Marshall, Morgan & Scott
(Publications) Ltd
Reprinted by special arrangement

First Zondervan printing 1977

Library of Congress Cataloging in Publication Data

Spurgeon, Charles Haddon, 1834-1892.
  Great verses from the Psalms.

  1. Bible.   O.T.   Psalms—Commentaries.   I. Title.
BS1430.S613 1977   223'.2'06   76-56100
ISBN 0-551-05547-2

Printed in the United States of America

Preface

'I like that Spurgeon. I can *understand* him.' No wonder six thousand people, from palace to poorhouse, used to crowd every week into the Metropolitan Tabernacle at Southwark. They came to hear a preacher who had a message for them from God, a command of homely English, and a heart filled with love for Jesus Christ.

Mark Guy Pearse, himself a famous preacher, once wrote to Spurgeon about listening to him in his student days. 'You used to wind me up like an eight-day clock. I was bound to go right for a week after listening to you.'

Charles Haddon Spurgeon was born at Kelvedon, Essex, a village on the Chelmsford–Colchester road, on 19 June 1834. His mother was only 19 at the time, and Charles was the first of seventeen children. His father, a coal-merchant's clerk during the week, entered the pulpit on Sundays as the minister of the Independent Church at Tollesbury.

When Charles was still a toddler he went to live for six years with his grandfather, James Spurgeon. He too was a minister, and served the Independent Church at Stambourne for 54 years. At Stambourne Charles taught himself to read from a copy of *Pilgrim's Progress* which he unearthed in the attic. He was encouraged to memorise the hymns of Isaac Watts (grandma paid him one penny a time), and to hunt rats (grandpa paid him one shilling a dozen).

Charles attended Mr Lewis's school at Colchester, where he won first prize for English, and then at 14 moved to All Saints' Agricultural College at Maidstone. He never found himself in either academy or university, though he would have excelled in both. Only a scholar of the first rank would have collected, as he did over the years, a fine theological library of 12,000 volumes. Of Dutch and Independent stock, Charles went to an Anglican school, was converted by a Primitive Methodist, and became a Baptist.

A year after his conversion (6 January 1850) Charles became pastor of Waterbeach Baptist Chapel. He was only 17. Three years later he was called to New Park Street Baptist Chapel in Southwark. Such crowds were soon pouring in that a new building became an urgent necessity. So the Metropolitan Tabernacle was opened in 1859. During the 38 years of his ministry in London nearly 15,000 members were added to the church. He preached for the last time on 7 June 1892 and died on 31 January the following year at Mentone in the south of France.

But Spurgeon was far from being simply a preacher of remarkable power and gifts. He began, and for years financed, what today are known as Spurgeon's College (for Baptist theological students) and Spurgeon's Homes (for orphans). His many other charitable organisations included temperance and clothing societies, and a colportage association to distribute Scriptures and tracts.

Through his pen Spurgeon's ministry extended all over the world. No less than 135 books came from his hand, and he edited another 28, an average of one volume every two or three months during the whole of his time at the Tabernacle. Every week a sermon of his, taken down in shorthand, was set up in type, proof-read, printed and published by the following Sunday.

But his most sustained literary effort was on the Book of Psalms. For over twenty years he laboured on *The Treasury of David*. It was published in seven volumes between 1869 and 1885. Before Spurgeon died, 120,000 copies of the *Treasury* had been sold. Afterwards it was issued in shilling monthly parts for even wider distribution.

This monumental work not only gave Spurgeon's own comments on every verse of every Psalm, but included extracts from hundreds of authors from all ages and denominations. 'There is nothing like it in all literature,' said one of his biographers, W. Y. Fullerton, who compared the research which had gone into the *Treasury* to a traveller's first sight of the Rocky Mountains: '*It is immense.*'

Benjamin Jowett (1817–1893), Master of Balliol College, Oxford, Regius Professor of Greek, and an Anglican clergyman, pronounced the work 'a marvellous exposition'. Spurgeon was 'not eclipsed even when set in the radiant succession of Calvin and Luther and Paul'. High praise.

The Scottish preacher and scholar James Stalker (1848–1927) was equally moved:

Not only do you everywhere feel the presence of a vigorous and vigilant mind, and a heart in thorough sympathy with the spirit of the Psalms, but I wish to say that I have often been perfectly astounded to observe how, without any parade of learning, he shows himself to be thoroughly acquainted with the results of the most modern scholarship. The truth is that there is scarcely a point in the Psalms of real importance—scarcely a point upon which scholarship can give us anything of real importance—as to which there are not sufficient hints to the intelligent reader in Mr Spurgeon's work.

Several times Spurgeon reveals his own thoughts. 'Only those,' he remarked, 'who have meditated profoundly upon the Psalms can have any adequate conception of the wealth they contain. Sometimes as I pondered over them holy fear fell upon me, and I shrank from the attempt to explain themes so sublime.'

The task seems to have increased in difficulty as he went on. It was remarkable how little material was available to be culled from other authors when he came to the later Psalms. But this meant that he re-doubled his own efforts at exposition. He gives a glimpse of the way he worked at the Psalms by quoting the method of his hero, John Bunyan, who said, 'As I pulled, it came.' 'We like to write after the same manner,' declared Spurgeon.

But Spurgeon confessed to much perplexity over Psalm 109, until the Bulgarian massacres (1876) sent shockwaves around the world. The news 'threw us into such a state of righteous indignation that while we were musing the fire burned, and we melted the sentences'.

The longest Psalm (119) occupies nearly 400 pages in the *Treasury*. Spurgeon's own comments on that Psalm were afterwards published separately under the title *The Golden Alphabet of the Praises of Holy Scripture*.

After spending over twenty years on the *Treasury*, Spurgeon finished the last page with mixed feelings. In the Preface to the final volume he wrote:

A tinge of sadness is on my spirit as I quit *The Treasury of David*, never to find on this earth a richer storehouse, though the whole palace of revelation is open to me. Blessed have been the days spent in meditating, mourning, hoping, believing, and exulting with David! Can I hope to spend hours more joyous on this side of the golden gates? Perhaps not. For the seasons have been very choice in which the harp of the great poet of the sanctuary has charmed my ears. Yet the training which has come of these heavenly contemplations may haply go far to create and sustain a peaceful spirit which will never be without aspirations after something higher than it yet has known.

And he concluded:

In these busy days it would be greatly to the spiritual profit of Christian men if they were more familiar with the Book of Psalms, in which they would find a complete armoury for life's battles, and a perfect supply for life's needs. Here we have both delight and usefulness, consolation and instruction. The Book supplies the babe in grace with penitent cries, and the perfected saint with triumphant songs. He who is acquainted with the marches of the Psalm-country knows that the land floweth with milk and honey, and he delights to travel therein. To such I have aspired to be a helpful companion.

It is given to very few books to be continuously in print for over a century, but such is the happy and deserved lot of Spurgeon's *Treasury of David*.

If the present selection from some of Spurgeon's own comments urges readers of another generation to reach for the complete *Treasury*, the editor's pleasant task will have been rewarded. But better by far if some word penned by Charles Haddon Spurgeon a century ago kindles faith and hope in the Lord he so remarkably laboured to serve.

Easter 1976   Norman Hillyer

GREAT
VERSES
from the
psalms
CHARLES H.
SPURGEON

GREAT VERSES FROM THE PSALMS

PSALM I

Blessed is the man that walketh not in the counsel of the ungodly, nor standeth in the way of sinners, nor sitteth in the seat of the scornful. *Psalm 1:1.*

Blessed. See how this Book of Psalms opens with a benediction! The word translated **blessed** is a very expressive one. The original word is plural. Hence we may learn the multiplicity of the blessings which shall rest upon the man whom God hath justified, and the perfection and greatness of the blessedness he shall enjoy. We might read it *Oh, the blessednesses!* and we may well regard it as a joyful acclamation of the gracious man's felicity. May the like benediction rest on us!

The gracious man **walketh not in the counsel of the ungodly.** He takes wiser counsel, and walks in the commandments of the Lord his God. It is a rich sign of inward grace when the outward walk is changed, and when ungodliness is put far from our actions. He **standeth not in the way of sinners.** His company is of a choicer sort than it was. Although a sinner himself, he is now a blood-washed sinner, quickened by the Holy Spirit, and renewed in heart. **Nor sitteth in the seat of the scornful.** He finds no rest in the atheist's scoffings. Let others make a mock of sin, of eternity, of hell and heaven, and of the Eternal God. This man has too much sense of God's presence to endure to hear his name blasphemed. The seat of the scorner may be very lofty, but it is very near to the gate of hell.

But his delight is in the law of the Lord; and in his law doth he meditate day and night. *Psalm 1:2.*

Mark the positive character of the blessed man: **His delight is in the law of the Lord.** He is not *under* the law as a curse and condemnation, but he is *in* it, and he delights to be in it as his rule of life. He delights, moreover, to **meditate** in it, to read it by **day,** and think upon it by **night.** He takes a text and carries it with him all day long. In the nightwatches, when sleep forsakes his eyelids, he museth upon the Word of God. In the **day** of his prosperity, he sings *psalms* out of the Word of God. In the **night** of his affliction, he comforts himself with *promises* out of the same book.

I

The law of the Lord is the daily bread of the true believer. And yet, in David's day, how small was the volume of inspiration! They had scarcely anything save the first five books of Moses. How much more, then, should we prize the whole written Word which it is our privilege to have in all our houses! But, alas, what ill-treatment is given to this angel from heaven. We are not all Berean searchers of the Scriptures. How few among us can lay claim to the benediction of the text! Perhaps some of you can claim a sort of negative purity, because you do not walk in the way of the ungodly. But let me ask you—Is your delight in the law of God? Do you study God's Word? Do you make it the man of your right hand—your best companion and hourly guide? If not, this blessing belongeth not to you.

PSALM 2

Serve the Lord with fear, and rejoice with trembling. Kiss the Son, lest he be angry, and ye perish from the way, when his wrath is kindled but a little. Blessed are all they that put their trust in him. *Psalm 2:11-12.*

Serve the Lord with fear. Let reverence and humility be mingled with your service. He is a great God, and ye are but puny creatures. Bend ye, therefore, in lowly worship, and let a filial fear mingle with all your obedience to the great Father of the Ages. **Rejoice with trembling.** There must ever be a holy fear mixed with the Christian's joy. This is a sacred compound, yielding a sweet smell. We must see to it that we burn no other upon the altar. Fear, without joy, is torment; and joy, without holy fear, would be presumption.

Mark the solemn argument for reconciliation and obedience. It is an awful thing to **perish** in the midst of sin, in the very **way** of rebellion. Yet how easily could **his wrath** destroy us suddenly. It needs not that his anger should be heated seven times hotter. Let the fuel kindle **but a little,** and we are consumed. O sinner! Take heed of the terrors of the Lord, for *our God is a consuming fire.* Note the benediction with which the Psalm closes: **Blessed are all they that put their trust in him.** Have we a share in this blessedness? Do we **trust in him**? Our faith may be slender as a spider's thread. But if it be real, we are in our measure blessed. The more we trust, the more fully shall we know this blessedness. *Lord, increase our faith.*

PSALM 3

Lord, how are they increased that trouble me! Many are they that rise up against me. *Psalm 3:1.*

The poor broken-hearted father complains of the multitude of his enemies. *The conspiracy was strong; for the people increased continually with Absalom*, while the troops of David constantly diminished! **Lord how are they increased that trouble me!** Here is a note of exclamation to express the wonder of woe which amazed and perplexed the fugitive father. Alas! I see no limit to my misery, for my troubles are enlarged! There was enough at first to sink me very low. But lo! my enemies multiply. When Absalom, my darling, is in rebellion against me, it is enough to break my heart. But lo! my faithful counsellors have turned their backs on me. Lo! my generals and soldiers have deserted my standard. **How are they increased that trouble me!** Troubles always come in flocks. Sorrow hath a numerous family.

Many are they that rise up against me. Their hosts are far superior to mine! Their numbers are too great for my reckoning! Innumerable hosts beset our Divine Redeemer. The legions of our sins, the armies of fiends, the crowd of bodily pains, the host of spiritual sorrows, and all the allies of death and hell, set themselves in battle against the Son of Man. O how precious to know and believe that he has routed their hosts, and trodden them down in his anger! They who would have troubled us he has removed into captivity. Those who would have risen up against us he has laid low. The dragon lost his sting when he dashed it into the soul of Jesus.

I laid me down and slept; I awaked; for the Lord sustained me. I will not be afraid of ten thousands of people, that have set themselves against me round about. Arise, O Lord; save me, O my God. *Psalm 3:5–7.*

David's faith enabled him to *lie down.* Anxiety would certainly have kept him on tiptoe, watching for an enemy. Yea, he was able to sleep, *to sleep* in the midst of trouble, surrounded by foes. There is a sleep of presumption. God deliver us from it! There is a sleep of holy confidence. God help us so to close our eyes! But David says he **awaked** also. Some sleep the sleep of death. But he, though exposed to many enemies, reclined his head on the bosom of his God, slept happily beneath the wing of Providence in sweet security, and then awoke in safety. **For the Lord sustained me.** He awoke conscious that the Lord had preserved him.

Buckling on his harness for the day's battle, our hero sings, **I will not be afraid of ten thousands of people, that have set themselves against me round about.** Observe that he does not attempt to underestimate the number or wisdom of his enemies. He reckons them at tens of thousands, and he views them as cunning huntsmen chasing him with cruel skill. Yet he trembles not, but looking his foeman in the face he is ready for the battle. There may be no way of escape. They may hem me in as the deer are surrounded by a circle of hunters. They may surround me on every side. But in the name of God I will dash through them. Or, if I remain in the midst of them, yet shall they not hurt me. I shall be free in my very prison. But David is too wise to venture to the battle without prayer. He therefore betakes himself to his knees, and cries aloud to Jehovah. **Arise, O Lord; save me, O my God.** His only hope is in his **God.** But that is so strong a confidence, that he feels the **Lord** hath but to **arise** and he is saved.

PSALM 4

I will both lay me down in peace, and sleep: for thou, Lord, only makest me dwell in safety. *Psalm 4:8.*

Sweet Evening Hymn! I shall not sit up to watch through fear, but I will **lay me down;** and then I will not lie awake listening to every rustling sound, but I will lie down **in peace and sleep,** for I have nought to fear. He that hath the wings of God above him needs no other curtain. Better than bolts or bars is the protection of the **Lord.** Armed men kept the bed of Solomon. But we do not believe that he slept more soundly than his father, whose bed was the hard ground, and who was haunted by blood-thirsty foes. Note the word **only,** which means that God alone was his keeper, and that though alone, without man's help, he was even then in good keeping, for he was alone with God. A quiet conscience is a good bedfellow.

How many of our sleepless hours might be traced to our untrusting and disordered minds. They slumber sweetly whom faith rocks to sleep. No pillow so soft as a promise; no coverlet so warm as an assured interest in Christ. O Lord, give us this calm repose on thee, that like David we may lie down in peace, and sleep each night while we live; and joyfully may we lie down in the appointed season, to sleep in death, to rest in God!

PSALM 5

Give ear to my words, O Lord, consider my meditation. *Psalm 5:1.*

There are two sorts of prayers—those expressed in words, and the unuttered longings which abide as silent meditations. Words are not the essence but the garments of prayer. Moses at the Red Sea cried to God, though he said nothing. Yet the use of language may prevent distraction of mind, may assist the powers of the soul, and may excite devotion. David, we observe, uses both modes of prayer, and craves for the one a *hearing*, and for the other a *consideration*. What an expressive word! **Consider my meditation.** If I have asked that which is right, give it to me. If I have omitted to ask that which I most needed, fill up the vacancy in my prayer. Let thy holy soul **consider** it as presented through my all-glorious Mediator. Then regard thou it in thy wisdom, weigh it in the scales, judge though of my sincerity, and of the true state of my necessities, and answer me in due time for thy mercy's sake!

There may be prevailing intercession where there are no words. Alas! there may be words where there is no true supplication. Let us cultivate the *spirit* of prayer which is even better than the *habit* of prayer. There may be seeming prayer where there is little devotion. We should begin to pray before we kneel down, and we should not cease when we rise up.

In the morning will I direct my prayer unto thee, and will look up. *Psalm 5:3.*

In the morning will I direct my prayer unto thee. Do we not miss very much of the sweetness and efficacy of prayer by a want of careful meditation before it, and of hopeful expectation after it? We too often rush into the presence of God without forethought or humility. We are like men who present themselves before a king without a petition, and what wonder is it that we often miss the end of prayer? We should be careful to keep the stream of meditation always running; for this is the water to drive the mill of prayer. It is idle to pull up the flood-gates of a dry brook, and then hope to see the wheel revolve. Prayer without fervency is like hunting with a dead dog, and prayer without preparation is hawking with a blind falcon. Prayer is the work of the Holy Spirit, but he works by means. God made man, but he used the dust of the earth as a material. The Holy Ghost is the author of prayer, but he employs the thoughts of a fervent soul as the gold with which to fashion the vessel. Let not our prayers and praises be the flashes of a hot and hasty brain, but the steady burning of a well-kindled fire.

But, furthermore, do we not forget to watch the result of our supplications? How can we expect the Lord to open the windows of his grace, and pour us out a blessing, if we will not open the windows of expectation and **look up** for the promised favour? Let holy preparation link hands with patient expectation, and we shall have far larger answers to our prayers.

PSALM 6

Have mercy upon me, O Lord; for I am weak: O Lord, heal me;

for my bones are vexed. My soul is also sore vexed: but thou, O Lord, how long? *Psalm 6:2–3.*

Have mercy upon me, O Lord; for I am weak. Though I deserve destruction, yet let thy mercy pity my frailty. This is the right way to plead with God if we would prevail. Urge not your goodness or your greatness, but plead your sin and your littleness. Cry, I am weak. Surely this is the plea that a sick man would urge to move the pity of his fellow if he were striving with him, 'Deal gently with me, for I am weak.' The original may be read, *I am one who droops*, or withered like a blighted plant.

O Lord, heal me; for my bones are vexed. Here he prays for *healing*, not merely the mitigation of the ills he endured, but their entire removal, and the curing of the wounds which had arisen therefrom. His bones were *shaken*, as the Hebrew has it. Ah, when the soul has a sense of sin, it is enough to make the bones shake. Lest, however, we should imagine that it was merely bodily sickness—although bodily sickness might be the outward sign—the Psalmist goes on to say, My soul is also sore vexed. Soul-trouble is the very soul of trouble. It matters not that the bones shake if the soul be firm, but when the soul itself is also sore vexed this is agony indeed. But thou, O Lord, how long? This sentence ends abruptly, for words failed, and grief drowned the little comfort which dawned upon him. The Psalmist had still, however, some hope. But that hope was only in his God. He therefore cries, O Lord, how long? The coming of Christ into the soul in his priestly robes of grace is the grand hope of the penitent soul. Indeed, in some form or other, Christ's appearance is, and ever has been, the hope of the saints.

Depart from me, all ye workers of iniquity; for the Lord hath heard the voice of my weeping. *Psalm 6:8.*

David has found peace, and rising from his knees he begins to sweep his house of the wicked. Depart from me, all ye workers of iniquity. The best remedy for us against an evil man is a long space between us both. 'Get ye gone; I can have no fellowship with you.' Repentance is a practical thing. It is not enough to bemoan the desecration of the temple of the heart, we must scourge out the buyers and sellers, and overturn the tables of the money changers. A pardoned sinner will hate the sins which cost the Saviour his blood. Grace and sin are quarrelsome neighbours, and one or the other must go to the wall.

For the Lord hath heard the voice of my weeping. What a fine Hebraism, and what grand poetry it is in English! Is there a voice in weeping? Does weeping speak? In what language doth it utter its

6

meaning? Why, in that universal tongue which is known and understood in all the earth, and even in heaven above. When a man weeps, whether he be a Jew or Gentile, Barbarian, Scythian, bond or free, it has the same meaning in it. Weeping is the eloquence of sorrow. It is an unstammering orator, needing no interpreter, but understood of all. Is it not sweet to believe that our tears are understood even when words fail! Let us learn to think of tears as liquid prayers, and of weeping as a constant dropping of importunate intercession which will wear its way right surely into the very heart of mercy, despite the stony difficulties which obstruct the way. My God, I will *weep* when I cannot plead, for thou hearest **the voice of my weeping.**

PSALM 7

O Lord my God, in thee do I put my trust: save me from all them that persecute me, and deliver me. *Psalm 7:1.*

David appears before God to plead with him against the Accuser, who had charged him with treason and treachery. The case is here opened with an avowal of confidence in God. Whatever may be the emergency of our condition, we shall never find it amiss to retain our reliance upon our God. **O Lord my God,** mine by a special covenant, sealed by Jesus' blood, and ratified in my own soul by a sense of union to thee. **In thee,** and in thee only, **do I put my trust,** even now in my sore distress. I shake, but my rock moves not. It is never right to distrust God, and never vain to trust him.

Now, with both divine relationship and holy trust to strengthen him, David utters the burden of his desire: **save me from all them that persecute me.** His pursuers were very many, and any one of them cruel enough to devour him. He cries, therefore, for salvation from them **all.** We should never think our prayers complete until we *ask for* preservation from *all* sin, and *all* enemies. **And deliver me,** extricate me from their snares, acquit me of their accusations, give a true and just deliverance in this trial of my injured character. See how clearly his case is stated. Let us see to it that we know what we would have when we are come to the throne of mercy. Pause a little while before you pray, that you may not offer the sacrifice of fools. Get a distinct idea of your need, and then you can pray with the more fluency of fervency.

Arise, O Lord, in thine anger, lift up thyself because of the rage of mine enemies: and awake for me to the judgment that thou hast commanded. So shall the congregation of the people compass thee about: for their sakes therefore return thou on high. *Psalm 7:6–7.*

7

Arise, O Lord, in thine anger. His sorrow makes the Psalmist view the Lord as a judge who had left the judgment-seat and retired to rest. Faith would move the Lord to avenge the quarrel of his saints. **Lift up thyself because of the rage of mine enemies**—a still stronger figure to express his anxiety that the Lord would assume his authority and mount the throne. Stand up, O God, rise thou above them all, and let thy justice tower above their villainies. **Awake for me to the judgment that thou hast commanded.** This is a bolder utterance still, for it implies sleep as well as inactivity. God never slumbers, yet he often seems to do so; for the wicked prevail, and the saints are trodden in the dust. God's silence is the patience of longsuffering, and if wearisome to the saints, they should bear it cheerfully in the hope that sinners may thereby be led to repentance.

So shall the congregation of the people compass thee about. As when a judge travels at the assizes, all men take their cases to his court that they may be heard, so will the righteous gather to their Lord. Here the Psalmist fortifies himself in prayer by pleading that if the Lord will mount the throne of judgment, multitudes of the saints would be blessed as well as himself. If I be too base to be remembered, yet **for their sakes,** for the love thou bearest to thy chosen people, come forth from thy secret pavilion, and sit in the gate dispensing justice among the people. When my suit includes the desires of all the righteous it shall surely speed, for *shall not God avenge his own elect?*

PSALM 8

O Lord our Lord how excellent is thy name in all the earth! who hast set thy glory above the heavens. *Psalm 8:1.*

O Lord, our Lord, how excellent is thy name in all the earth! No heart can measure, no tongue can utter, the half of the greatness of Jehovah. The whole creation is full of his glory and radiant with the excellency of his power. His goodness and his wisdom are manifested on every hand. The countless myriads of terrestrial beings, from man the head, to the creeping worm at the foot, are all supported and nourished by the Divine bounty. The solid fabric of the universe leans upon his eternal arm. Universally is he present, and everywhere is his name excellent. God worketh ever and everywhere. *There is no place where God is not.* God is there in a thousand wonders, upholding yon rocky barriers, filling the flowercups with their perfume, and refreshing the lonely pines with the breath of his mouth. Descend, if you will, into the lowest depths of the ocean, where undisturbed the water sleeps, and the very sand is motionless in unbroken quiet, but the glory of the Lord is

8

there, revealing its excellence in the silent palace of the sea. Borrow the wings of the morning and fly to the uttermost parts of the sea, but God is there.

Who hast set thy glory above the heavens. Nor on earth alone is Jehovah extolled, for his brightness shines forth in the firmament above the earth. His glory exceeds the glory of the starry heavens. Above the region of the stars he hath set fast his everlasting throne, and there he dwells in light ineffable. Let us adore him *who alone spreadeth out the heavens, and treadeth upon the waves of the sea; who maketh Arcturus, Orion, and Pleiades, and the chambers of the south.*

PSALM 9

I will praise thee, O Lord, with my whole heart; I will show forth all thy marvellous works. *Psalm 9:1.*

With a holy resolution the songster begins his hymn **I will praise thee, O Lord.** It sometimes needs all our determination to face the foe and bless the Lord in the teeth of his enemies; vowing that whoever else may be silent *we* will bless his name. Here, however, the overthrow of the foe is viewed as complete, and the song flows with sacred fullness of delight. It is our duty to praise the Lord. Let us perform it as a privilege. Observe that David's praise is all given to the Lord. Praise is to be offered to God alone. We may be grateful to the intermediate agent, but our thanks must have long wings and mount aloft to heaven. **With my whole heart.** Half heart is no heart.

I will show forth. There is true praise in the thankful telling forth to others of our heavenly Father's dealings with us. This is one of the themes upon which the godly should speak often to one another. It will not be casting pearls before swine if we make even the ungodly hear of the lovingkindness of the Lord to us. **All thy marvellous works.** Gratitude for one mercy refreshes the memory as to thousands of others. One silver link in the chain draws up a long series of tender remembrances. Here is eternal work for us, for there can be no end to the showing forth of *all* his deeds of love. If we consider our own sinfulness and nothingness, we must feel that every work of preservation, forgiveness, conversion, deliverance, and sanctification, which the Lord has wrought for us, or in us is a **marvellous** work. Even in heaven, divine lovingkindness will doubtless be as much a theme of surprise as of rapture.

The Lord also will be a refuge for the oppressed, a refuge in times of trouble. And they that know thy name will put their

trust in thee: for thou, Lord, hast not forsaken them that seek thee.
Psalm 9:9-10.

There are many forms of oppression, both from man and from Satan. For all its forms, **a refuge** is provided in the Lord Jehovah. There were cities of refuge under the law. God is our refuge-city under the gospel. As the ships when vexed with tempest make for harbour, so do the oppressed hasten to the wings of a just and gracious God. He is a high tower so impregnable, that the hosts of hell cannot carry it by storm, and from its lofty heights faith looks down with scorn upon her enemies.

Ignorance is worst when it amounts to ignorance of God, and knowledge is best when it exercises itself upon the **name** of God. This most excellent knowledge leads to the most excellent grace of faith. O, to learn more of the attributes and character of God. Unbelief, that hooting nightbird, cannot live in the light of divine knowledge. It flies before the sun of God's great and gracious name. If we read this verse literally, there is, no doubt, a glorious fullness of assurance in the names of God. By knowing his name is also meant an experimental acquaintance with the attributes of God, which are every one of them anchors to hold the soul from drifting in seasons of peril. The Lord may hide his face for a season from his people. But he never has utterly, finally, really, or angrily, **forsaken them that seek him.** Let the poor seekers draw comfort from this fact, and let the finders rejoice yet more exceedingly, for what must be the Lord's faithfulness to those who find if he is so gracious to those who seek.

Arise, O Lord; let not man prevail: let the heathen be judged in thy sight. Put them in fear, O Lord: that the nations may know themselves to be but men. *Psalm 9:19-20.*

Prayers are the believer's weapons of war. When the battle is too hard for us, we call in our great ally, who, as it were, lies in ambush until faith gives the signal by crying out, **Arise, O Lord.** Although our cause be all but lost, it shall be soon won again if the Almighty doth but bestir himself. He will not suffer man to prevail over God, but with swift judgments will confound their gloryings. In the very sight of God the wicked will be punished, and he who is now all tenderness will have no compassion for them, since they had no tears of repentance while their day of grace endured.

One would think that men would not grow so vain as to deny themselves to be **but men.** But it appears to be a lesson which only a divine schoolmaster can teach to some proud spirits. Crowns leave their wearers **but men.** Degrees of eminent learning make their owners not more than **men.** Valour and conquest cannot elevate beyond the dead level of **but men.** All the wealth of Croesus, the wisdom of Solomon, the power of Alexander, the eloquence of Demosthenes, if added together, would leave the possessor but a man. May we ever remember this, lest like those in the text, we should be **put in fear.**

PSALM 10

Why standest thou afar off, O Lord? why hidest thou thyself in times of trouble? *Psalm 10:1.*

To the tearful eye of the sufferer the Lord seemed to *stand* still, as if he calmly looked on, and did not sympathise with his afflicted one. Nay, more, the Lord appeared to be **afar off,** no longer *a very present help in trouble,* but an inaccessible mountain, which no man could climb. The presence of God is the joy of his people. But any suspicion of his absence is distracting beyond measure. Let us, then, ever remember that the Lord *is* nigh us. The refiner is never far from the mouth of the furnace, when his gold is in the fire. The Son of God is always walking in the midst of the flames, when his holy children are cast into them. Yet we find it hard to bear the apparent neglect of the Lord when he forbears to work our deliverance.

Why hidest thou thyself in times of trouble? It is not the trouble, but the hiding of our Father's face, which cuts us to the quick. When our sun is eclipsed, it is dark indeed. If we need an answer to the question **Why hidest thou thyself?** it is to be found in the fact that there is a needs-be, not only for trial, but for heaviness of heart under trial (1 *Pet.* 1:6). But how could this be the case, if the Lord should shine upon us while he is afflicting us? Should the parent comfort his child while he is correcting him, where would be the use of the chastening? A smiling face and a rod are not fit companions. God bares the back that the blow may be felt. It is only *felt* affliction which can become *blest* affliction. If we are carried in the arms of God over every stream, where would be the trial and where the experience, which trouble is meant to teach us?

PSALM 11

The Lord is in his holy temple, the Lord's throne is in heaven. *Psalm 11:4.*

Jehovah is in his holy temple. The heavens are above our heads in

11

all regions of the earth, and so is the Lord ever near to us in every state and condition. This is a very strong reason why we should not adopt the vile suggestions of distrust. There is one who pleads his precious blood in our behalf **in the temple** above, and there is one upon the throne who is never deaf to the intercession of his Son. Why, then, should we fear? What plots can men devise which Jesus will not discover? Satan has doubtless desired to have us, that he may sift us as wheat, but Jesus is in the temple praying for us, and how can our faith fail? What attempts can the wicked make which Jehovah shall not behold? And since he is in his holy temple, delighting in the sacrifice of his Son, will he not defeat every device, and send us a sure deliverance?

Jehovah's throne is in the heavens. He reigns supreme. Nothing can be done in heaven, or earth, or hell, which he doth not ordain and over-rule. He is the world's great Emperor. Wherefore, then, should we flee? If we trust this King of kings, is not this enough? Cannot he deliver us without our cowardly retreat? Yes, blessed be the Lord our God, we can salute him as Jehovah-nissi. In his name we set up our banners, and, instead of flight, we once more raise the shout of war.

The righteous Lord loveth righteousness; his countenance doth behold the upright. *Psalm 11:7.*

The righteous Lord loveth righteousness. It is not only his *office* to defend it, but his *nature* to love it. He would deny himself if he did not defend the just. Fear not, then, the end of all your trials, but be just, and fear not. God approves, and, if men oppose, what matters it? **His countenance doth behold the upright.** We need never be out of countenance, for God countenances us. He observes, he approves, he delights in the upright. He sees his own image in them, an image of his own fashioning, and therefore with complacency he regards them. Shall we dare to put forth our hand unto iniquity in order to escape affliction? Let us have done with by-ways and short turnings. Let us keep to that fair path of right along which Jehovah's smile shall light us. Are we tempted to put our light under a bushel, to conceal our religion from our neighbours? Is it suggested to us that there are ways of avoiding the cross, and shunning the reproach of Christ?

Let us not hearken to the voice of the charmer, but seek an increase of faith, that we may wrestle with principalities and powers, and follow the Lord, fully going without the camp, bearing his reproach. Mammon, the flesh, the devil, will all whisper in our ear, *Flee as a bird to your mountain!* But let us come forth and defy them all. *Resist the devil, and he will flee from you.* There is no room or reason for retreat. Advance! Let the vanguard push on! To the front! all ye powers and passions of our soul. On! on! in God's name, on! for *the Lord of hosts is with us; the God of Jacob is our refuge.*

PSALM 12

Help, Lord. *Psalm 12:1.*

A short, but sweet, suggestive, seasonable, and serviceable prayer; a kind of angel's sword, to be turned every way, and to be used on all occasions. The word rendered **help** is largely used for all manner of saving, helping, delivering, preserving. Thus it seems that the prayer is very full and instructive. The Psalmist sees the extreme danger of his position, for a man had better be among lions than among liars. He feels his own inability to deal with such sons of Belial, for *he who shall touch them must be fenced with iron.* He therefore turns himself to his all-sufficient Helper, the **Lord,** whose help is never denied to his servants, and whose aid is enough for all their needs.

Help, Lord is a very useful ejaculation which we may dart up to heaven on occasions of emergency, whether in labour, learning, suffering, fighting, living, or dying. As small ships can sail into harbours which larger vessels, drawing more water, cannot enter, so our brief cries and short petitions may trade with heaven when our soul is wind-bound, and business-bound, as to longer exercises of devotion, and when the stream of grace seems at too low an ebb to float a more laborious supplication.

For the oppression of the poor, for the sighing of the needy, now will I arise, saith the Lord; I will set him in safety from him that puffeth at him. *Psalm 12:5.*

The mere **oppression** of saints, however silently they bear it, is in itself a cry to God. Moses was heard at the Red Sea, though he said nothing. Hagar's affliction was heard despite her silence. Jesus feels with his people, and their smarts are mighty orators with him. By-and-by, however, *they* begin to sigh and express their misery, and then relief comes post-haste. Nothing moves a father like the cries of his children. He bestirs himself, wakes up his manhood, overthrows the enemy, and sets his beloved in safety. A *puff* is too much for the child to bear, and the foe is so haughty, that he laughs the little one to scorn. But the Father comes. Then it is the child's turn to laugh, when he is set above the rage of his tormentor.

What virtue is there in a poor man's sighs, that they should move the

13

Almighty God to arise from his throne. The needy did not dare to speak, and could only sigh in secret, but the Lord heard, and could rest no longer, and girded on his sword for the battle. Man's extremity is God's opportunity. Jesus will come to deliver just when his needy ones shall sigh, as if all hope had gone for ever. O Lord, set thy **now** near at hand, and rise up speedily to our help. He who promises to **set** us **in safety** means thereby preservation on earth, and eternal salvation in heaven.

The words of the Lord are pure words: as silver tried in a furnace of earth, purified seven times. *Psalm 12:6.*

What a contrast between the vain words of man, and the **pure words** of Jehovah. Man's words are yea and nay, but the Lord's promises are yea and amen. For truth, certainty, holiness, faithfulness, **the words of the Lord** are pure as well-refined **silver.** In the original there is an allusion to the most severely-purifying process known to the ancients, through which silver was passed when the greatest possible purity was desired. The dross was all consumed, and only the bright and precious metal remained. So clear and free from all alloy of error or unfaithfulness is the book of **the words of the Lord.**

The Bible has passed through the furnace of persecution, literary criticism, philosophic doubt, and scientific discovery, and has lost nothing but those human interpretations which clung to it as alloy to precious ore. The experience of saints has tried it in every conceivable manner. Not a single doctrine or promise has been consumed in the most excessive heat. What God's words are, the words of his children should be. If we would be Godlike in conversation, we must watch our language, and maintain the strictest purity of integrity and holiness in all our communications.

PSALM 13

How long wilt thou forget me, O Lord? for ever? How long wilt thou hide thy face from me? *Psalm 13:1.*

How long? This question is repeated no less than four times in two verses. It betokens very intense desire for deliverance, and great anguish of heart. And what if there be some impatience mingled therewith? Is not this the more true a portrait of our own experience? It is not easy to prevent desire from degenerating into impatience. O for grace that, while we wait on God, we may be kept from indulging a murmuring spirit! The gold which is long in the fire must have had much dross to be consumed, hence the question **how long?** may suggest deep searching of heart. **How long wilt thou forget me?** Ah, David! how like a fool thou talkest! Can God *forget?* Can Omniscience fail in memory? Above all, can Jehovah's heart forget his own beloved child?

For ever? Oh, dark thought! It was surely bad enough to suspect a temporary forgetfulness. But shall we ask the ungracious question, and imagine that the Lord will for ever cast away his people? No, his anger may endure for a night, but his love shall abide eternally. **How long wilt thou hide thy face from me?** This is a far more rational question, for God may hide his face, and yet he may remember still. A hidden face is no sign of a forgetful heart. It is in love that his face is turned away. Yet to a real child of God, this hiding of his Father's face is terrible. He will never be at ease until once more he hath his Father's smile.

But I have trusted in thy mercy; my heart shall rejoice in thy salvation. I will sing unto the Lord, because he hath dealt bountifully with me. *Psalm 13:5–6.*

David's heart was more often out of tune than his harp. He begins many of his Psalms sighing, and ends them singing. Joy is all the greater because of previous sorrow, as calm is all the more delightful in recollection of the preceding tempest. Here is his avowal of his confidence: **But I have trusted in thy mercy.** For many a year it had been his wont to make the Lord his castle and tower of defence, and he smiles from behind the same bulwark still. Had he doubted the reality of his trust in God, he would have blocked up one of the windows through which the sun of heaven delights to shine. Faith is now in exercise, and consequently is readily discovered. There is never a doubt about the existence of faith while it is in action. All the powers of his enemies had not driven the Psalmist from his stronghold. As the shipwrecked mariner clings to the mast, so did David cling to his faith. He neither could nor would give up his confidence in the Lord his God.

Now hearken to the music which faith makes in the soul. The bells of the mind are all ringing, **My heart shall rejoice in thy salvation.** Sweet is the music which sounds from the strings of the heart. But this is not all. *The voice* joins itself in the blessed work, and the tongue keeps tune with the soul, while the writer declares, **I will sing unto the Lord.** The Psalm closes with a sentence which is a refutation of the charge of forgetfulness which David had uttered in the first verse: **He hath dealt bountifully with me.** So shall it be with us, if we wait awhile. The complaint which in our haste we utter shall be joyfully retracted, and we shall witness that the Lord hath dealt bountifully with us.

The fool hath said in his heart, There is no God. They are corrupt, they have done abominable works, there is none that doeth good. *Psalm 14:1*.

The fool. The atheist is *the* fool pre-eminently, and *a* fool universally. He would not deny God if he were not a fool by nature, and having denied God it is no marvel that he becomes a fool in practice. Sin is always folly. As it is the height of sin to attack the very existence of the Most High, so is it also the greatest imaginable folly. To say there is no God is to belie the plainest evidence, which is *obstinacy*; to oppose the common consent of mankind, which is *stupidity*; to stifle consciousness, which is *madness*. If the sinner could by his atheism destroy the God whom he hates there were some sense, although much wickedness, in his infidelity. But as denying the existence of fire does not prevent its burning a man who is in it, so doubting the existence of God will not stop the Judge of all the earth from destroying the rebel who breaks his laws. Nay, this atheism is a crime which much provokes heaven, and will bring down terrible vengeance on the fool who indulges it.

Would to God the mischief stopped even there. But alas! one fool makes hundreds, and a noisy blasphemer spreads his horrible doctrines as lepers spread the plague. The word here used is *nabal*, which has the signification of fading, dying, or falling away, as a withered leaf or flower. It is a title given to the foolish man as having lost the juice and sap of wisdom, reason, honesty, and godliness. With what earnestness should we shun the appearance of doubt as to the presence, activity, power and love of God, for all such mistrust is of the nature of folly, and who among us would wish to be ranked with the fool in the text? Yet let us never forget that all unregenerate men are more or less such fools.

The Lord looked down from heaven upon the children of men, to see if there were any that did understand, and seek God. *Psalm 14:2*.

The Lord looked down from heaven upon the children of men. As from a watchtower, or other elevated place of observation, the Lord is represented as gazing intently upon men. He will not punish blindly, nor like a tyrant command an indiscriminate massacre because a rumour of rebellion has come up to his ears. What condescending interest and impartial justice are here imagined! Behold the eyes of Omniscience ransacking the globe, and prying among every people and nation,

to see if there were any that did understand, and seek God. The objects of the Lord's search are not wealthy men, great men, or learned men. These, with all they can offer, cannot meet the demands of the great Governor. At the same time, he is not looking for superlative eminence in virtue. He seeks for **any that did understand** themselves, their state, their duty, their destiny, their happiness. He looks for any that **seek God,** who, if there be a God, are willing and anxious to find him out.

Surely this is not too great a matter to expect. If men have not yet known God, if they have any right understanding, they will seek him. Alas! even this low degree of good is not to be found even by him who sees all things. Men love the hideous negation of *No God*, and with their backs to their Creator, who is the sun of their life, they journey into the dreary region of unbelief and alienation. That is a land of darkness as darkness itself, and of the shadow of death without any order and where the light is as darkness.

There were they in great fear: for God is in the generation of the righteous. *Psalm 14:5.*

Oppressors have it not all their own way. They have their fits of trembling and their appointed seasons of overthrow. **There**—where they denied God and hectored against his people; **there**—where they thought of peace and safety, they were made to quail. **There were they**—these very loud-mouthed, iron-handed, proud-hearted Nimrods and Herods, these heady, high-minded sinners—**there were they in great fear.** A panic terror seized them: *they feared a fear*, as the Hebrew puts it. An undefinable, horrible, mysterious dread crept over them. The most hardened of men have their periods when conscience casts them into a cold sweat of alarm. As cowards are cruel, so all cruel men are at heart cowards. The ghost of past sin is a terrible spectre to haunt any man, and though unbelievers may boast as loudly as they will, a sound is in their ears which makes them ill at ease.

For God is in the generation of the righteous. This makes the company of godly men so irksome to the wicked, because they perceive that God is with them. Shut their eyes as they may, they cannot but perceive the image of God in the character of his truly gracious people, nor can they fail to see that he works for their deliverance. The sinner feels the influence of the believer's true nobility and quails before it, for God is there. Let scoffers beware, for they persecute the Lord Jesus when they molest his people. The union is very close between God and his people. It amounts to a mysterious indwelling, **for God is in the generation of the righteous.**

17

Lord, who shall abide in thy tabernacle? who shall dwell in thy holy hill? *Psalm 15:1.*

Thou high and holy One, who shall be permitted to have fellowship with thee? The heavens are not pure in thy sight. Where angels bow with veiled faces, how shall man be able to worship at all? The unthinking many imagine it to be a very easy matter to approach the Most High. But truly humbled souls often shrink under a sense of utter unworthiness. They would not dare to approach the throne of the God of holiness if it were not for him, our Lord, our Advocate, who can abide in the heavenly temple, because his righteousness endureth for ever.

Who shall abide in thy tabernacle? Who shall be admitted to be one of the household of God, to sojourn under his roof, and enjoy communion with himself? **Who shall dwell in thy holy hill?** Who shall be a citizen of Zion, and an inhabitant of the heavenly Jerusalem? The question is raised, because it is a question. All men have not this privilege. Even among professors there are aliens from the commonwealth, who have no secret intercourse with God. On the grounds of law no mere man can dwell with God, for there is not one upon earth who answers to the just requirements mentioned in the succeeding verses. The questions in the text are asked of the **Lord,** as if none but the Infinite Mind could answer them so as to satisfy the unquiet conscience. We must know from the Lord of the tabernacle what are the qualifications for his service. When we have been taught of him, we shall clearly see that only our spotless Lord Jesus, and those who are conformed unto his image, can ever stand with acceptance before the Majesty on high.

Preserve me, O God: for in thee do I put my trust. *Psalm 16:1.*

Preserve me, *keep,* or *save me,* or *guard me,* even as bodyguards surround their monarch, or as shepherds protect their flocks. Tempted in all points like as we are, the Lord Jesus did not confide in purity of nature, but as an example to his followers, looked to the Lord, his **God,** for preservation. It had been promised to the Lord Jesus in express words, that he should be preserved: *Thus saith the Lord, the Redeemer of Israel, and his Holy One, to him whom man despiseth, to him whom the nation abhorreth, I will preserve thee, and give thee for a covenant of the people* (Isaiah 49:7–8). This promise was to the letter fulfilled, by both providential deliverance and sustaining power, in the case of our Lord. Being preserved himself, he is able to restore the preserved of Israel, for we are *preserved in Christ Jesus and called.*

The intercession recorded in John is but an amplification of this cry: *Holy Father, keep through thine own name those whom thou hast given me, that they may be one, as we are.* But while we rejoice in the fact that the Lord Jesus used this prayer for his members, we must not forget that he employed it most surely for himself. He had so emptied himself, and so truly taken upon him the form of a servant, that as man he needed divine keeping even as we do, and often cried unto the Strong for strength. Frequently on the mountain-top he breathed forth this desire, and on one occasion in almost the same words, he publicly prayed, *Father, save me from this hour.* If Jesus looked out of himself for protection, how much more must we, his erring followers, do so!

The lines are fallen unto me in pleasant places; yea, I have a goodly heritage. *Psalm 16:6.*

Jesus found the way of obedience to lead into **pleasant places.** Notwithstanding all the sorrows which marred his countenance, he exclaimed, *Lo, I come: in the volume of the book it is written of me, I delight to do thy will, O my God: yea, thy law is within my heart.* It may seem strange, but while no other man was ever so thoroughly acquainted with grief, no other man ever experienced so much joy and delight in service, for no other served so faithfully and with such great results in view as his recompense of reward. The joy which was set before him must have sent some of its beams of splendour a-down the rugged places where he endured the cross, despising the shame, and must have made them in some respects **pleasant places** to the generous heart of the Redeemer.

He asks no more **goodly heritage** than that his own beloved may be with him where he is and behold his glory. All the saints can use the language of this verse. The more thoroughly they can enter into its contented, grateful, joyful spirit, the better for themselves, and the more glorious to their God. Our Lord was poorer than we are, for he had not where to lay his head, and yet when he mentioned his poverty he never used a word of murmuring. Discontented spirits are as unlike Jesus as the croaking raven is unlike the cooing dove. Some divines think that discontent was the first sin, the rock which wrecked our race in paradise. Certainly there can be no paradise where this evil spirit has power. Its slime will poison all the flowers of the garden.

For thou wilt not leave my soul in hell; neither wilt thou suffer thine Holy One to see corruption. *Psalm 16:10.*

19

Our Lord Jesus was not disappointed in his hope. He declared his Father's faithfulness in the words, **thou wilt not leave my soul in hell.** That faithfulness was proven on the resurrection morning. Among the departed and disembodied Jesus was not left. He had believed in the resurrection, and he received it on the third day, when his body rose in glorious life, according as he had said in joyous confidence, **neither wilt thou suffer thine Holy One to see corruption.** Into the outer prison of the grave his body might go, but into the inner prison of **corruption** he could not enter. He who in soul and body was pre-eminently God's **Holy One,** was loosed from the pains of death, because it was not possible that he should be holden of it.

This is noble encouragement to all the saints. Die they must, but rise they shall. Though in their case they shall see corruption, yet they shall rise to everlasting life. Christ's resurrection is the cause, the earnest, the guarantee, and the emblem of the rising of all his people. Let them, therefore, go to their graves as to their beds, resting their flesh among the clods as they now do upon their couches. Wretched will that man be who, when the Philistines of death invade his soul, shall find that, like Saul, he is forsaken of God. But blessed is he who has the Lord at his right hand. He shall fear no ill, but shall look forward to an eternity of bliss.

PSALM 17

Hear the right, O Lord, attend unto my cry, give ear unto my prayer, that goeth not out of feigned lips. *Psalm 17:1.*

Hear the right, O Lord. It is well if our case is good in itself and can be urged as a **right** one, for right shall never be wronged by our right-eous Judge. But if our suit be marred by our infirmities, it is a great privilege that we may make mention of the righteousness of our Lord Jesus, which is ever prevalent on high. **Right** has a voice which Jehovah always hears; and if my wrongs clamour against me with great force and fury, I will pray the Lord to hear that still louder and mightier voice of the right, and the rights of his dear Son. *Hear, O God, the just One.* **Attend unto my cry.** This shows the vehemence and earnestness of the petitioner. He is no mere talker, he weeps and laments. Who can resist a cry? A cry is our earliest utterance, and in many ways the most natural of human sounds. If our prayer should like the infant's cry be more natural than intelligent, and more earnest than elegant, it will be none the less eloquent with God. There is a mighty power in a child's cry to prevail with a parent's heart.

Give ear unto my prayer. Some repetitions are not vain, but like the repeated blow of a hammer hitting the same nail on the head to fix it the more effectually, or the continued knocking of a beggar at the gate who cannot be denied an alms. **That goeth not out of feigned lips.** Sincerity is a *sine qua non* in prayer. Our sincerity in prayer has no merit in it, any more than the earnestness of a mendicant in the street. But at the same time the Lord has regard to it, through Jesus, and will not long refuse his ear to an honest and fervent petitioner.

Hold up my goings in thy paths, that my footsteps slip not. *Psalm 17:5.*

Under trial it is not easy to behave ourselves aright. In evil times prayer is peculiarly needful, and wise men resort to it at once. Plato said to one of his disciples, 'When men speak ill of thee, live so that no one will believe them.' Good enough advice; but he did not tell us how to carry it out. If we would be preserved, we must cry to the Preserver, and enlist divine support upon our side. **Hold up my goings**—as a careful driver holds up his horse when going down hill. We have all sorts of paces, both fast and slow, and the road is never long of one sort, but with God to hold up our goings, nothing in the pace or in the road can cast down. He who has been down once and cut his knees sadly had need redouble his zeal when using this prayer. All of us, since we are so weak on our legs through Adam's fall, had need use it every hour of the day.

    In thy paths. Forsaking Satan's paths, he prayed to be upheld in God's paths. We cannot keep *from* evil without keeping *to* good. If the bushel be not full of wheat, it may soon be once more full of chaff. In all the appointed ordinances and duties of our most holy faith, may the Lord enable us to run through his upholding grace! **That my footsteps slip not.** What! slip in God's ways? Yes, the road is good, but our feet are evil, and therefore slip, even on the King's highway. One may trip over an ordinance as well as over a temptation. Jesus Christ himself is a stumbling-block to some, and the doctrines of grace have been the occasion of offence to many. Grace alone can hold up our goings in the paths of truth.

Keep me as the apple of the eye, hide me under the shadow of thy wings. *Psalm 17:8.*

Keep me as the apple of the eye. No part of the body more precious, more tender, and more carefully guarded than the **eye.** And of the eye, no portion is more peculiarly to be protected than the central **apple,** the pupil, or, as the Hebrew calls it, *the daughter of the eye.* The all-wise

Creator has placed the eye in a well-protected position. It stands surrounded by projecting bones like Jerusalem encircled by mountains. Moreover, its great Author has surrounded it with many tunics of inward covering, besides the hedge of the eyebrows, the curtain of the eyelids, and the fence of the eyelashes. In addition to this, he has given to every man so high a value for his eyes, and so quick an apprehension of danger, that no member of the body is more faithfully cared for than the organ of sight. Thus, Lord, **keep** thou **me,** for I trust I am one with Jesus, and so a member of his mystical body.

Hide me under the shadow of thy wings. Even as the parent bird completely shields her brood from evil, and meanwhile cherishes them with the warmth of her own heart, by covering them with her wings, so do thou with me, most condescending God, for I am thine offspring, and thou hast a parent's love in perfection. This last clause is in the Hebrew in the future tense, as if to show that what the writer had asked for but a moment before he was now sure would be granted to him. Confident expectation should keep pace with earnest supplication.

PSALM 18

The Lord is my rock, and my fortress, and my deliverer; my God, my strength, in whom I will trust; my buckler, and the horn of my salvation, and my high tower. *Psalm 18:2.*

The Lord is my rock and my fortress. Dwelling among the crags and mountain fastnesses of Judea, David had escaped the malice of Saul, and here he compares his God to such a place of concealment and security. The clefts of the Rock of Ages are safe abodes. **My deliverer,** interposing in my hour of peril. When almost captured the Lord's people are rescued from the hand of the mighty by him who is mightier still. **My God** means my perpetual, unchanging, infinite, eternal good. He who can say truly **my God,** may well add, *my heaven, my all.* **My strength.** This word is really *my rock* in the sense of strength and immobility. My sure, unchanging, eternal confidence and support. Thus the word *rock* occurs twice. The first time it is a rock for *concealment,* but here a rock for *firmness* and *immutabilty.* **In whom I will trust.** Faith must be exercised, or the preciousness of God is not truly known; and God must be the object of faith, or faith is mere presumption.

My buckler, warding off the blows of my enemy, shielding me from arrow or sword. The Lord furnishes his warriors with weapons both offensive and defensive. Our armoury is completely stored, so that none need go to battle unarmed. **The horn of my salvation,** enabling

22

me to push down my foes, and to triumph over them with holy exultation. **My high tower,** a citadel high planted on a rocky eminence beyond the reach of my enemies, from the heights of which I look down upon their fury without alarm, and survey a wide landscape of mercy reaching even unto the goodly land beyond Jordan.

In my distress I called upon the Lord, and cried unto my God: he heard my voice out of his temple, and my cry came before him, even into his ears. *Psalm 18:6.*

In my distress I called upon the Lord, and cried unto my God. Prayer is that postern gate which is left open even when the city is straitly besieged by the enemy. Observe that he *calls,* and then *cries.* Prayer grows in vehemence as it proceeds. Note also that he first invokes his God under the name of Jehovah, and then advances to a more familiar name, **my God.** Thus faith increases by exercise, and he whom we at first viewed as Lord is soon seen to be our God in covenant. It is never an ill time to pray. No distress should prevent us from using the divine remedy of supplication. Above the noise of the raging billows of death, or the barking dogs of hell, the feeblest cry of a true believer will be heard in heaven.

 He heard my voice out of his temple, and my cry came before him, even into his ears. Far up within the bejewelled walls, and through the gates of pearl, the cry of the suffering suppliant was heard. Music of angels and harmony of seraphs availed not to drown or even to impair the voice of that humble call. The King heard it in his palace of light unsufferable, and lent a willing ear to the cry of his own beloved child. O honoured prayer, to be able thus through Jesus' blood to penetrate the very ears and heart of Deity! The **voice** and the **cry** are themselves heard directly by the Lord, and not made to pass through the medium of saints and intercessors. **My cry came before** *him.* The operation of prayer with God is immediate and personal. We may cry with confident and familiar importunity, while our Father himself listens.

He brought me forth also into a large place; he delivered me, because he delighted in me. *Psalm 18:19.*

He brought me forth also into a large place. After pining a while in the prison-house, Joseph reached the palace. From the cave of Adullam, David mounted to the throne. Sweet is pleasure after pain. Enlargement is the more delightful after a season of pinching poverty and sorrowful confinement. Besieged souls delight in the broad fields of the promise, when God drives off the enemy and sets open the gates of the environed city. The Lord does not leave his work half done. Having routed the foe, he leads out the captive into liberty. **Large** indeed is the possession and place of the believer in Jesus. There need be no limit to his peace, for there is no bound to his privilege.

He delivered me, because he delighted in me. Free grace lies at the foundation. Rest assured, if we go deep enough, sovereign grace is the truth which lies at the bottom of every well of mercy. Deep sea fisheries in the ocean of divine bounty always bring the pearls of electing, discriminating love to light. Why Jehovah should delight in us is an answerless question, and a mystery which angels cannot solve. But that he does delight in his beloved is certain, and the fruitful root of favours as numerous as they are precious.

Thou wilt light my candle: the Lord my God will enlighten my darkness. *Psalm 18:28.*

Thou wilt light my candle. Even the children of the day sometimes need candle-light. In the darkest hour light will arise. A candle shall be lit. It will be comfort such as we may fittingly use without dishonesty— it will be our own candle. Yet God himself will find the holy fire with which the candle shall burn. Our evidences are our own, but their comfortable light is from above. Candles which are lit by God, the devil cannot blow out. All candles are not shining, and so there are some graces which yield no present comfort. But it is well to have candles which may by-and-by be lit, and it is well to possess graces which may yet afford us cheering evidences.

The metaphor of the whole verse is founded upon the dolorous nature of **darkness** and the delightfulness of **light**. *Truly the light is sweet, and a pleasant thing it is for the eyes to behold the sun.* Even so the presence of the Lord removes all the gloom of sorrow, and enables the believer to rejoice with exceeding great joy. The lighting of the lamp is a cheerful moment in the winter's evening. But the lifting up of the light of God's countenance is happier by far. It is said that the poor in Egypt will stint themselves of bread to buy oil for the lamp, so that they may not sit in darkness. We could well afford to part with all earthly comforts, if the light of God's love could but constantly gladden our souls.

Thy gentleness hath made me great. *Psalm 18:35.*

The word is capable of being translated, **thy** *goodness* **hath made me great.** David saw much of benevolence in God's action towards him, and he gratefully ascribed all his greatness not to his own goodness, but to the goodness of God. *Thy providence* is another reading, which is indeed nothing more than goodness in action. Goodness is the bud of which providence is the flower; or goodness is the seed of which providence is the harvest. Some render it *thy help*, which is but another word for providence; providence being the firm ally of the saints, aiding them in the service of their Lord. Certain learned annotators tell us that the text means, *thy humility* **hath made me great.**

Thy condescension may, perhaps, serve as a comprehensive reading, combining the ideas already mentioned, as well as that of humility. It is God's making himself little which is the cause of our being made great. We are so little that if God should manifest his greatness without condescension, we should be trampled under his feet. But God, who must stoop to view the skies and bow to see what angels do, looks to the lowly and contrite, and makes them great. While these are the translations which have been given to the adopted text of the original, we find that the Septuagint reads *thy discipline*—thy fatherly correction— **hath made me great.** David ascribes all his own greatness to the condescending goodness and graciousness of his Father in heaven. Let us all feel this sentiment in our own hearts, and confess that whatever of goodness or greatness God may have put upon us, we must cast our crowns at his feet, and cry, **thy gentleness hath made me great.**

PSALM 19

The heavens declare the glory of God. *Psalm 19:1.*

The heavens are plural for their variety, comprising the *watery* heavens with their clouds of countless forms, the *aerial* heavens with their calms and tempests, the *solar* heavens with all the glories of the day, and the *starry* heavens with all the marvels of the night. What the *Heaven of heavens* must be hath not entered into the heart of man, but there in chief all things are telling the glory of God. The heavens **declare, or** *are declaring*, for the continuance of their testimony is intended by the participles employed. Every moment God's existence, power, wisdom, and goodness, are being sounded abroad by the heavenly heralds which shine upon us from above. He who would guess at divine sublimity should gaze upward into the starry vault. He who would imagine infinity must peer into the boundless expanse. He who desires to see divine wisdom should consider the balancing of the orbs. He who would know divine fidelity must mark the regularity of the planetary motions. He who would attain some conceptions of divine power, greatness, and majesty, must estimate the forces of attraction, the magnitude of the fixed stars, and the brightness of the whole celestial train.

It is not merely *glory* that the heavens declare, but the **glory of God,** for they deliver to us unanswerable arguments for a conscious, intelligent, planning, controlling, and presiding Creator. Yet for all this, to what avail is the loudest declaration to a deaf man, or the clearest showing to one spiritually blind? God the Holy Ghost must illuminate us. All the suns in the Milky Way never will.

The law of the Lord is perfect, converting the soul. *Psalm 19:7.*

The law of the Lord is perfect: not merely the law of Moses but the doctrine of God, the whole run and rule of sacred Writ. The doctrine revealed by God he declares to be perfect. Yet David had but a very small part of the Scriptures, and if a fragment, and that the darkest and most historical portion, be **perfect,** what must the entire volume be? The gospel is a complete scheme or law of gracious salvation, presenting to the needy sinner everything that his terrible necessities can possibly demand. There are no redundancies and no omissions in the Word of God, and in the plan of grace. Why then do men try to paint this lily and gild this refined gold? The gospel is perfect in all its parts, and perfect as a whole. It is a crime to add to it, treason to alter it, and felony to take from it.

Converting the soul—making the man to be returned or restored to the place from which sin had cast him. The practical effect of the Word of God is to turn the man to himself, to his God, and to holiness; and the turn or conversion is not outward alone, **the soul** is moved and renewed. The great means of the conversion of sinners is the Word of God, and the more closely we keep to it in our ministry the more likely are we to be successful. It is God's Word rather than man's comment on God's Word, which is made mighty with souls. Try men's depraved nature with philosophy and reasoning, and it laughs your efforts to scorn. But the Word of God soon works a transformation.

The testimony of the Lord is sure, making wise the simple. *Psalm 19:7.*

The testimony of the Lord is sure. God bears his **testimony** against sin, and on behalf of righteousness. He testifies of our fall and of our restoration. This testimony is plain, decided, and infallible, and is to be accepted as sure. God's witness in his Word is so **sure** that we may draw solid comfort from it both for time and eternity, and so sure that no attacks made upon it, however fierce or subtle, can ever weaken its force. What a blessing that in a world of uncertainties we have something sure to rest upon! We hasten from the quicksands of human speculations to the *terra firma* of Divine Revelation.

Making wise the simple. Humble, candid, teachable minds receive the word, and are made wise unto salvation. Things hidden from the wise and prudent are revealed unto babes. The persuadable grow wise, but the cavillers continue fools. As a law or plan the Word of God converts, and then as a testimony it instructs. It is not enough for us to be converts, we must continue to be disciples. And if we have felt the power of truth, we must go on to prove its certainty by experience. The perfection of the gospel converts, but its sureness edifies. If we would be edified, it becomes us not to stagger at the promise through unbelief, for a doubted gospel cannot make us wise. But truth of which we are assured will be our establishment.

Who can understand his errors? cleanse thou me from secret faults. *Psalm 19:12.*

Who can understand his errors? A question which is its own answer. It rather requires a note of exclamation than of interrogation. By the law is the knowledge of sin, and in the presence of divine truth, the Psalmist marvels at the number and heinousness of his sins. He best knows himself who best knows the Word. But even such an one will be in a maze of wonder as to what he does *not* know, rather than on the mount of congratulation as to what he does know. **Cleanse thou me from secret faults.** Thou canst mark in me faults entirely hidden from myself. It were hopeless to expect to see all my spots. Therefore, O Lord, wash away in the atoning blood even those sins which my conscience has been unable to detect. Secret sins, like private conspirators, must be hunted out, or they may do deadly mischief. It is well to be much in prayer concerning them.

Why, if we could receive pardon for all our sins by telling every sin we have committed in one hour, there is not one of us who would be able to enter heaven, since, besides the sins that are known to us and that we may be able to confess, there are a vast mass of sins, which are as truly sins as those which we lament, but which are secret, and come not beneath our eyes. If we had eyes like those of God, we should think very differently of ourselves. The transgressions which we see and confess are but like the farmer's small samples which he brings to market, when he has left his granary full at home. We have but a very few sins which we can observe and detect, compared with those which are hidden from ourselves and unseen by our fellow-creatures.

The Lord hear thee in the day of trouble. *Psalm 20:1.*

All loyal subjects pray for their sovereign, and most certainly citizens of Zion have good cause to pray for the Prince of Peace. In times of conflict loving subjects redouble their pleas, and surely in the sorrows of our Lord his church could not but be in earnest. All the Saviour's days were days of **trouble,** and he also made them days of prayer. The church joins her intercession with her Lord's, and pleads that he may be heard in his cries and tears. The agony in the garden was especially a gloomy hour, but he was heard in that he feared. He knew that his Father heard him always, yet in that troublous hour no reply came until thrice he had fallen on his face in the garden. Then sufficient strength was given in answer to prayer, and he rose a victor from the conflict.

On the cross also his prayer was not unheard, for in the twenty-second Psalm he tells us, *Thou hast heard me from the horns of the unicorns.* The church in this verse implies that her Lord would be himself much given to prayer. In this he is our example, teaching us that if we are to receive any advantage from the prayers of others, we must first pray for ourselves. What a mercy that we *may* pray in the day of trouble, and what a still more blessed privilege that no trouble can prevent the Lord from hearing us! Troubles roar like thunder, but the believer's voice will be heard above the storm. O Jesus, when thou pleadest for us in our hour of trouble, the Lord Jehovah will hear thee. This is a most refreshing confidence, and it may be indulged in without fear.

We will rejoice in thy salvation, and in the name of our God we will set up our banners: the Lord fulfil all thy petitions. *Psalm 20:5.*

We will rejoice in thy salvation. The people in this Psalm, before their king went to battle, felt sure of victory, and therefore began to rejoice beforehand. How much more ought we to do this who have seen the victory completely won! Unbelief begins weeping for the funeral before the man is dead. Why should not faith commence piping before the dance of victory begins? Buds are beautiful, and promises not yet fulfilled are worthy to be admired. If joy were more general among the Lord's people, God would be more glorified among men. The happiness of the subjects is the honour of the sovereign.

And in the name of our God we will set up our banners. We lift the standard of defiance in the face of the foe, and wave the flag of victory over the fallen adversary. Some proclaim war in the name of one king and some of another. But the faithful go to war in Jesu's name, the name of the incarnate God, Immanuel, God with us. So long as Jesus lives and reigns in his church, we need not furl our banners in fear, but advance them with sacred courage. The church cannot forget that Jesus is her advocate before the throne, and therefore she sums up the desires already expressed in the short sentence, **The Lord fulfil all thy petitions.** Be it never forgotten that among those petitions is that choice one, *Father, I will that they also whom thou hast given me be with me where I am.*

Some trust in chariots, and some in horses: but we will remember the name of the Lord our God. *Psalm 20:7.*

Some trust in chariots, and some in horses. Chariots and **horses** make an imposing show, and with their rattling, and dust, and fine caparisons, make so great a figure that vain man is much taken with them. Yet the discerning eye of faith sees more in an invisible God than in all these. The most dreaded war-engine of David's day was the war-chariot, armed with scythes, which mowed down men like grass: this was the boast and glory of the neighbouring nations. But the saints considered **the name** of Jehovah to be a far better defence. As the Israelites might not keep horses, it was natural for them to regard the enemy's cavalry with more than usual dread. It is, therefore, all the greater evidence of faith that the bold songster can here disdain even the horse of Egypt in comparison with the Lord of hosts.

Alas, how many in our day who profess to be the Lord's are as abjectly dependent upon their fellow-men or upon an arm of flesh in some shape or other, as if they had never known the name of Jehovah at all. Jesus, be thou alone our rock and refuge, and never may we mar the simplicity of our faith. **We will remember the name of the Lord our God. Our God** in covenant, who has chosen us and whom we have chosen; this is **our God.** The **name** of our God is JEHOVAH, and this should never be forgotten. The self-existent, independent, immutable, ever-present, all-filling I AM. Let us adore that matchless name, and never dishonour it by distrust or creature-confidence.

PSALM 21

Thou hast made him most blessed for ever: thou hast made him exceeding glad with thy countenance. *Psalm 21:6.*

Thou hast made him most blessed for ever. He is most blessed in himself, for he is God over all, **blessed for ever.** But this relates to him as our Mediator, in which capacity blessedness is given to him as **a**

reward. The margin has it, *thou hast set him to be blessings*. He is an over-flowing wellspring of blessings to others, a sun filling the universe with light. According as the Lord sware unto Abraham, the promised seed is an everlasting source of blessings to all the nations of the earth. He is set for this, ordained, appointed, made incarnate with this very design, that he may bless the sons of men. Oh that sinners had sense enough to use the Saviour for that end to which he is ordained, viz., to be a Saviour to lost and guilty souls!

Thou hast made him exceeding glad with thy countenance. He who is a blessing to others cannot but be glad himself. The unbounded good-doing of Jesus ensures him unlimited joy. The loving favour of his Father, the countenance of God, gives Jesus exceeding joy. This is the purest stream to drink of, and Jesus chooses no other. His joy is full. Its source is divine. Its continuance eternal. Its degree exceeding all bounds. The **countenance** of God makes the Prince of Heaven glad. How ought we to seek it, and how careful should we be lest we should provoke him by our sins to hide his face from us! Our anticipations may cheerfully fly forward to the hour when the joy of our Lord shall be shed abroad on all the saints, and the countenance of Jehovah shall shine upon all the blood-bought. So shall we enter into the joy of our Lord.

They intended evil against thee: they imagined a mischievous device, which they are not able to perform. *Psalm 21:11.*

They intended evil against thee. God takes notice of intentions. He who would, but could not, is as guilty as he who did. Christ's church and cause are not only attacked by those who do not understand it, but there are many who have the light and yet hate it. Intentional **evil** has a virus in it which is not found in sins of ignorance. Now as ungodly men with malice aforethought attack the gospel of Christ, their crime is great, and their punishment will be proportionate. The words **against thee** show us that he who intends evil against the poorest believer means ill to the King himself: let persecutors beware.

They imagined a mischievous device, which they are not able to perform. Want of power is the clog on the foot of the haters of the Lord Jesus. They have the wickedness to *imagine*, and the cunning to *devise*, and the malice to *plot* mischief, but blessed be God, they fail in ability. Yet they shall be judged as to their hearts, and the will shall be taken for the deed in the great day of account. When we read the boastful threatenings of the enemies of the gospel at the present day, we may close our reading by cheerfully repeating, **which they are not able to perform.** The serpent may hiss, but his head is broken. The

30

lion may worry, but he cannot devour. The tempest may thunder, but cannot strike.

My God, my God, why hast thou forsaken me? *Psalm 22:1.*

This was the startling cry of Golgotha: *Eloi, Eloi, lama sabachthani.* Nailed to the tree we behold our great Redeemer in extremities, and what see we? First, our Lord keeps his hold upon his God with both hands and cries twice, **My God, my God!** Oh that we could imitate this cleaving to an afflicting God! Nor does the sufferer distrust the power of God to sustain him, for the title used—*El*—signifies *strength,* and is the name of the Mighty God. He knows the Lord to be the all-sufficient support and succour of his spirit, and therefore appeals to him in the agony of grief, but not in the misery of doubt.

Why hast thou forsaken me? We must lay the emphasis on every word of this saddest of all utterances. **Why?** what is the great cause of such a strange fact as for God to leave his own Son at such a time and in such a plight? **Hast:** it is done, and the Saviour is feeling its dread effect as he asks the question. It was no *threatening* of forsaking which made the great Surety cry aloud. He endured that forsaking in very deed. **Thou:** I can understand why traitorous Judas and timid Peter should be gone, but *thou,* my God, my faithful friend, how canst thou leave me? This is worst of all. Hell itself has for its fiercest flame the separation of the soul from God. **Forsaken:** if thou hadst chastened I might bear it, for thy face would shine. But to forsake me utterly, ah! why is this? **Me:** thine innocent, obedient, suffering Son, why leavest thou *me* to perish? A sight of self seen by penitence, and of Jesus on the cross seen by faith, will best expound this question. Jesus is forsaken because our sins had separated between us and our God.

He trusted on the Lord that he would deliver him: let him deliver him, seeing he delighted in him. *Psalm 22:8.*

Here the taunt is cruelly aimed at the sufferer's faith in God, which is the tenderest point in a good man's soul, the very apple of his eye. They must have learned the diabolical art from Satan himself, for they made rare proficiency in it. According to Matthew 27:39–44, there were five forms of taunt hurled at the Lord Jesus; this special piece of mockery is probably mentioned in this psalm because it is the most bitter of the whole. It has a biting, sarcastic irony in it, which gives it a peculiar venom. It must have stung the Man of Sorrows to the quick.

When we are tormented in the same manner, let us remember him who endured such contradiction of sinners against himself, and we shall be comforted.

On reading these verses one is ready to ask, Is this a prophecy or a history? for the description is so accurate. We must not lose sight of the truth which was unwittingly uttered by the Jewish scoffers. They themselves are witnesses that Jesus of Nazareth **trusted** in God. Why then was he permitted to perish? Jehovah had aforetime delivered those who rolled their burdens upon him. Why was this man deserted? Oh that they had understood the answer! Note further, that their ironical jest, **seeing he delighted in him,** was true. The Lord did delight in his dear Son, and when he was found in fashion as a man, and became obedient unto death, he still was well pleased in him. Strange mixture! Jehovah delights in him, and yet bruises him; is well pleased, and yet slays him.

He hath not despised nor abhorred the affliction of the afflicted; neither hath he hid his face from him; but when he cried unto him, he heard. *Psalm 22:24.*

He hath not despised nor abhorred the affliction of the afflicted. Here is good matter and motive for praise. The experience of our covenant Head and Representative should encourage all of us to bless the God of grace. Never was man so afflicted as our Saviour in body and soul from friends and foes, by heaven and hell, in life and death. He was the foremost in the ranks of the **afflicted.** But all those afflictions were sent in love, and not because his Father despised and abhorred him. 'Tis true that justice demanded that Christ should bear the burden which as a substitute he undertook to carry. But Jehovah always loved him, and in love laid that load upon him with a view to his ultimate glory and to the accomplishment of the dearest wish of his heart.

Under all his woes our Lord was honourable in the Father's sight, the matchless jewel of Jehovah's heart. **Neither hath he hid his face from him.** That is to say, the hiding was but temporary, and was soon removed. It was not final and eternal. **But when he cried unto him, he heard.** Jesus was heard in that he feared. Every child of God should seek refreshment for his faith in this testimony of the Man of Sorrows. What Jesus here witnesses is as true today as when it was first written. It shall never be said that any man's affliction or poverty prevented his being an accepted suppliant at Jehovah's throne of grace. The meanest applicant is welcome at mercy's door.

The Lord is my shepherd. *Psalm 23:1.*

What condescension is this, that the Infinite **Lord** assumes towards his people the office and character of a **Shepherd!** It should be the subject of grateful admiration that the great God allows himself to be compared to anything which will set forth his great love and care for his own people. David had himself been a keeper of sheep, and understood both the needs of the sheep and the many cares of a shepherd. He compares himself to a creature weak, defenceless, and foolish, and he takes God to be his Provider, Preserver, Director, and, indeed, his everything.

No man has a right to consider himself the Lord's sheep unless his nature has been renewed, for the scriptural description of unconverted men does not picture them as sheep, but as wolves or goats. A sheep is an object of property, not a wild animal. Its owner sets great store by it, and frequently it is bought with a great price. It is well to know, as certainly as David did, that we belong to the Lord. There is a noble tone of confidence about this sentence. There is no *if* nor *but*, nor even *I hope so*. But he says, **The Lord** *is* **my shepherd.** We must cultivate the spirit of assured dependence upon our heavenly Father. The sweetest word of the whole is that monosyllable, **my.** He does not say, The Lord is the shepherd of the world at large, and leadeth forth the multitude as his flock, but **The Lord is** *my* **shepherd.** If he be a Shepherd to no one else, he is a Shepherd to *me.* He cares for *me*, watches over *me*, and preserves *me.* The words are in the present tense. Whatever be the believer's position, he is even now under the pastoral care of Jehovah.

He maketh me to lie down in green pastures: he leadeth me beside the still waters. *Psalm 23:2.*

The Christian life has two elements in it, the contemplative and the active, and both are richly provided for. First, the contemplative, **He maketh me to lie down in green pastures.** What are these **green pastures** but the Scriptures of truth—always fresh, always rich, and never exhausted? There is no fear of biting the bare ground where the grass is long enough for the flock to lie down in it. Sweet and full are the doctrines of the gospel. Fit food for souls, as tender grass is natural nutriment for sheep. When by faith we are enabled to find rest in the promises, we are like the sheep that lie down in the midst of the pasture. We find at the same moment provender and peace, rest and refreshment, serenity and satisfaction. But observe: **He** *maketh* **me to**

lie down. It is the Lord who graciously enables us to perceive the preciousness of his truth, and to feed upon it. How grateful ought we to be for the power to appropriate the promises!

The second part of a vigorous Christian's life consists in gracious activity. We not only think, but we act. We are not always lying down to feed, but are journeying onward towards perfection. Hence we read, **he leadeth me beside the still waters.** What are these **still waters** but the influences and graces of his blessed Spirit? His spirit attends us in various operations, like **waters**—in the plural—to cleanse, to refresh, to fertilise, to cherish. They are *still* **waters,** for the Holy Ghost loves peace, and sounds no trumpet of ostentation in his operations. He is a dove, not an eagle; the dew, not the hurricane. Our Lord leads us beside these **still waters.** We could not go there of ourselves, we need his guidance, therefore is it said, **he leadeth me.**

Yea, though I walk through the valley of the shadow of death, I will fear no evil: for thou art with me; thy rod and thy staff they comfort me. *Psalm 23:4.*

Yea, though I *walk,* as if the believer did not quicken his pace when he came to die, but still calmly *walked* with God. To **walk** indicates the steady advance of a soul which knows its road, knows its end, resolves to follow the path, feels quite safe, and is therefore perfectly calm and composed. Observe that it is not walking *in* the valley, but *through* the valley. Death is not the house but the porch. The dying article is called **a valley.** The storm breaks on the mountain, but the valley is the place of quietude. And, then, it is not *the valley of death*, but **the valley of the** *shadow* **of death,** for **death** in its substance has been removed, and only the **shadow** of it remains. Someone has said that when there is a shadow there must be light somewhere, and so there is. Nobody is afraid of a shadow, for a shadow cannot stop a man's pathway even for a moment. The shadow of a dog cannot bite. The shadow of a sword cannot kill. The shadow of death cannot destroy us. Let us not, therefore, be afraid.

I will fear no evil, not even the Evil One himself. I will not dread the last enemy. I will look upon him as a conquered foe, an enemy to be destroyed. **For thou art with me.** This is the joy of the Christian! I have in having thee, all that I can crave: I have perfect comfort and absolute security, **for** *thou* **art with me. Thy rod and thy staff,** by which thou governest and rulest thy flock, the ensigns of thy sovereignty and of thy gracious care—**they comfort me.** I will believe that thou reignest still. The rod of Jesse shall still be over me as the sovereign succour of my soul.

The earth is the Lord's, and the fullness thereof. *Psalm 24:1.*

Man lives upon the earth, and parcels out its soil among his mimic kings and autocrats. But the earth is not man's. He is but a tenant at will, a leaseholder upon most precarious tenure, liable to instantaneous ejectment. The great Landowner and true Proprietor holds his court above the clouds and laughs at the title-deeds of worms of the dust. The fee-simple is not with the lord of the manor nor the freeholder, but with the Creator.

The **fullness** of the earth may mean its harvests, its wealth, its life, or its worship. In all these senses the Most High God is Possessor of all. The earth is full of God. He made it full and he keeps it full, notwithstanding all the demands which living creatures make upon its stores. The sea is full, despite all the clouds which rise from it. The air is full, notwithstanding all the lives which breathe it. The soil is full, though millions of plants derive their nourishment from it. Under man's tutored hand the world is coming to a greater fullness than ever, but it is all the Lord's. The field and the fruit, the earth, and all earth's wonders are Jehovah's. We look also for a sublimer fullness when the true ideal of a world for God shall have been reached in millennial glories, and then most clearly the earth will be the Lord's, and the fullness thereof. These words are upon London's Royal Exchange. They shall one day be written in letters of light across the sky.

Who shall ascend into the hill of the Lord? or who shall stand in his holy place? He that hath clean hands, and a pure heart; who hath not lifted up his soul unto vanity, nor sworn deceitfully. *Psalm 24:3-4.*

Who shall ascend into the hill of the Lord? It is uphill work for the creature to reach the Creator. Where is the mighty climber who can scale the towering heights? Nor is it height alone; it is glory too. Whose eye shall see the King in his beauty and dwell in his palace? In heaven he reigns most gloriously; who shall be permitted to enter into his royal presence? Who shall be able to **stand** or continue there? Who is he that can gaze upon the Holy One, and can abide in the blaze of his glory? Certainly none may venture to commune with God upon the footing of the law, but grace can make us meet to behold the vision of the divine presence. Those who draw near to God must have **clean hands**. If our hands are now unclean, let us wash them in Jesu's precious blood, and so let us pray unto God, lifting up pure hands. But clean hands would not suffice, unless they were connected with **a pure**

heart. True religion is heart-work. There must be a work of grace in the core of the heart as well as in the palm of the hand, or our religion is a delusion. Dirt in the heart throws dust in the eyes.

The man who is born for heaven **hath not lifted up his soul unto vanity.** He who is content with the husks will be reckoned with the swine. But the saint loves more substantial things; like Jehoshaphat, he is lifted up in the ways of the Lord. **Nor sworn deceitfully.** The Christian man's word is his only oath. But that is as good as twenty oaths of other men. Every liar is a child of the devil, and will be sent home to his father.

PSALM 25

Unto thee, O Lord, do I lift up my soul. *Psalm 25:1.*

Unto thee, O Lord. See how the holy soul flies to its God like a dove to its cote. When the storm-winds are out, the Lord's vessels put about and make for their well-remembered harbour of refuge. What a mercy that the Lord will condescend to hear our cries in time of trouble, although we may have almost forgotten him in our hours of fancied prosperity. **Unto thee, O Jehovah, do I lift up my soul.** It is but mockery to uplift the hands and the eyes unless we also bring our souls into our devotions. True prayer may be described as the soul rising from earth to have fellowship with heaven. It is taking a journey upon Jacob's ladder, leaving our cares and fears at the foot, and meeting with a covenant God at the top.

Very often the soul cannot rise. She has lost her wings, and is heavy and earth-bound, more like a burrowing mole than a soaring eagle. At such dull seasons we must not give over prayer, but must, by God's assistance, exert all our power to lift up our hearts. Let faith be the lever and grace be the arm, and the dead lump will yet be stirred. But what a lift it has sometimes proved! With all our tugging and straining we have been utterly defeated, until the heavenly loadstone of our Saviour's love has displayed its omnipotent attractions. Then our hearts have gone up to our Beloved like mounting flames of fire.

Good and upright is the Lord: therefore will he teach sinners in the way. The meek will he guide in judgment: and the meek will he teach his way. *Psalm 25:8–9.*

Good and upright is the Lord: therefore will he teach sinners in the way. As a good man naturally endeavours to make others like himself, so will the Lord our God in his compassion bring sinners into the way of holiness and conform them to his own image. Let those who desire to be delivered from sin take comfort from this. God himself will be the teacher of sinners. God's teaching is practical. He teaches sinners not only the doctrine, but **the way**.

The meek will he guide in judgment. Meek spirits are in high favour with the Father of the meek and lowly Jesus, for he sees in them the image of his only-begotten Son. They know their need of guidance, and are willing to submit their own understandings to divine will. Therefore the Lord condescends to be their guide. Humble spirits are in this verse endowed with a rich inheritance. Let them be of good cheer. Trouble puts gentle spirits to their wits' ends, and drives them to act without discretion. But grace comes to the rescue, enlightens their mind to follow that which is just, and helps them to discern the way in which the Lord would have them to go. Proud of their own wisdom fools will not learn, and therefore miss their road to heaven. But lowly hearts sit at Jesu's feet, and find the gate of glory, for **the meek will he teach his way**. Blessed teacher! Favoured scholar! Divine lesson!

The secret of the Lord is with them that fear him; and he will show them his covenant. *Psalm 25:14.*

The secret of the Lord is with them that fear him. Some read it *the friendship*. It signifies familiar intercourse, confidential intimacy, and select fellowship. This is a great secret. Carnal minds cannot guess what is intended by it. Even believers cannot explain it in words, for it must be felt to be known. The higher spiritual life is necessarily a path which the eagle's eye hath not known, and which the lion's whelp has not travelled. Neither wisdom nor strength can force a door into this inner chamber. Saints have the key of heaven's hieroglyphics. They can unriddle celestial enigmas. They are initiated into the fellowship of the skies. They have heard words which it is not possible for them to repeat to their fellows.

And he will show them his covenant. Its antiquity, security, righteousness, fullness, graciousness and excellence shall be revealed to their hearts and understandings. Above all, their own part in it shall be sealed to their souls by the witness of the Holy Spirit. The designs of love which the Lord has to his people in the covenant of grace, he has been pleased to show to believers in the Book of Inspiration. By his Spirit he leads us into the mystery, even the hidden mystery of redemption. He who does not know the meaning of this verse, will never learn it from a commentary. Let him look to the cross, for the secret lies there.

Examine me, O Lord, and prove me; try my reins and my heart.
Psalm 26:2.

There are three modes of trial here challenged, which in the original refer to trial by touch, trial by smell, and trial by fire. The Psalmist was so clear from the charge laid against him, that he submitted himself unconditionally to any form of examination which the Lord might see fit to employ. **Examine me, O Lord.** Look me through and through. Make a minute survey. Put me to the question. Cross-examine my evidence. **And prove me.** Put me again to trial; and see if I would follow such wicked designs as my enemies impute to me.

Try my reins and my heart. Assay me as metals are assayed in the furnace, and do this to my most secret parts, where my affections hold their court. See, O God, whether or no I love murder, and treason, and deceit. All this is a very bold appeal. Made by a man like David, who feared the Lord exceedingly, it manifests a most solemn and complete conviction of innocence. The expressions here used should teach us the thoroughness of the divine judgment, and the necessity of being in all things profoundly sincere, lest we be found wanting at the last. Our enemies are severe with us with the severity of spite, and this a brave man endures without a fear. But God's severity is that of unswerving right. Who shall stand against such a trial? The sweet singer asks *Who can stand before his cold?* We may well enquire, *Who can stand before the heat of his iustice?*

Lord, I have loved the habitation of thy house, and the place where thine honour dwelleth. *Psalm 26:8.*

Lord, I have loved the habitation of thy house. Into the abodes of sin the Psalmist would not enter, but the **house** of God he had long loved, and loved it still. We were sad children if we did not love our Father's dwelling-place. Though we own no sacred buildings, yet the church of the living God is the house of God, and true Christians delight in her ordinances, services, and assemblies. O that all our days were Sabbaths!

And the place where thine honour dwelleth. In his church where God is had in **honour** at all times, where he reveals himself in the glory of his grace, and is proclaimed by his people as the Lord of all. We come not together as the Lord's people to honour the preacher, but to give glory to God. Such an occupation is most pleasant to the saints of the Most High. What are those gatherings where God is not honoured? Are they not an offence to his pure and holy eyes? Are they not a sad stumbling-block to the people of God? It brings the scalding-tear upon our cheek to hear sermons in which the honour of God is so far from being the preacher's object, that one might almost imagine that the preacher worshipped the dignity of manhood, and thought more of it than of the Infinite Majesty of God.

PSALM 27

The Lord is my light and my salvation; whom shall I fear? the Lord is the strength of my life; of whom shall I be afraid? *Psalm 27:1.*

Here is personal interest, **my light, my salvation.** The soul is assured of it, and therefore, declaring it boldly. **My light.** Into the soul at the new birth divine **light** is poured as the precursor of salvation. **Salvation** finds us in the dark, but it does not leave us there. After conversion our God is our joy, comfort, guide, teacher, and in every sense our light. He is light within, light around, light reflected from us, and light to be revealed to us. Note, it is not said merely that the Lord gives light, but that he *is* light. Nor that he gives salvation, but that he *is* salvation. He, then, who by faith has laid hold upon God, has all covenant blessings in his possession.

Whom shall I fear? A question which is its own answer. The powers of darkness are not to be feared, for the Lord, our light, destroys them. The damnation of hell is not to be dreaded by us, for the Lord is our salvation. This is a very different challenge from that of boastful Goliath, for it is based upon a very different foundation. It rests not upon the conceited vigour of an arm of flesh, but upon the real power of the omnipotent I AM. **The Lord is the strength of my life.** Here is a third glowing epithet, to show that the writer's hope was fastened with a threefold cord which could not be broken. Our life derives all its strength from him who is the author of it. If he deigns to make us strong, we cannot be weakened by all the machinations of the adversary. **Of whom shall I be afraid?** The bold question looks into the future as well as the present. If God be for us, who can be against us, either now or in time to come?

In the time of trouble he shall hide me in his pavilion: in the secret of his tabernacle shall he hide me; he shall set me up upon a rock. *Psalm 27:5.*

This verse gives an excellent reason for the Psalmist's desire after communion with God, namely, that he was thus secured in the hour of peril. **In the time of trouble,** that needy time, that time when others forsake me, **he shall hide me in his pavilion:** he shall give me the best of shelter in the worst of danger. The royal pavilion was erected in the centre of the army, and around it all the mighty men kept guard at all hours. Thus in that divine sovereignty, which almighty power is sworn to maintain, the believer peacefully is hidden, hidden not by himself furtively, but by the king, who hospitably entertains him.

In the secret of his tabernacle shall he hide me. Sacrifice aids sovereignty in screening the elect from harm. No one of old dared to enter the most holy place on pain of death. If the Lord has hidden his people there, what foe shall venture to molest them? **He shall set me up upon a rock.** Immutability, eternity, and infinite power here come to the aid of sovereignty and sacrifice. How blessed is the standing of the man whom God himself sets on high above his foes, upon an impregnable rock which never can be stormed! Well may we desire to dwell with the Lord who so effectually protects his people.

Wait on the Lord: be of good courage, and he shall strengthen thine heart: wait, I say, on the Lord. *Psalm 27:14.*

Wait on the Lord. Wait at his door with prayer. Wait at his foot with humility. Wait at his table with service. Wait at his window with expectancy. Suitors often win nothing but the cold shoulder from earthly patrons after long and obsequious waiting. He speeds best whose patron is in the skies. **Be of good courage.** A soldier's motto. Be it mine. Courage we shall need, and for the exercise of it we have as much reason as necessity, if we are soldiers of King Jesus. **And he shall strengthen thine heart.** He can lay the plaister right upon the weak place. Let the heart be strengthened, and the whole machine of humanity is filled with power. A strong heart makes a strong arm.

What strength is this which God himself gives to the heart? Read *The Book of Martyrs,* and see its glorious deeds of prowess. Go to God rather, and get such power thyself. **Wait, I say, on the Lord.** David, in the words **I say,** sets his own private seal to the word which, as an inspired man, he had been moved to write. It is *his* testimony as well as the command of God. Indeed, he who writes these scanty notes has himself found it so sweet, so reviving, so profitable to draw near to God, that on his own account *he* also feels bound to write, **Wait, I say, on the Lord.**

PSALM 28

Unto thee will I cry, O Lord my rock; be not silent to me, lest, if

thou be silent to me, I become like them that go down into the pit. *Psalm 28:1.*

Unto thee will I cry, O Lord my rock. To cry to man is to waste our entreaties upon the air. The immutable Jehovah is our **rock,** the immovable foundation of all our hopes and our refuge in time of trouble. We are fixed in our determination to flee to him as our stronghold in every hour of danger. It will be in vain to call to the rocks in the day of judgment, but our Rock attends to our cries. **Be not silent to me.** Mere formalists may be content without answers to their prayers, but genuine suppliants cannot. They are not satisfied with the results of prayer itself in calming the mind and subduing the will. They must go further and obtain actual replies from heaven, or they cannot rest. And those replies they long to receive at once, if possible. They dread even a little of God's silence. When God seems to close his ear, we must not therefore close our mouths, but rather cry with more earnestness. When our note grows shrill with eagerness and grief, he will not long deny us a hearing.

What a dreadful case should we be in if the Lord should become for ever silent to our prayers! This thought suggested itself to David, and he turned it into a plea, thus teaching us to argue and reason with God in our prayers. **Lest, if thou be silent to me, I become like them that go down into the pit.** Deprived of the God who answers prayer, we should be in a more pitiable plight than the dead in the grave, and should soon sink to the same level as the lost in hell. We *must* have answers to prayer. Ours is an urgent case of dire necessity. Surely the Lord will speak peace to our agitated minds, for he never can find it in his heart to permit his own elect to perish.

The Lord is my strength and my shield; my heart trusted in him, and I am helped: therefore my heart greatly rejoiceth; and with my song will I praise him. *Psalm 28:7.*

The Lord is my strength. The Psalmist, by an act of appropriating faith, takes the omnipotence of Jehovah to be his own. Dependence upon the invisible God gives great independence of spirit, inspiring us with confidence more than human. **And my shield.** Thus David found both sword and shield in his God. The Lord preserves his people from unnumbered ills. The Christian warrior, sheltered behind his God, is far more safe than the hero when covered with his shield of brass or triple steel. **My heart trusted to him, and I am helped.** Heart work is sure work. Heart trust is never disappointed. Faith must come before help, but help will never be long behindhand. Every day the believer may say, *I am helped,* for the divine assistance is vouchsafed us every moment, or we should go back unto perdition. When more manifest help is needed, we have but to put faith into exercise, and it will be given us.

Therefore my heart greatly rejoiceth; and with my song will I praise him. The **heart** is mentioned twice to show the truth of his faith and his joy. Observe the adverb **greatly.** We need not be afraid of being too full of rejoicing at the remembrance of grace received. We serve a great God. Let us greatly rejoice in him. A song is the soul's fittest method of giving vent to its happiness. It were well if we were more like the singing lark, and less like the croaking raven. When the heart is glowing, the lips should not be silent. When God blesses us, we should bless him with all our heart.

PSALM 29

Give unto the Lord, O ye mighty, give unto the Lord glory and strength. Give unto the Lord the glory due unto his name; worship the Lord in the beauty of holiness. *Psalm 29:1–2.*

Give, ascribe. Neither men nor angels can confer anything upon Jehovah. But they should recognise his glory and might, and ascribe it to him in their songs and in their hearts. **Unto the Lord,** and unto him alone, must honour be given. Natural causes, as men call them, are God in action, and we must not ascribe power to them, but to the infinite Invisible who is the true source of all. **O ye mighty.** You great ones of earth and of heaven, kings and angels, join in rendering worship to the blessed and only Potentate. **Give unto the Lord glory and strength,** both of which men are too apt to claim for themselves, although they are the exclusive prerogatives of the self-existent God. Let crowns and swords acknowledge their dependence upon God. *All worship be to God only.* Let this be emblazoned on every coat of arms.

Give unto the Lord the glory due unto his name. A third time the admonition is given, for men are backward in glorifying God. Unbelief and distrust, complaining and murmuring, rob God of his honour. In this respect, even the saints fail to **give the glory due** to their King. **Worship the Lord.** Bow before him with devout homage and sacred awe, and let your worship be such as he appoints. Of old, worship was cumbered with ceremonial, and men gathered around one dedicated building, whose solemn pomp was emblematic of **the beauty of holiness.** But now our worship is spiritual, The architecture of the house and the garments of the worshippers are matters of no importance. The spiritual beauty of inward purity and outward holiness is far more precious in the eyes of our thrice holy God.

The Lord sitteth upon the flood; yea, the Lord sitteth King for ever. The Lord will give strength unto his people; the Lord will bless his people with peace. *Psalm 29:10–11.*

The Lord sitteth upon the flood. Flood follows tempest, but Jehovah is ready for the emergency. No deluge can undermine the foundation of his throne. He is calm and unmoved, however much the deep may roar and be troubled. His government rules the most unstable and boisterous of created things. Far out on the wild waste of waters, Jehovah *plants his footsteps in the sea, and rides upon the storm.* **Yea, the Lord sitteth King for ever.** Jesus has the government upon his shoulders eternally. Our interests in the most stormy times are safe in his hands. Satan is not king, but Jehovah Jesus is. Therefore, let us worship him, and rejoice evermore.

Power was displayed in the hurricane whose course this Psalm so grandly pictures. Now, in the cool calm after the storm, that power is promised to be the strength of the chosen. He who wings the unerring bolt, will give to his redeemed the wings of eagles. He who shakes the earth with his voice, will terrify the enemies of his saints, and give his children **peace.** Why are we weak when we have divine strength to flee to? Why are we troubled when the Lord's own peace is ours? Jesus the mighty God is our peace. What a blessing is this today! What a blessing it will be to us in that day of the Lord which will be in darkness and not light to the ungodly! Is not this a noble Psalm to be sung in stormy weather? Can you sing amid the thunder?

PSALM 30

I will extol thee, O Lord; for thou hast lifted me up, and hast not made my foes to rejoice over me. *Psalm 30:1.*

I will extol thee. Others may forget thee, murmur at thee, despise thee, blaspheme thee, but **I will extol thee,** for I have been favoured above all others. I will extol thy name, thy character, thine attributes, thy mercy to me, thy great forbearance. But, especially will I speak well of **thee.** This shall be my cheerful and constant employ. **For thou hast lifted me up.** Here is an antithesis: *I will exalt thee, for thou hast exalted me.* I would render according to the benefit received. The Psalmist's praise was reasonable. He had a reason to give for the praise that was in his heart. He had been drawn up like a prisoner from a dungeon, like Joseph out of the pit, and therefore he loved his deliverer.

Grace has uplifted us from the pit of hell, from the ditch of sin, from the Slough of Despond, from the bed of sickness, from the bondage of doubts and fears. Have we no song to offer for all this? How high has our Lord lifted us? Lifted us up into the children's place, to be adopted into the family. Lifted us up into union with Christ, *to sit together with him in heavenly places*. Lift high the name of our God, for he has lifted us above the stars. **And hast not made my foes to rejoice over me.** This was the judgment which David most feared out of the three evils. He said, let me fall into the hand of the Lord, and not into the hand of man (1 *Chron.* 21). Terrible indeed were our lot if we were delivered over to the will of our enemies. Blessed be the Lord, we have been preserved from so dire a fate. The devil and all our spiritual enemies have not been permitted to rejoice over us.

O Lord my God, I cried unto thee, and thou hast healed me. *Psalm 30:2.*

If we must have a physician, let it be so. But still let us go to our God first of all. Above all, remember that there can be no power to heal in medicine of itself. The healing energy must flow from the divine hand. If our watch is out of order, we take it to the watchmaker. If body or soul be in an evil plight, let us resort to him who created them, and has unfailing skill to put them in right condition. As for our spiritual diseases, nothing can heal these evils but the touch of the Lord Christ. If we do but touch the hem of his garment, we shall be made whole. If we embrace all other physicians in our arms, they can do us no service. **O Lord my God.** Observe the covenant name which faith uses: **my God.** Thrice happy is he who can claim the Lord himself to be his portion. Note how David's faith ascends the scale. He sang *O Lord* in the first verse, but it is **O Lord my God** in the second. Heavenly heart-music is an ascending thing, like the pillars of smoke which rose from the altar of incense.

I cried unto thee. I could hardly pray, but I cried. I poured out my soul as a little child pours out its desires. I cried to my God. I knew to whom to cry. I did not cry to my friends, or to any arm of flesh. Hence the sure and satisfactory result: **Thou hast healed me.** I know it. I am sure of it. I have the evidence of spiritual health within me now. Glory be to thy name! Every humble suppliant with God who seeks release from the disease of sin, shall speed as well as the Psalmist did. But those who will not so much as seek a cure, need not wonder if their wounds putrefy and their soul dies.

His anger endureth but a moment; in his favour is life: weeping may endure for a night, but joy cometh in the morning. *Psalm 30:5.*

His anger endureth but a moment. David here alludes to those dispensations of God's providence which are the chastisement ordered in his paternal government towards his erring children, such as the plague which fell upon Jerusalem for David's sins. These are but short judgments, and they are removed as soon as real penitence sues for pardon and presents the great and acceptable sacrifice. What a mercy is this, for if the Lord's wrath smoked for a long season, flesh would utterly fail before him. God puts up his rod with great readiness as soon as its work is done. He is slow *to* anger and swift to end it. **In his favour is life.** As soon as the Lord looked favourably upon David, the city lived, and the king's heart lived too. We die like withered flowers when the Lord frowns. But his sweet smile revives us as the dews refresh the fields. His favour not only sweetens and cheers life, but it is life itself, the very essence of life. Who would know life, let him seek the favour of the Lord.

Weeping may endure for a night. But nights are not for ever. Even in the dreary winter the day-star lights his lamp. **But joy cometh in the morning.** When the Sun of Righteousness comes, we wipe our eyes, and joy chases out intruding sorrow. Who would not be joyful that knows Jesus? The first beams of the morning bring us comfort when Jesus is the day-dawn, and all believers know it to be so. Mourning only lasts till **morning.** When the night is gone the gloom shall vanish. This is adduced as a reason for saintly singing, and forcible reason it is. Short nights and merry days call for the psaltery and harp.

PSALM 31

Into thine hand I commit my spirit: thou hast redeemed me, O Lord God of truth. *Psalm 31:5.*

Into thine hand I commit my spirit. These living words of David were our Lord's dying words. Be assured that they are good, choice, wise, and solemn words. We may use them now and in the last tremendous hour. Observe, the object of the good man's solicitude in life and death is not his body or his estate, but his spirit. This is his jewel, his secret treasure. If this be safe, all is well. See what he does with his pearl! He commits it to the hand of his God. It came from him. It is his own. He has aforetime sustained it. He is able to keep it, and it is most fit that he should receive it. All things are safe in Jehovah's hands. What we entrust to the Lord will be secure, both now and in that day of days towards which we are hastening. Without reservation the good man yields himself to his heavenly Father's hand. It is enough for him to be there. It is peaceful living and glorious dying to repose in the care of heaven. At all times we should commit and continue to commit our all to Jesus' sacred care. Then, though life may hang on a thread, and adversities may multiply as the sands of the sea, our soul shall dwell at ease, and delight itself in quiet resting places.

Thou hast redeemed me, O Lord God of truth. Redemption is a solid basis for confidence. David had not known Calvary as we have done, but temporal redemption cheered him. Shall not eternal redemption yet more sweetly console us? Past deliverances are strong pleas for present assistance. What the Lord has done he will do again, for he changes not. He is faithful to his promises, and gracious to his saints. He will not turn away from his people.

But I trusted in thee, O Lord: I said, Thou art my God. My times are in thy hand: deliver me from the hand of mine enemies, and from them that persecute me. *Psalm 31:14–15.*

But I trusted in thee, O Lord. Notwithstanding all afflicting circumstances, David's faith maintained its hold. So long as our faith, which is our shield, is safe, the battle may go hard, but its ultimate result is no matter of question. If that could be torn from us, we should be as surely slain as were Saul and Jonathan upon the high places of the field. **I said, Thou art my God.** He proclaimed aloud his determined allegiance to Jehovah. He was no fair-weather believer. He could hold to his faith in a sharp frost, and wrap it about him as a garment fitted to keep out all the ills of time. He who can say what David did need not envy Cicero his eloquence. **Thou art my God** has more sweetness in it than any other utterance which human speech can frame. Note that this adhesive faith is here mentioned as an argument with God to honour his own promise by sending a speedy deliverance.

My times are in thy hand. The sovereign arbiter of destiny holds in his power all the issues of our life. We are not waifs and strays upon the ocean of fate, but are steered by infinite wisdom towards our desired haven. Providence is a soft pillow for anxious heads, an anodyne for care, a grave for despair. **Deliver me from the hand of mine enemies, and from them that persecute me.** It is lawful to desire escape from persecution if it be the Lord's will. When this may not be granted us in the form which we desire, sustaining grace will give us deliverance in another form, by enabling us to laugh to scorn all the fury of the foe.

Oh how great is thy goodness, which thou hast laid up for them that fear thee; which thou hast wrought for them that trust in thee before the sons of men! *Psalm 31:19.*

46

Oh how great is thy goodness! When faith led David to his God, she set him singing at once. He does not tell us how great was God's goodness, for he could not. If we cannot measure, we can marvel. Though we may not calculate with accuracy, we can adore with fervency. **Which thou hast laid up for them that fear thee.** In the treasury of the covenant, in the field of redemption, in the caskets of the promises, in the granaries of providence, the Lord has provided for all the needs which can possibly occur to his chosen. We ought often to consider the laid-up goodness of God which has not yet been distributed to the chosen, but is already provided for them. If we are much in such contemplations, we shall be led to feel devout gratitude, such as glowed in the heart of David.

Which thou hast wrought for them that trust in thee before the sons of men. Heavenly mercy is not all hidden in the storehouse. In a thousand ways it has already revealed itself on behalf of those who are bold to avow their confidence in God. Before their fellow-men this goodness of the Lord has been displayed, that a faithless generation might stand rebuked. Overwhelming are the proofs of the Lord's favour to believers. History teems with amazing instances, and our own lives are full of prodigies of grace. We serve a good Master. Faith receives a large reward even now, but looks for her full inheritance in the future. Who would not desire to take his lot with the servants of a Master whose boundless love fills all holy minds with astonishment?

PSALM 32

Blessed is he whose transgression is forgiven, whose sin is covered. *Psalm 32:1.*

Blessed. This is the second psalm of benediction. Psalm 1 describes the result of holy blessedness. Psalm 32 details the cause of it. The first pictures the tree in full growth. This depicts it in its first planting and watering. He who in the first Psalm is a reader of God's book, is here a suppliant at God's throne accepted and heard. **Blessed is he whose transgression is forgiven.** He is now blessed, and ever shall be. Pardoning mercy is of all things in the world most to be prized, for it is the only and sure way to happiness. Blessedness is not in this case ascribed to the man who has been a diligent lawkeeper, for then it would never come to us, but rather to a lawbreaker, who by grace most rich and free has been forgiven. The word rendered **forgiven** is in the original *taken off*, or *taken away*, as a burden is lifted or a barrier removed. What a lift is here! It cost our Saviour a sweat of blood to bear

47

our load. Yea, it cost him his life to bear it quite away. Samson carried the gates of Gaza; but what was that to the weight which Jesus bore on our behalf?

Whose sin is covered. Covered by God, as the ark was covered by the mercy-seat, as Noah was covered from the flood. What a cover must that be which hides away for ever from the sight of the all-seeing God all the filthiness of the flesh and of the spirit! He who has once seen **sin** in its horrible deformity, will appreciate the happiness of seeing it no more for ever. Christ's atonement is the propitiation, the covering, the making an end of sin. It is clear from the text that a man may *know* that he is pardoned. Where would be the blessedness of an unknown forgiveness?

I acknowledged my sin unto thee, and mine iniquity have I not hid. I said, I will confess my transgressions unto the Lord; and thou forgavest the iniquity of my sin. *Psalm 32:5.*

I acknowledged my sin unto thee. After long lingering, the broken heart bethought itself of what it ought to have done at the first, and laid bare its bosom before the Lord. The least thing we can do, if we would be pardoned, is to acknowledge our fault. If we are too proud for this we doubly deserve punishment. **And mine iniquity have I not hid.** We must confess the guilt as well as the fact of sin. It is useless to conceal it, for it is well known to God. It is beneficial to us to own it, for a full confession softens and humbles the heart. We must as far as possible unveil the secrets of the soul, dig up the hidden treasure of Achan, and by weight and measure bring out our sins.

I said. This was his fixed resolution. **I will confess my transgressions unto the Lord.** Not to my fellow-men or to the high priest, but unto Jehovah. Even in those days of symbol, the faithful looked to God alone for deliverance from sin's intolerable load; much more now, when types and shadows have vanished at the appearance of the dawn. When the soul determines to lay low and plead guilty, absolution is near at hand. Hence we read, **And thou forgavest the iniquity of my sin.** Not only was the sin itself pardoned, but the iniquity of it. The virus of its guilt was put away, and that at once, so soon as the acknowledgement was made. God's pardons are deep and thorough. The knife of mercy cuts at the roots of the ill weed of sin.

For this shall every one that is godly pray unto thee in a time when thou mayest be found: surely in the floods of great waters they shall not come nigh unto him. *Psalm 32:6.*

For this shall every one that is godly pray unto thee in a time when thou mayest be found. If the Psalmist means that *on account* of God's mercy others would become hopeful, his witness is true. Remarkable answers to prayer very much quicken the prayerfulness of other godly persons. Where one man finds a golden nugget others feel inclined to dig. Perhaps the Psalmist meant *for* this favour or the like all godly souls would seek. Here, again, we can confirm his testimony, for all will draw near to God in the same manner as he did when godliness rules their heart. There is, however, a set time for prayer, beyond which it will be unavailing. The godly pray while the Lord has promised to answer. The ungodly postpone their petitions till the Master of the house has risen up and shut the door, and then their knocking is too late. What a blessing to be led to seek the Lord before the great devouring floods leap forth from their lairs, for then when they do appear we shall be safe.

Surely in the floods of great waters they shall not come nigh unto him. The floods shall come, and the waves shall rage, and toss themselves like Atlantic billows. But the praying man shall be at a safe distance, most surely secured from every ill. David was familiar with those great land-floods which fill up, with rushing torrents, the beds of rivers which at other times are almost dry. These overflowing waters often did great damage, and were sufficient to sweep away whole armies. From sudden and overwhelming disasters, thus set forth in metaphor, the true suppliant will certainly be held secure. He who is saved from sin has no need to fear anything else.

Be glad in the Lord, and rejoice, ye righteous: and shout for joy, all ye that are upright in heart. *Psalm 32:11.*

Be glad. Happiness is not only our privilege, but our duty. Truly we serve a generous God, since he makes it a part of our obedience to be joyful. How sinful are our rebellious murmurings! How natural does it seem that a man blest with forgiveness should be glad! **In the Lord.** Here is the directory by which gladness is preserved from levity. We are not to be glad in sin, or to find comfort in corn, and wine, and oil, but in our God. That there is such a God, and that he is our Father and our reconciled Lord, is matter enough for a never-ending Psalm of rapturous joy. **And rejoice, ye righteous.** Redouble your rejoicing, peal upon peal. Since God has clothed his choristers in the white garments of holiness, let them not restrain their joyful voices, but sing aloud.

And shout for joy, all ye that are upright in heart. Our happiness should be demonstrative. Men whisper their praises decorously where a hearty outburst of song would be far more natural. Note how the pardoned are represented as upright, righteous, and without guile. A man may have many faults and yet be saved, but a false heart is everywhere the damning mark. A man of twisting, shifty ways of a crooked, crafty nature, is not saved, and in all probability never will be. The ground which brings forth a harvest when grace is sown in it, may be weedy and waste. But our Lord tells us it is *honest* and good ground. Our observation has been that men of double tongues and tricky ways are the least likely of all men to be saved. Certainly where grace comes it restores man's mind to its perpendicular, and delivers him from being doubled up with vice, twisted with craft, or bent with dishonesty.

PSALM 33

Rejoice in the Lord, O ye righteous: for praise is comely for the upright. *Psalm 33:1.*

Rejoice in the Lord. Joy is the soul of praise. To delight ourselves in God is most truly to extol him, even if we let no notes of song proceed from our lips. That God is, and that he is such a God, and our God, ours for ever and ever, should wake within us an unceasing and overflowing joy. To rejoice in temporal comforts is dangerous. To rejoice in self is foolish. To rejoice in sin is fatal. But to rejoice in God is heavenly. He who would have a double heaven must begin below to rejoice like those above. **O ye righteous.** This is peculiarly *your* duty. Your obligations are greater, and your spiritual nature more adapted to the work. Be ye then first in the glad service. Even the righteous are not always glad, and have need to be stirred up to enjoy their privileges.

For praise is comely for the upright. God has an eye to things which are becoming. When saints wear their choral robes, they look fair in the Lord's sight. A harp suits a blood-washed hand. No jewel more ornamental to a holy face than sacred praise. Praise is not comely from unpardoned professional singers. It is like a jewel of gold in a swine's snout. Crooked hearts make crooked music. But the upright are the Lord's delight. Praise is the dress of saints in heaven. It is meet that they should fit it on below.

Sing unto him a new song; play skilfully with a loud noise. *Psalm 33:3.*

Sing unto him a new song. All songs of praise should be **unto him.**

50

Singing for singing's sake is nothing worth. We must carry our tribute to the King, and not cast it to the winds. Do most worshippers mind this? Our faculties should be exercised when we are magnifying the Lord, so as not to run in an old groove without thought. We ought to make every hymn of praise **a new song.** To keep up the freshness of worship is a great thing, and in private it is indispensable. Let us not present old worn-out praise, but put life, and soul, and heart, into every song, since we have new mercies every day, and see new beauties in the work and word of our Lord.

Play skilfully. It is wretched to hear God praised in a slovenly manner. He deserves the best that we have. Every Christian should endeavour to sing according to the rules of the art, so that he may keep time and tune with the congregation. The sweetest tunes and the sweetest voices, with the sweetest words, are all too little for the Lord our God. Let us not offer him limping rhymes, set to harsh tunes, and growled out by discordant voices. **With a loud noise.** Heartiness should be conspicuous in divine worship. Well-bred whispers are disreputable here. It is not that the Lord cannot hear us, but that it is natural for great exultation to express itself in the loudest manner. Men shout at the sight of their kings. Shall we offer no loud hosannahs to the Son of David?

The counsel of the Lord standeth for ever, the thoughts of his heart to all generations. *Psalm 33:11.*

The counsel of the Lord standeth for ever. He changes not his purpose. His decree is not frustrated. His designs are accomplished. God has a predestination according to the counsel of his will, and none of the devices of his foes can thwart his decree for a moment. Men's purposes are blown to and fro like the thread of the gossamer or the down of the thistle. But the eternal purposes are firmer than the earth.

The thoughts of his heart to all generations. Men come and go. Sons follow their sires to the grave. But the undisturbed mind of God moves on in unbroken serenity, producing ordained results with unerring certainty. No man can expect his will or plan to be carried out from age to age. The wisdom of one period is the folly of another. But the Lord's wisdom is always wise, and his designs run on from century to century. His power to fulfil his purposes is by no means diminished by the lapse of years. He who was absolute over Pharaoh in Egypt is not one whit the less today the King of kings and Lord of lords. Still do his chariot wheels roll onward in imperial grandeur, none being for a moment able to resist his eternal will.

I will bless the Lord at all times: his praise shall continually be in my mouth. *Psalm 34:1.*

I will bless the Lord at all times. He is resolved and fixed: **I will.** Let others do as they may. He knows to whom the praise is due, and what is due, and for what and when. To Jehovah, and not to second causes our gratitude is to be rendered. **The Lord** hath by right a monopoly in his creatures' praise. **At all times,** in every situation, under every circumstance, before, in and after trials, in bright days of glee, and dark nights of fear. He would never have done praising, because never satisfied that he had done enough, always feeling that he fell short of the Lord's deservings. Happy is he whose fingers are wedded to his harp. He who praises God for mercies shall never want a mercy for which to praise. To bless the Lord is never unseasonable.

His praise shall continually be in my mouth. Not in my heart merely, but in my mouth too. Our thankfulness is not to be a dumb thing. It should be one of the daughters of music. Our tongue is our glory, and it ought to reveal the glory of God. What a blessed mouthful is God's praise! How sweet, how purifying, how perfuming! If men's mouths were always thus filled, there would be no repining against God, or slander of neighbours. If we continually rolled this dainty morsel under our tongue, the bitterness of daily affliction would be swallowed up in joy.

O fear the Lord, ye his saints: for there is no want to them that fear him. The young lions do lack, and suffer hunger: but they that seek the Lord shall not want any good thing. *Psalm 34:9–10.*

O fear the Lord, ye his saints. Pay to him humble childlike reverence, walk in his laws, have respect to his will, tremble to offend him, hasten to serve him. Fear not the wrath of men, neither be tempted to sin through the virulence of their threats. Fear God and fear nothing else. **For there is no want to them that fear him.** Jehovah will not allow his faithful servants to starve. He may not give luxuries, but the promise binds him to supply necessaries, and he will not run back from his word. Many whims and wishes may remain ungratified, but real wants the Lord will supply. Men seek a patron and hope to prosper. He prospers surely who hath the Lord of Hosts to be his friend and defender.

The young lions do lack, and suffer hunger. They are fierce, cunning, strong, in all the vigour of youth. Yet they sometimes howl in their ravenous hunger. Even so, crafty, designing, and oppressing men, with all their sagacity and unscrupulousness, often come to want. Yet simple-minded believers, who dare not act as the greedy lions of earth, are fed with food convenient for them. To trust God is better policy than the craftiest politicians can teach or practise. **But they that seek the Lord shall not want any good thing.** No really **good thing** shall be denied to those whose first and main end in life is to seek the Lord. Men may call them fools, but the Lord will prove them wise. They shall win where the world's wiseacres lose their all, and God shall have the glory of it.

Many are the afflictions of the righteous: but the Lord delivereth him out of them all. *Psalm 34:19.*

Many are the afflictions of the righteous. Thus are they made like Jesus their covenant Head. Scripture does not flatter us like the story books with the idea that goodness will secure us from trouble. On the contrary, we are again and again warned to expect tribulation while we are in this body. Our afflictions come from all points of the compass, and are as many and as tormenting as the mosquitoes of the tropics. It is the earthly portion of the elect to find thorns and briers growing in their pathway, yea, to lie down among them, finding their rest broken and disturbed by sorrow. **But,** blessed **but.** How it takes the sting out of the previous sentence!

But the Lord delivereth him out of them all. Through troops of ills Jehovah shall lead his redeemed scatheless and triumphant. There is an end to the believer's affliction, and a joyful end too. None of his trials can hurt so much as a hair of his head, neither can the furnace hold him for a moment after the Lord bids him come forth of it. Hard would be the lot of the righteous if this promise, like a bundle of camphire, were not bound up in it. But this sweetens all. The same Lord who sends the afflictions will also recall them, when his design is accomplished. But he will never allow the fiercest of them to rend and devour his beloved.

PSALM 35

Take hold of shield and buckler, and stand up for mine help. Draw out also the spear, and stop the way against them that persecute me: say unto my soul, I am thy salvation. *Psalm 35:2–3.*

Take hold of shield and buckler, and stand up for mine help. In vivid metaphor the Lord is pictured as coming forth armed for battle, and interposing himself between his servant and his enemies. This poetic imagery shows how the Psalmist realised the existence and power of God, and thought of him as a real and actual personage, truly working for his afflicted.

Draw out also the spear, and stop the way against them that persecute me. Before the enemy comes to close quarters the Lord can push them off as with a long spear. To stave off trouble is no mean act of lovingkindness. As when some valiant warrior with his lance blocks up a defile, and keeps back a host until his weaker brethren have made good their escape, so does the Lord often hold the believer's foes at bay until the good man has taken breath, or clean fled from his foes. He often gives the foes of Zion some other work to do, and so gives rest to his church. What a glorious idea is this of Jehovah blocking the way of persecutors, holding them at the pike's end, and giving time for the hunted saint to elude their pursuit! **Say unto my soul, I am thy salvation.** Besides holding off the enemy, the Lord can also calm the mind of his servant by express assurance from his own mouth, that he is, and shall be, safe under the Almighty wing. An inward persuasion of security in God is of all things the most precious in the furnace of persecution. One word from the Lord quiets all our fears.

Let them shout for joy, and be glad, that favour my righteous cause: yea, let them say continually, Let the Lord be magnified, which hath pleasure in the prosperity of his servant. And my tongue shall speak of thy righteousness and of thy praise all the day long. *Psalm 35:27–28.*

Let them shout for joy, and be glad, that favour my righteous cause. Even those who could not render him active aid, but in their hearts favoured him, David would have the Lord reward most abundantly. Men of tender heart set great store by the good wishes and prayers of the Lord's people. Jesus also prizes those whose hearts are with his cause. The day is coming when shouts of victory shall be raised by all who are on Christ's side, for the battle will turn, and the foes of truth shall be routed. **Yea, let them say continually, Let the Lord be magnified.** He would have their gladness contributory to the divine glory. They are not to shout to David's praise, but for the honour of Jehovah.

Which hath pleasure in the prosperity of his servant. They recognised David as the Lord's servant, and saw with pleasure the Lord's favour to him. We can have no nobler title than servant of God, and no greater reward than for our Master to delight in our **prosperity.** What true prosperity may be we are not always best able to judge. We must leave that in Jesus' hand. He will not fail to rule all things

54

for our highest good. **All the day long.** Unceasing praise is here vowed to the just and gracious God. From morning till evening the grateful tongue would talk and sing, and glorify the Lord. O for such a resolve carried out by us all!

PSALM 36

Thy mercy, O Lord, is in the heavens; and thy faithfulness reacheth unto the clouds. *Psalm 36: 5.*

Thy mercy, O Lord, is in the heavens. Clear sky is evermore above, and **mercy** calmly smiles above the din and smoke of this poor world. Darkness and clouds are but of earth's lower atmosphere: the heavens are evermore serene, and bright with innumerable stars. Divine mercy abides in its vastness of expanse, and matchless patience, all unaltered by the rebellions of man. When we can measure **the heavens,** then shall we bound the mercy of the Lord. Towards his own servants especially, in the salvation of the Lord Jesus, he has displayed grace higher than the heaven of heavens, and wider than the universe. O that the atheist could but see this. How earnestly would he long to become a servant of Jehovah!

Thy faithfulness reacheth unto the clouds. Far, far above all comprehension is the truth and faithfulness of God. He never fails, nor forgets, nor falters, nor forfeits his word. Afflictions are like **clouds,** but the divine truthfulness is all around them. While we are under the cloud we are in the region of God's **faithfulness.** When we mount above it we shall not need such an assurance. To every word of threat, or promise, prophecy, or covenant, the Lord has exactly adhered, for he is not a man that he should lie, nor the son of man that he should repent.

Thy righteousness is like the great mountains; thy judgments are a great deep. *Psalm 36: 6.*

Thy righteousness is like the great mountains. Firm and unmoved, lofty and sublime. As winds and hurricanes shake not an Alp, so the **righteousness** of God is never in any degree affected by circumstances. He is always just. Who can bribe the Judge of all the earth, or who can, by threatening, compel him to pervert judgment? Not even to save his elect would the Lord suffer his righteousness to be set aside. No awe inspired by mountain scenery can equal that which fills the soul when it beholds the Son of God slain as a victim to vindicate the justice of the Inflexible Lawgiver.

Thy judgments are a great deep. God's dealings with men are not to be fathomed by every boaster who demands to see a why for every wherefore. The Lord is not to be questioned by us as to why this and why that. He has reasons. But he does not choose to submit them to our foolish consideration. Far and wide, terrible and irresistible like the ocean, are the providential dispensations of God. At one time, they appear as peaceful as the unrippled sea of glass; at another, tossed with tempest and whirlwind, but evermore most glorious and full of mystery. Yet as the deep mirrors the sky, so the mercy of the Lord is to be seen reflected in all the arrangements of his government on earth, and over the profound depth the covenant rainbow casts its arch of comfort, for the Lord is faithful in all that he doeth.

PSALM 37

Fret not thyself because of evildoers, neither be thou envious against the workers of iniquity. *Psalm 37:1.*

It is alas! too common for believers in their hours of adversity to think themselves harshly dealt with when they see persons utterly destitute of religion and honesty, rejoicing in abundant prosperity. Much needed is the command, **Fret not thyself because of evildoers.** To **fret** is to worry, to have the heart-burn, to fume, to become vexed. Nature is very apt to kindle a fire of jealousy when it sees lawbreakers riding on horses, and obedient subjects walking in the mire. It is a lesson learned only in the school of grace, when one comes to view the most paradoxical providences with the devout complacency of one who is sure that the Lord is righteous in all his acts. It seems hard to carnal judgments that the best meat should go to the dogs, while loving children pine for want of it.

Neither be thou envious against the workers of iniquity. The same advice under another shape. When one is poor, despised, and in deep trial, our old Adam naturally becomes **envious** of the rich and great. And when we are conscious that we have been more righteous than they, the devil is sure to be at hand with blasphemous reasonings. Stormy weather may curdle even the cream of humanity. Evil men instead of being envied, are to be viewed with horror and aversion. Yet their loaded tables, and gilded trappings, are too apt to fascinate our poor half-opened eyes. Who envies the fat bullock the ribbons and garlands which decorate him as he is led to the shambles? Yet the case is a parallel one; for ungodly rich men are but as beasts fattened for the slaughter.

Trust in the Lord, and do good; so shalt thou dwell in the land, and verily thou shalt be fed. *Psalm 37:3.*

Trust in the Lord. Faith cures fretting. Sight is cross-eyed, and views things only as they seem; hence her envy. Faith has clearer optics to behold things as they really are; hence her peace. **And do good.** True faith is actively obedient. Doing good is a fine remedy for fretting. There is a joy in holy activity which drives away the rust of discontent. **So shalt thou dwell in the land.** In the land which floweth with milk and honey; the Canaan of the covenant. Thou shalt not wander in the wilderness of murmuring, but abide in the promised land of content and rest. *We which have believed do enter into rest.* Very much of our outward depends upon the inward. Where there is heaven in the heart there will be heaven in the house.

And verily thou shalt be fed, or *shepherded.* To integrity and faith necessaries are guaranteed. The good shepherd will exercise his pastoral care over all believers. In truth they shall be fed, and fed on truth. The promise of God shall be their perpetual banquet. They shall neither lack in spirituals nor in temporals. Some read this as an exhortation, *Feed on truth.* Certainly this is good cheer, and banishes for ever the hungry heart-burnings of envy.

Rest in the Lord, and wait patiently for him: fret not thyself because of him who prospereth in his way, because of the man who bringeth wicked devices to pass. *Psalm 37:7.*

Rest in the Lord. To hush the spirit, to be silent before the Lord, to wait in holy patience the time for clearing up the difficulties of Providence—this is what every gracious heart should aim at. 'Aaron held his peace' . . . 'I opened not my mouth, because thou didst it.' A silent tongue in many cases not only shows a wise head, but a holy heart. **And wait patiently for him.** Time is nothing to him. Let it be nothing to thee. God is worth waiting for. He never is before his time. He never is too late. In a story we wait for the end to clear up the plot. We ought not to prejudge the great drama of life, but stay till the closing scene, and see to what a finish the whole arrives. **Fret not thyself because of him who prospereth in his way, because of the man who bringeth wicked devices to pass.** There is no good, but much evil, in worrying your heart about the present success of graceless plotters. Be not enticed into premature judgments —they dishonour God, they weary yourself. Determine, let the wicked succeed as they may, that you will treat the matter with indifference. Never allow a question to be raised as to the righteousness and goodness of the Lord. What if wicked devices succeed and your own plans are defeated? There is more of the love of God in your defeats than in the successes of the wicked.

I have been young, and now am old; yet have I not seen the righteous forsaken, nor his seed begging bread. *Psalm 37:25.*

This was David's observation. It is not *my* observation just as it stands, for I have relieved the children of undoubtedly good men, who have appealed to me as common mendicants. But this does not cast a doubt upon the observation of David. He lived under a dispensation more outward, and more of this world than the present rule of personal faith. Never are the **righteous forsaken.** That is a rule without exception.

Seldom indeed are their **seed begging bread.** Although it does occasionally occur, through dissipation, idleness, or some such causes on the part of their sons, yet doubtless it is so rare a thing that there are many alive who never saw it. Go into the union house and see how few are the children of godly parents. Enter the gaol and see how much rarer still is the case. Poor ministers' sons often become rich. I am not **old,** but I have seen the families of the poor godly become rich, and have seen the Lord reward the faithfulness of the father in the success of the son, so that I have often thought that the best way to endow one's seed with wealth is to become poor for Christ's sake.

The mouth of the righteous speaketh wisdom, and his tongue talketh of judgment. The law of his God is in his heart; none of his steps shall slide. *Psalm 37:30–31.*

The mouth of the righteous speaketh wisdom. A man's tongue is no ill index of his character. **The mouth** betrays the heart. Good men, as a rule, speak that which is to edifying, sound speech, religious conversation, consistent with the divine illumination which they have received. Righteousness is wisdom in action. Hence all *good* men are practically *wise* men, and well may the speech be wise. **His tongue talketh of judgment.** He advocates justice, gives an honest verdict on things and men, and he foretells that God's **judgment** will come upon the wicked, as in the former days. His talk is neither foolish nor ribald, neither vapid nor profane. Our conversation is of far more consequence than some men imagine.

The law of his God is in his heart; none of his steps shall slide. The best thing in the best place, producing the best results. Well might the man's talk be so admirable when his heart was so well stored. To love holiness, to have the motives and desires sanctified, to be in one's inmost nature obedient to the Lord—this is the surest method of making the whole run of life efficient for its great ends, and even for securing the details of it, our **steps** from any serious mistake. To keep the even tenor of one's way, in such times as these, is given only to those whose hearts are sound towards God, who can, as in the text, call God their God. Policy slips and trips, it twists and tacks, and after all is worsted in the long run. Sincerity plods on its plain pathway, and reaches the goal.

The salvation of the righteous is of the Lord: he is their strength in the time of trouble. And the Lord shall help them, and deliver them: he shall deliver them from the wicked, and save them, because they trust in him. *Psalm 37:39–40.*

But the salvation of the righteous is of the Lord. Sound doctrine this. The very marrow of the gospel of free grace. By **salvation** is meant deliverance of every kind; not only the salvation which finally lands us in glory, but all the minor rescues of the way. These are all to be ascribed unto **the Lord,** and to him alone. Let him have glory from those to whom he grants salvation. **He is their strength in the time of trouble.** While **trouble** overthrows the wicked, it only drives the righteous to their strong Helper, who rejoices to uphold them.

And the Lord shall help them. In all future time Jehovah will stand up for his chosen. Our Great Ally will bring up his forces in the heat of the battle. **He shall deliver them from the wicked.** As he rescued Daniel from the lions, so will he preserve his beloved from their enemies. They need not therefore fret, nor be discouraged. **And save them, because they trust in him.** Faith shall ensure the safety of the elect. It is the mark of the sheep by which they shall be separated from the goats. Not their merit, but their believing, shall distinguish them. Who would not try the walk of faith? Whoever truly believes in God will be no longer fretful against the apparent irregularities of this present life. He will rest assured that what is mysterious is nevertheless just, and what seems hard, is, beyond a doubt, ordered in mercy. Happy they who can thus sing themselves out of ill frames into gracious conditions.

PSALM 38

My heart panteth, my strength faileth me: as for the light of mine eyes, it also is gone from me. *Psalm 38:10.*

My heart panteth. Here begins another tale of woe. The Psalmist was so dreadfully pained by the unkindness of friends that his heart was in a state of perpetual palpitation. Sharp and quick were the beatings of his heart. He was like a hunted roe, filled with distressing alarms, and ready to fly out of itself with fear. The soul seeks sympathy in sorrow. If it finds none, its sorrowful heart-throbs are incessant. **My strength faileth me.** What with disease and distraction, he was weakened and ready to expire. A sense of sin, and a clear perception that none can help us in our distress, are enough to bring a man to death's door, especially if there be none to speak a gentle word, and point the broken spirit to the beloved Physician.

As for the light of mine eyes, it also is gone from me. Sweet **light** departed from his bodily eye, and consolation vanished from his soul. Those who were the very light of his eyes forsook him. Hope, the last lamp of night, was ready to go out. What a plight was the poor convict in! Yet here we have some of us been. Here should we have perished had not infinite mercy interposed. Now, as we remember the lovingkindness of the Lord, we see how good it was for us to find our own strength fail us. It drove us to the strong for strength. How right it was that our light should all be quenched, that the Lord's light should be all in all to us.

Forsake me not, O Lord: O my God, be not far from me. Make haste to help me, O Lord my salvation. *Psalm 38:21–22.*

Forsake me not, O Lord. Now is the time I need thee most. When sickness, slander, and sin, all beset a saint, he requires the especial aid of heaven, and he shall have it too. He is afraid of nothing while God is with him, and God is with him evermore. **Be not far from me.** Withhold not the light of thy near and dear love. Reveal thyself to me. Stand at my side. Let me feel that though friendless besides, I have a most gracious and all-sufficient friend in thee.

Make haste to help me. Delay would prove destruction. The poor pleader was far gone and ready to expire, only speedy help would serve his turn. See how sorrow quickens the importunity of prayer! Here is one of the sweet results of affliction. It gives new life to our pleading, and drives us with eagerness to our God. **O Lord my salvation.** Not my Saviour only, but my **salvation.** He who has the Lord on his side has salvation in present possession. Faith foresees the blessed issue of all her pleas, and in this verse begins to ascribe to God the glory of the expected mercy. We shall not be left of the Lord. His grace will succour us most opportunely. In heaven we shall see that we had not one trial too many, or one pang too severe. A sense of sin shall melt into the joy of salvation. Grief shall lead on to gratitude, and gratitude to joy unspeakable and full of glory.

I said, I will take heed to my ways, that I sin not with my tongue. *Psalm 39:1.*

I said. I steadily resolved and registered a determination. In his great perplexity his greatest fear was lest he should sin. Therefore, he cast about for the most likely method for avoiding it. He determined to be silent. It is right excellent when a man can strengthen himself in a good course by the remembrance of a well and wisely-formed resolve. *What I have written I have written*, or *what I have spoken I will perform*, may prove a good strengthener to a man in a fixed course of right.

I will take heed to my ways. To avoid sin one had need be very circumspect, and keep one's actions as with a guard or garrison. Unguarded ways are generally unholy ones. Heedless is another word for graceless. In times of sickness or other trouble we must watch against the sins peculiar to such trials, especially against murmuring and repining. **That I sin not with my tongue.** Tongue sins are great sins. Like sparks of fire, ill-words spread and do great damage. If believers utter hard words of God in times of depression, the ungodly will take them up and use them as a justification for their sinful courses. If a man's own children rail at him, no wonder if his enemies' mouths are full of abuse. Our tongue always wants watching. It is restive as an ill-broken horse. But especially must we hold it in when the sharp cuts of the Lord's rod excite it to rebel.

I was dumb with silence, I held my peace, even from good; and my sorrow was stirred. *Psalm 39:2.*

I was dumb with silence. He was as strictly speechless as if he had been tongueless—not a word escaped him. He was as silent as the dumb. **I held my peace, even from good.** Neither bad nor good escaped his lips. Perhaps he feared that if he began to talk at all, he would be sure to speak amiss, and, therefore, he totally abstained. It was an easy, safe, and effectual way of avoiding sin, if it did not involve a neglect of the duty which he owed to God to speak well of his name. Our divine Lord was silent before the wicked. But not altogether so, for before Pontius Pilate he witnessed a good confession, and asserted his kingdom. A sound course of action may be pushed to the extreme, and become a fault.

And my sorrow was stirred. Inward grief was made to work and ferment by want of vent. The pent-up floods were swollen and agitated. Utterance is the natural outlet for the heart's anguish, and silence is, therefore, both an aggravation of the evil and a barrier against its cure.

In such a case the resolve to hold one's peace needs powerful backing, and even this is most likely to give way when grief rushes upon the soul. Before a flood gathering in force and foaming for outlet the strongest banks are likely to be swept away. Nature may do her best to silence the expression of discontent, but unless grace comes to her rescue, she will be sure to succumb.

Deliver me from all my transgressions: make me not the reproach of the foolish. *Psalm 39:8.*

Deliver me from all my transgressions. How fair a sign it is when the Psalmist no longer harps upon his sorrows, but begs freedom from his sins! What is *sorrow* when compared with *sin*! Let but the poison of sin be gone from the cup, and we need not fear its gall, for the bitter will act medicinally. None can deliver a man from his transgressions but the blessed One who is called Jesus, because he saves his people from their sins. And when he once works this great deliverance for a man from the cause, the consequences are sure to disappear too. The thorough cleansing desired is well worthy of note. To be saved from *some* **transgressions** would be of small benefit. Total and perfect deliverance is needed.

Make me not the reproach of the foolish. The wicked are **the foolish** here meant: such are always on the watch for the faults of saints, and at once make them the theme of ridicule. It is a wretched thing for a man to be suffered to make himself the butt of unholy scorn by apostasy from the right way. Alas, how many have thus exposed themselves to well-deserved **reproach**! Sin and shame go together and from both David would fain be preserved.

PSALM 40

I waited patiently for the Lord; and he inclined unto me, and heard my cry. *Psalm 40:1.*

I waited patiently for the Lord. Patient *waiting* upon God was a special characteristic of our Lord Jesus. Impatience never lingered in his heart, much less escaped his lips. All through his agony in the garden, his trial of cruel mockings before Herod and Pilate, and his passion on the tree, he waited in omnipotence of patience. No glance of wrath, no word of murmuring, no deed of vengeance came from God's patient Lamb. He waited and waited on; was patient, and patient to perfection, far excelling all others who have according to their measure glorified God in the fires. The Christ of God wears the imperial crown among the patient. Did the Only Begotten wait, and shall we be petulant and rebellious?

And he inclined unto me, and heard my cry. Neither Jesus the head, nor any one of the members of his body, shall ever wait upon the Lord in vain. Mark the figure of *inclining*, as though the suppliant cried out of the lowest depression, and condescending love stooped to hear his feeble moans. What a marvel is it that our Lord should have to cry as we do, and wait as we do, and should receive the Father's help after the same process of faith and pleading as must be gone through by ourselves! The Saviour's prayers among the midnight mountains and in Gethsemane expound this verse. The Son of David was brought very low, but he rose to victory. Here he teaches us how to conduct our conflicts so as to succeed after the same glorious pattern of triumph. Let us arm ourselves with the same mind; and panoplied in patience, armed with prayer, and girt with faith, let us maintain the Holy War.

He brought me up also out of an horrible pit, out of the miry clay, and set my feet upon a rock, and established my goings. *Psalm 40:2.*

He brought me up also out of an horrible pit. When our Lord bore in his own person the terrible curse which was due to sin, he was so cast down as to be like a captive, forgotten of all mankind, immured amid horror, darkness, and desolation. Yet the Lord Jehovah made him to ascend from all his abasement. He retraced his steps from that deep hell of anguish into which he had been cast as our substitute. He who thus delivered our surety *in extremis*, will not fail to liberate us from our far lighter griefs. **Out of the miry clay.** The sufferer was as one who cannot find a foothold, but slips and sinks. Once give a man good foothold, and a burden is greatly lightened. But to be loaded, and to be placed on slimy, slippery clay, is to be tried doubly.

And set my feet upon a rock, and established my goings. The Redeemer's work is done. He reposes on the firm ground of his accomplished engagements. He can never suffer again. For ever does he reign in glory. What a comfort to know that Jesus our Lord and Saviour stands on a sure foundation in all that he is and does for us. His goings forth in love are not liable to be cut short by failure in years to come, for God has fixed him firmly. He is for ever and eternally able to save unto the uttermost them that come unto God by him, seeing that in the highest heavens he ever liveth to make intercession for them. Jesus is the true Joseph taken from the pit to be Lord of all.

If we are cast like our Lord into the lowest pit of shame and sorrow, we shall by faith rise to stand on the same elevated, sure, and everlasting rock of divine favour and faithfulness.

Many, O Lord my God, are thy wonderful works which thou hast done, and thy thoughts which are to us-ward: they cannot be reckoned up in order unto thee: if I would declare and speak of them, they are more than can be numbered. *Psalm 40:5.*

Many, O Lord my God, are thy wonderful works which thou hast done. Wonders of grace beyond all enumeration take their rise from the cross: adoption, pardon, justification, and a long chain of godlike miracles of love proceed from it. **My God.** The man Christ Jesus claimed for himself and us a covenant relationship with Jehovah. Let our interest in our God be ever to us our peculiar treasure. **And thy thoughts which are to us-ward.** The divine thoughts march with the divine acts, for it is not according to God's wisdom to act without deliberation and counsel. God's thoughts of love are very many, very wonderful, very practical! God's thoughts of you are many. Let not yours be few in return. **They cannot be reckoned up in order unto thee.** Their sum is so great as to forbid alike analysis and numeration. How sweet to be outdone, overcome, and overwhelmed by the astonishing grace of the Lord our God!

    If I would declare and speak of them, and surely this should be be the occupation of my tongue at all seasonable opportunities, **they are more than can be numbered.** Far beyond all human arithmetic they are multiplied. Thoughts from all eternity, thoughts of my fall, my restoration, my redemption, my conversion, my pardon, my upholding, my perfecting, my eternal reward: the list is too long for writing, and the value of the mercies too great for estimation. Yet, if we cannot show forth all the works of the Lord, let us not make this an excuse for silence; for our Lord, who is in this our best example, often spake of the tender thoughts of the great Father.

I delight to do thy will, O my God: yea, thy law is within my heart. *Psalm 40:8.*

I delight to do thy will, O my God. No outward formal devotion was rendered by Christ. His heart was in his work, holiness was his element, the Father's **will** his meat and drink. We must each of us be like our Lord in this, or we shall lack the evidence of being his disciples. Where there is no heart work, no pleasure, no **delight** in God's law, there can be no acceptance. Let the devout reader adore the Saviour for the spontaneous and hearty manner in which he undertook the great work of our salvation.

Yea, thy law is within my heart. The law is too broad for such poor creatures as we are to hope to fulfil it to the uttermost. But Jesus not only did the Father's will, but found a delight therein. From old eternity he had desired the work set before him. In his human life he was straitened till he reached the baptism of agony in which he magnified the law. Even in Gethsemane itself he chose the Father's will, and set aside his own. Herein is the essence of obedience, namely, in the soul's cheerful devotion to God. Our Lord's obedience, which is our righteousness, is in no measure lacking in this eminent quality. Notwithstanding his measureless griefs, our Lord found delight in his work, and for *the joy that was set before him he endured the cross, despising the shame*.

Let all those that seek thee rejoice and be glad in thee: let such as love thy salvation say continually, The Lord be magnified. *Psalm 40:16.*

Let all those that seek thee, rejoice and be glad in thee. Here our Lord pronounces benedictions on his people. Note who the blessed objects of his petitions are: not all men, but some men. He pleads for *seekers.* And what does he entreat for them? It is that they may be doubly glad, intensely happy, emphatically joyful, for such the repetition of terms implies. Jesus would have all seekers made happy by finding what they seek after, and by winning peace through his grief. As deep as were his sorrows, so high would he have their joys. He groaned that we might sing, and was covered with a bloody sweat that we might be anointed with the oil of gladness.

Let such as love thy salvation say continually, The Lord be magnified. Another result of the Redeemer's passion is the promotion of the glory of God by those who gratefully delight in his salvation. Our Lord's desire should be our directory. We love with all our hearts his great salvation. Let us then, with all our tongues, proclaim the glory of God which is resplendent therein. Never let his praises cease. As the heart is warm with gladness, let it incite the tongue to perpetual praise. If we cannot do what we would for the spread of the kingdom, at least let us desire and pray for it. Be it ours to make God's glory the chief end of every breath and pulse. The suffering Redeemer regarded the consecration of his people to the service of heaven as a grand result of his atoning death. It is the joy which was set before him. That God is glorified is the reward of the Saviour's travail.

65

Blessed is he that considereth the poor: the Lord will deliver him in time of trouble. *Psalm 41:1.*

Blessed is he that considereth the poor. The **poor** intended are such as are poor in substance, weak in bodily strength, despised in repute, and desponding in spirit. These are mostly avoided and frequently scorned. Such as have been made partakers of divine grace receive a tenderer nature, and are not hardened against their own flesh and blood. They do not toss them a penny and go on their way, but enquire into their sorrows, sift out their cause, study the best ways for their relief, and practically come to their rescue. Such as these have the mark of the divine favour plainly upon them, and are as surely the sheep of the Lord's pasture as if they wore a brand upon their foreheads. They are not said to have considered the poor years ago, but they still do so. Stale benevolence, when boasted of, argues present churlishness.

First and foremost, yea, far above all others put together in tender compassion for the needy, is our Lord Jesus, who so remembered our low estate, that though he was rich, for our sakes he became poor. He weighed our case and came in the fullness of wisdom to execute the wonderful work of mercy by which we are redeemed from our destructions. He still considereth us; his mercy is always in the present tense, and so let our praises be. **The Lord will deliver him in time of trouble.** God measures to us with our own bushel. Days of trouble come even to the most generous, and they have made the wisest provision for rainy days who have lent shelter to others when times were better with them. The promise is not that the generous saint shall have no trouble, but that he shall be preserved in it, and in due time brought out of it.

I said, Lord, be merciful unto me: heal my soul; for I have sinned against thee. *Psalm 41:4.*

I said—said it in earnest prayer—**Lord, be merciful unto me.** No appeal is made to justice; the petitioner but hints at the promised reward, but goes straightforward to lay his plea at the feet of mercy. **Heal my soul.** My time of languishing is come, now do as thou hast said, and strengthen me, especially in my soul. We ought to be far more earnest for the soul's healing than for the body's ease. We hear much of the cure of souls, but we often forget to care about it.

For I have sinned against thee. Here was the root of sorrow. Sin and suffering are inevitable companions. Observe that by the Psalmist sin was felt to be mainly evil because directed against God. This is of the essence of true repentance. How strangely evangelical is the argument: heal me, not for I am innocent, but **I have sinned.** How contrary is this to all self-righteous pleading! How consonant with grace! How inconsistent with merit! A direct appeal is made to mercy on the ground of great sin. Here is a divinely revealed precedent for thee. Be not slow to follow it.

As the hart panteth after the water brooks, so panteth my soul after thee, O God. *Psalm 42:1.*

As after a long drought the poor fainting hind longs for the streams, or rather as the hunted hart instinctively seeks after the river to lave its smoking flanks and to escape the dogs, even so my weary, persecuted soul pants after the Lord my God. Debarred from public worship, David was heartsick. Ease he did not seek, honour he did not covet, but the enjoyment of communion with God was an urgent need of his soul; he viewed it not merely as the sweetest of all luxuries, but as an absolute necessity, like water to a stag. Like the parched traveller in the wilderness, whose skin bottle is empty, and who finds the wells dry, he must drink or die—he must have his God or faint.

His **soul,** his very self, his deepest life, was insatiable for a sense of the divine presence. As the hart brays so his soul prays. Give him his God and he is as content as the poor deer which at length slakes its thirst and is perfectly happy; but deny him his Lord, and his heart heaves, his bosom palpitates, his whole frame is convulsed, like one who gasps for breath, or pants with long running. The next best thing to living in the light of the Lord's love is to be unhappy till we have it, and to pant hourly after it—hourly, did I say? thirst is a perpetual appetite, and not to be forgotten, and even thus continual is the heart's longing after God. When it is as natural for us to long for God as for an animal to thirst, it is well with our souls, however painful our feelings.

The Lord will command his lovingkindness in the daytime, and in the night his song shall be with me, and my prayer unto the God of my life. *Psalm 42:8.*

The Lord will command his lovingkindness in the daytime. Come what may, there shall be a certain secret something to sweeten all. **Lovingkindness** is a noble lifebelt in a rough sea. The day may darken into a strange and untimely midnight, but the love of God, ordained of old to be the portion of the elect, shall be by sovereign decree meted out to them. No day shall ever dawn on an heir of grace and find him altogether forsaken of his Lord. The Lord reigneth. As a sovereign he will with authority command mercy to be reserved for his chosen.

And in the night. Both divisions of the day shall be illuminated with special love, and no stress of trial shall prevent it. Our God is God of the nights as well as the days. None shall find his Israel unprotected, be the hour what it may. **His song shall be with me.** Songs of praise for blessings received shall cheer the gloom of night. No music sweeter than this. The belief that we shall yet glorify the Lord for mercy given in extremity is a delightful stay to the soul. Affliction may put out our candle. But if it cannot silence our song, we will soon light the candle again. **And my prayer unto the God of my life. Prayer** is yoked with praise. He who is the living God, is the God of our life, from him we derive it, with him in prayer and praise we spend it, to him we devote it, in him we shall perfect it. To be assured that our sighs and songs shall both have free access to our glorious Lord is to have reason for hope in the most deplorable condition.

PSALM 43

O send out thy light and thy truth: let them lead me; let them bring me unto thy holy hill, and to thy tabernacles. *Psalm 43:3.*

O send out thy light and thy truth. The joy of thy presence and the faithfulness of thy heart: let both of these be manifest to me. Reveal my true character by **thy light,** and reward me according to thy truthful promise. As the sun darts forth his beams, so does the Lord send forth his favour and his faithfulness towards all his people. As all nature rejoices in the sunshine, even so the saints triumph in the manifestation of the love and fidelity of their God, which, like the golden sunbeam, lights up even the darkest surroundings with delightful splendour. **Let them lead me.** Be these my star to guide me to my rest. Be these my Alpine guides to conduct me over mountains and precipices to the abodes of grace.

Let them bring me unto thy holy hill, and to thy tabernacle. First in thy mercy bring me to thine earthly courts, and end my weary exile, and then in due time admit me to thy celestial palace above. We seek not **light** to sin by, nor **truth** to be exalted by it, but that they may become our practical guides to the nearest communion with God. Only such light and truth as are sent us from God will do this. Common light is not strong enough to show the road to heaven, nor will mere moral or physical truths assist to the holy hill. But the light of the

Holy Spirit, and the truth as it is in Jesus, these are elevating, sanctifying, perfecting; and hence their virtue in leading us to the glorious presence of God. It is beautiful to observe how David's longing to be away from the oppression of man always leads him to sigh more intensely for communion with God.

Why art thou cast down, O my soul? and why art thou disquieted within me? hope in God: for I shall yet praise him, who is the health of my countenance, and my God. *Psalm 43:5.*

Why art thou cast down, O my soul? If God be thine, why this dejection? If he uplifts thee, why art thou so near the ground? The dew of love is falling, O withering heart, revive. **And why art thou disquieted within me?** What cause is there to break the repose of thy heart? Wherefore indulge unreasonable sorrows, which benefit no one, fret thyself, and dishonour thy God? Why overburden thyself with forebodings? **Hope in God,** or *wait for God.* There is need of patience. But there is ground for hope. The Lord cannot but avenge his own elect. The heavenly Father will not stand by and see his children trampled on for ever. As surely as the sun is in the heavens, light must arise for the people of God, though for awhile they may walk in darkness. Why, then, should we not be encouraged, and lift up our head with comfortable hope?

For I shall yet praise him. Times of complaint will soon end, and seasons of praise will begin. Come, my heart, look out of the window, and sweeten thy chamber with sprigs of the sweet herb of hope. **Who is the health of my countenance, and my God.** My God will clear the furrows from my brow, and the tear-marks from my cheek. Therefore will I lift up my head and smile in the face of the storm.

PSALM 44

We have heard with our ears, O God, our fathers have told us, what work thou didst in their days, in the times of old. *Psalm 44:1.*

We have heard with our ears, O God. Among the godly Israelites the biography of their nation was preserved by oral tradition, with great diligence and accuracy. This mode of preserving and transmitting history has its disadvantages, but it certainly produces a more vivid impression on the mind than any other. To hear with the ears affects us more sensitively than to read with the eyes. We ought to note this and seize every possible opportunity of telling abroad the gospel of our Lord Jesus *viva voce*, since this is the most telling mode of communication. **Heard with our ears.** Too many have ears but hear not. Happy are they who, having ears, have learned to hear.

Our fathers have told us. They could not have had better informants. Schoolmasters are well enough. But godly fathers are, both by the order of nature and grace, the best instructors of their sons. Nor can they delegate the sacred duty. When fathers are tongue-tied religiously with their offspring, need they wonder if their children's hearts remain sin-tied? Religious conversation need not be dull. Indeed it could not be if, as in this case, it dealt more with facts and less with opinions. **What work thou didst in their days, in the times of old.** They began with what their own eyes had witnessed, and then passed on to what were the traditions of their youth. A nation tutored as Israel was in a history so marvellous as their own, always had an available argument in pleading with God for aid in trouble, since he who never changes gives in every deed of grace a pledge of mercy yet to come. The traditions of our past experience are powerful pleas for present help.

Thou art my King, O God: command deliverances for Jacob. *Psalm 44:4.*

Thou art my King, O God. Knowing right well thy power and grace, my heart is glad to own thee for her sovereign prince. Who among the mighty are so illustrious as thou art? To whom, then, should I yield my homage or turn for aid? God of my fathers in the olden time, thou art my soul's monarch and liege Lord. **Command deliverances.** To whom should a people look but to their king? He it is who, by virtue of his office, fights their battles for them. In the case of our King, how easy it is for him to scatter all our foes! O Lord, the King of kings, with what ease canst thou rescue thy people! A word of thine can do it. Give but the command and thy persecuted people shall be free.

For Jacob. Jacob's long life was crowded with trials and deliverances. His descendants are here called by his name, as if to typify the similarity of their experience to that of their great forefather. He who would win the blessings of Israel must share the sorrows of Jacob. This verse contains a personal declaration and an intercessory prayer. Those can pray best who make most sure of their personal interest in God. Those who have the fullest assurance that the Lord is their God should be the foremost to plead for the rest of the tried family of the faithful.

Through thee will we push down our enemies: through thy name will we tread them under that rise up against us. *Psalm 44:5.*

Through thee will we push down our enemies. The fight was very close. Bows were of no avail, and swords failed to be of service. It came to daggers drawing, and hand to hand wrestling, pushing and tugging. Jacob's God was renewing in the seed of Jacob their father's wrestling. And how fared it with faith then? Could she stand foot to foot with her foe and hold her own? Yea, verily, she came forth victorious from the encounter, for she is great at a close push, and overthrows all her adversaries, the Lord being her helper.

Through thy name will we tread them under that rise up against us. The Lord's name served instead of weapons. It enabled those who used it to leap on their foes and crush them with jubilant valour. In union and communion with God, saints work wonders. If God be for us, who can be against us? Mark well that all the conquests of these believers are said to be *through thee*, **through thy name.** Never let us forget this, lest going to warfare at our own charges, we fail most ignominiously. Let us not, however, fall into the equally dangerous sin of distrust, for the Lord can make the weakest of us equal to any emergency. Though today we are timid and defenceless as sheep, he can by his power make us strong as the firstling of his bullock, and cause us to push as with the horns of unicorns, until those who rose up against us shall be so crushed and battered as never to rise again. Those who of themselves can scarcely keep their feet, but like little babes totter and fall, are by divine assistance made to overthrow their foes, and set their feet upon their necks.

Thou sellest thy people for nought, and dost not increase thy wealth by their price. *Psalm 44:12.*

Thou sellest thy people for nought. As men sell merchandise to anyone who cares to have it, so the Lord seemed to hand over his people to any nation who might choose to make war upon them. Meanwhile no good result was perceptible from all the miseries of Israel. So far as the Psalmist could discover, the Lord's name received no honour from the sorrows of his people. They were given away to their foes as if they were so little valued as not to be worth the ordinary price of slaves, and the Lord did not care to gain by them so long as they did but suffer. The woe expressed in this line is as vinegar mingled with gall. The expression is worthy of the weeping prophet.

And dost not increase thy wealth by their price. If Jehovah had been glorified by all this wretchedness, it could have been borne patiently. But it was the reverse. The Lord's name had, through the nation's calamities, been despised by the insulting heathen, who counted the overthrow of Israel to be the defeat of Jehovah himself.

71

It always lightens a believer's trouble when he can see that God's great name will be honoured thereby. But it is a grievous aggravation of misery when we appear to be tortured in vain. For our comfort let us rest satisfied that in reality the Lord is glorified. When no revenue of glory is manifestly rendered to him, he none the less accomplishes his own secret purposes, of which the grand result will be revealed in due time. We do not suffer for nought, nor are our griefs without result.

PSALM 45

Thou art fairer than the children of men: grace is poured into thy lips: therefore God hath blessed thee for ever. *Psalm 45:2.*

Thou art fairer than the children of men. The Hebrew word is doubled: *Beautiful, beautiful art thou.* Jesus is so emphatically lovely that words must be doubled, strained, yea, exhausted before he can be described. In Jesus we behold every feature of a perfect character in harmonious proportion. He is lovely everywhere, and from every point of view. But never more so than when we view him in conjugal union with his church. Then love gives a ravishing flush of glory to his loveliness. **Grace is poured into thy lips.** Beauty and eloquence make a man majestic when they are united. They both dwell in perfection in the all fair, all eloquent Lord Jesus. Whoever in personal communion with the Well-beloved has listened to his voice will feel that *never man spake like this man.* Well did the bride say of him, *His lips are like lilies dropping sweet-smelling myrrh.* Oftentimes a sentence from his lips has turned our own midnight into morning, our winter into spring.

Therefore God hath blessed thee for ever. Christ is blessed, blessed of God, **blessed for ever.** This is to us one great reason for his beauty, and the source of the gracious words which proceed out of his lips. The rare endowments of the man Christ Jesus are given him of the Father, that by them his people may be blessed with all spiritual blessings in union with himself. The Father has blessed the Mediator as a reward for all his gracious labours. Right well does he deserve the recompense. Whom God blesses we should bless, and the more so because all his blessedness is communicated to us.

Thy throne, O God, is for ever and ever: the sceptre of thy kingdom is a right sceptre. *Psalm 45:6.*

Thy throne, O God, is for ever and ever. To whom can this be spoken but our Lord? The Psalmist cannot restrain his adoration. His

72

enlightened eye sees in the royal Husband of the church, **God,** God to be adored, God reigning, God reigning **for ever and ever.** Blessed sight! Blind are the eyes that cannot see God in Christ Jesus! We never appreciate the tender condescension of our King in becoming one flesh with his church, and placing her at his right hand, until we have fully rejoiced in his essential glory and deity. What a mercy for us that our Saviour is God, for who but a God could execute the work of salvation? What a glad thing it is that he reigns on a **throne** which will never pass away, for we need both sovereign grace and eternal love to secure our happiness. Could Jesus cease to reign we should cease to be blessed, and were he not God, and therefore eternal, this must be the case. No throne can endure for ever, but that on which God himself sitteth.

The sceptre of thy kingdom is a right sceptre. He is the lawful monarch of all things that be. His rule is founded in right. Its law is right. Its result is right. Our King is no usurper and no oppressor. Even when he shall break his enemies with a rod of iron, he will do no man wrong. His vengeance and his grace are both in conformity with justice. Hence we trust him without suspicion. He cannot err. No affliction is too severe, for he sends it. No judgment too harsh, for he ordains it. O blessed hands of Jesus! The reigning power is safe with you. All the just rejoice in the government of the King who reigns in righteousness.

So shall the king greatly desire thy beauty: for he is thy Lord; and worship thou him. *Psalm 45:11.*

So shall the king greatly desire thy beauty. Whole-hearted love is the duty and bliss of the marriage state in every case, but especially so in this lofty, mystic marriage. The church must forsake all others and cleave to Jesus only, or she will not please him nor enjoy the full manifestation of his love. What less can he ask, what less may she dare propose than to be wholly his? Jesus sees a **beauty** in his church, a beauty which he delights in most when it is not marred by worldliness. He has always been most near and precious to his saints when they have cheerfully taken up his cross and followed him without the camp. His Spirit is grieved when they mingle themselves among the people and learn their ways. No great and lasting revival of religion can be granted us till the professed lovers of Jesus prove their affection by coming out from an ungodly world, being separated, and touching not the unclean thing.

For he is thy Lord; and worship thou him. He has royal rights still; his condescending grace does not lessen but rather enforce his authority. Our Saviour is also our Ruler. The husband is the head of the wife. The love he bears her does not lessen but strengthen her obligation to obey. The church must reverence Jesus, and bow before him in prostrate adoration. His tender union with her gives her liberty, but not licence. It frees her from all other burdens, but places his easy yoke upon her neck. Who would wish it to be otherwise? The service of God is heaven in heaven, and perfectly carried out it is heaven upon earth. Bear with us, and work by thy Spirit in us till thy will is done by us on earth as it is in heaven.

I will make thy name to be remembered in all generations: therefore shall the people praise thee for ever and ever. *Psalm 45:17.*

I will make thy name to be remembered in all generations. Jehovah by the prophet's mouth promises to the Prince of Peace eternal fame as well as a continuous progeny. His **name** is his fame, his character, his person. These are dear to his people now—they never can forget them; and it shall be so as long as men exist. Names renowned in one generation have been unknown to the next era. But the laurels of Jesus shall ever be fresh, his renown ever new. God will see to this. His providence and his grace shall make it so. The fame of Messiah is not left to human guardianship. The Eternal guarantees it, and his promise never fails. All down the ages the memories of Gethsemane and Calvary shall glow with unextinguishable light. Nor shall the lapse of time, the smoke of error, or the malice of hell be able to dim the glory of the Redeemer's fame.

Therefore shall the people praise thee for ever and ever. They shall confess thee to be what thou art, and shall render to thee in perpetuity the homage due. **Praise** is due from every heart to him who loved us, and redeemed us by his blood. This praise will never be fully paid, but will be ever a standing and growing debt. His daily benefits enlarge our obligations. Let them increase the number of our songs. Age to age reveals more of his love. Let every year swell the volume of the music of earth and heaven. Let thunders of song roll up in full diapason to the throne of him that liveth, and was dead, and is alive for evermore, and hath the keys of hell and of death.

PSALM 46

God is our refuge and strength, a very present help in trouble. *Psalm 46:1.*

God is our refuge and strength. Not our armies, or our fortresses. Israel's boast is in Jehovah, the only living and true God. Others

74

vaunt their impregnable castles, placed on inaccessible rocks and secured with gates of iron. But **God** is a far better **refuge** from distress than all these. And when the time comes to carry the war into the enemy's territories, the Lord stands his people in better stead than all the valour of legions or the boasted strength of chariot and horse. Soldiers of the cross, remember this, and count yourselves safe, and make yourselves strong in God. Forget not the personal possessive word **our**. Make sure each one of your portion in God, that you may say, 'He is *my* refuge and strength.' Neither forget the fact that God is our refuge just now, in the immediate present, as truly as when David penned the word. God alone is our all in all. All other refuges are refuges of lies, all other strength is weakness, for power belongeth unto God. But as God is all-sufficient, our defence and might are equal to all emergencies.

A very present help in trouble, or *in distresses he has so been found,* he has been tried and proved by his people. He never withdraws himself from his afflicted. He is their **help,** truly, effectually, constantly. He is **present** or near them, close at their side and ready for their succour. This is emphasised by the word **very** in our version. He is more present than friend or relative can be, yea, more nearly present than even the trouble itself.

God is in the midst of her; she shall not be moved: God shall help her, and that right early. *Psalm 46:5.*

God is in the midst of her. His help is therefore sure and near. Is the city besieged? Then he is himself besieged within her, and we may be certain that he will break forth upon his adversaries. How near is the Lord to the distresses of his saints, since he sojourns in their midst! Let us take heed that we do not grieve him. Let us have such respect to him as Moses had when he felt the sand of Horeb's desert to be holy, and put off his shoes from off his feet when the Lord spake from the burning bush. **She shall not be moved.** How can she **be moved** unless her enemies move her Lord also? His presence renders all hope of capturing and demolishing the city utterly ridiculous. The Lord is in the vessel, and she cannot, therefore, be wrecked.

God shall help her. Within her he will furnish rich supplies. Outside her walls he will lay her foes in heaps, like the armies of Sennacherib when the angel went forth and smote them. **And that right early.** As soon as the first ray of light proclaims the coming day, at the turning of the morning God's right arm shall be outstretched for his people. The Lord is up betimes. We are slow to meet him. But he is never tardy in helping us. Impatience complains of divine delays. But in very deed the Lord is not slack concerning his promise. Man's haste is often folly. But God's apparent delays are ever wise, and, when rightly viewed, are no delays at all.

Be still, and know that I am God: I will be exalted among the heathen, I will be exalted in the earth. The Lord of hosts is with us; the God of Jacob is our refuge. *Psalm 46:10–11.*

Be still, and know that I am God. Hold off your hands, ye enemies! Sit down and wait in patience, ye believers! Acknowledge that Jehovah is God, ye who feel the terrors of his wrath! Adore him, and him only, ye who partake in the protections of his grace! Since none can worthily proclaim his nature, let 'expressive silence muse his praise'. The boasts of the ungodly and the timorous forebodings of the saints should certainly be hushed by a sight of what the Lord has done in past ages. **I will be exalted among the heathen.** They forget God. They worship idols. But Jehovah will yet be honoured by them. Let no man's heart fail him; the solemn declarations of this verse must be fulfilled. **I will be exalted in the earth,** among all people, whatever may have been their wickedness or their degradation. Either by terror or love God will subdue all hearts to himself. The whole earth shall yet reflect the light of his majesty. All the more because of the sin, and obstinacy, and pride of man shall God be glorified when grace reigns unto eternal life in all corners of the world.

The Lord of hosts is with us; the God of Jacob is our refuge. It is a truth of which no believer wearies, a fact too often forgotten, a precious privilege which cannot be too often considered. Reader, is the Lord on thy side? Is Emmanuel, God with us, thy Redeemer? Is there a covenant between thee and God as between God and Jacob? If so, thrice happy art thou. Show thy joy in holy song, and in times of trouble play the man by still making music for thy God.

PSALM 47

O clap your hands, all ye people; shout unto God with the voice of triumph. *Psalm 47:1.*

O clap your hands. The most natural and most enthusiastic tokens of exultation are to be used in view of the victories of the Lord, and his universal reign. Our joy in God may be demonstrative, and yet he will not censure it. **All ye people.** The joy is to extend to all nations. Israel may lead the van, but all the Gentiles are to follow in the march of triumph. They have an equal share in that Kingdom where there is neither Greek nor Jew, but Christ is all and in all. Even now if they did but know it, it is the best hope of all nations that Jehovah ruleth over them. If they cannot all speak the same tongue, the symbolic language of the **hands** they can all use. All people will be ruled by the Lord in the latter days, and will exult in that rule. Were they wise, they would submit to it now, and rejoice to do so. Yea, they would clap their hands in rapture at the thought.

Shout. Let your voices keep tune with your hands. **Unto God.** Let him have all the honours of the day. Let them be loud, joyous, universal, and undivided. **With the voice of triumph.** With gladsome sounds, consonant with such splendid victories, so great a King, so excellent a rule, and such gladsome subjects. Many are human languages, and yet the nations may triumph as with one voice. Faith's view of God's government is full of transport. The prospect of the universal reign of the Prince of Peace is enough to make the tongue of the dumb sing. What will the reality be?

He shall choose our inheritance for us, the excellency of Jacob whom he loved. *Psalm 47:4.*

While as yet we see not all things put under him, we are glad to put ourselves and our fortunes at his disposal. **He shall choose our inheritance for us.** We feel his reign to be so gracious that we even now ask to be in the fullest degree the subjects of it. We submit our will, our choice, our desire, wholly to him. Our heritage here and hereafter we leave to him. Let him do with us as seemeth him good.

The excellency of Jacob whom he loved. He gave his ancient people their portion. He will give us ours, and we ask nothing better. This is the most spiritual and real manner of clapping our hands because of his sovereignty, namely, to leave all our affairs in *his* hands, for then *our* hands are empty of all care for self, and free to be used in his honour. He was the boast and glory of Israel, he is and shall be ours. He loved his people, and became their greatest glory. He loves us, and he shall be our exceeding joy. As for the latter days, we ask nothing better than to stand in our appointed lot, for if we have but a portion in our Lord Jesus, it is enough for our largest desires. Our beauty, our boast, our best treasure, lies in having such a God to trust in, such a God to love us.

The princes of the people are gathered together, even the people of the God of Abraham: for the shields of the earth belong unto God: he is greatly exalted. *Psalm 47:9.*

The princes of the people are gathered together. The prophetic eye of the Psalmist sees the willing subjects of the great King assembled to celebrate his glory. Not only the poor and the men of low estate are there, but nobles bow their willing necks to his sway. *All kings shall bow down before him.* No people shall be unrepresented. How august will be the parliament where the Lord Jesus shall open the court, and princes shall rise up to do him honour! **Even the people of the God of Abraham.** That same God, who was known only to here and there a patriarch like the father of the faithful, shall be adored by a seed as many as the stars of heaven. The covenant promise shall be fulfilled. *In thee and in thy seed shall all the nations of the earth be blessed. Shiloh shall come and to him shall the gathering of the people be.*

For the shields of the earth belong unto God. The insignia of pomp, the emblems of rank, the weapons of war—all must pay loyal homage to the King of all. Right honourables must honour Jesus, and majesties must own him to be far more majestic. Those who are earth's protectors, **the shields** of the commonwealth, derive their might from him, and are his. All principalities and powers must be subject unto Jehovah and his Christ, for **he is greatly exalted.** In nature, in power, in character, in glory, there is none to compare with him. Oh, glorious vision of a coming era! Make haste, ye wheels of time! Meanwhile, ye saints, *Be ye steadfast, unmovable, always abounding in the work of the Lord, forasmuch as ye know that your labour is not in vain in the Lord.*

PSALM 48

Great is the Lord, and greatly to be praised in the city of our God, in the mountain of his holiness. *Psalm 48:1.*

Great is the Lord. He is *great* in the deliverance of his people, *great* in their esteem who are delivered, and *great* in the hearts of those enemies whom he scatters by their own fears. There is none great in the church but the Lord. Jesus is *the great Shepherd,* he is *a Saviour, and a great one,* our *great God and Saviour,* our *great High Priest.* His Father has divided him *a portion with the great,* and his *name shall be great* unto the ends of the earth. **And greatly to be praised.** According to his nature should his worship be. It cannot be too constant, too laudatory, too earnest, too reverential, too sublime. There is none like the Lord, and there should be no praises like his praises.

In the city of our God. He is great there, and should be greatly praised there. If all the world beside renounced Jehovah's worship, the chosen people in his favoured city should continue to adore him, for in their midst and on their behalf his glorious power has been so manifestly revealed. In the church the Lord is to be extolled though all the nations rage against him. Jerusalem was the peculiar abode of the God of Israel, the seat of the theocratic government, and the centre of prescribed worship. Even thus is the church the place of divine manifestation. **In the mountain of his holiness,** where his holy temple, his holy priests, and his holy sacrifices might continually be seen. Zion was a mount, and as it was the most renowned part of the city, it is mentioned as a synonym for the city itself. The church of God is a mount for elevation and for conspicuousness, and it should be adorned with holiness. Only by holy men can the Lord be fittingly praised, and they should be incessantly occupied with his worship.

Beautiful for situation, the joy of the whole earth, is mount Zion, on the sides of the north, the city of the great King. *Psalm 48:2.*

Beautiful for situation. Jerusalem was so naturally. She was styled the Queen of the East. The church is so spiritually, being placed near God's heart, within the mountains of his power, upon the hills of his faithfulness, in the centre of providential operations. The elevation of the church is her beauty. The more she is above the world, the fairer she is. **The joy of the whole earth is mount Zion.** Jerusalem was the world's star. Whatever light lingered on earth was borrowed from the oracles preserved by Israel. An ardent Israelite would esteem the holy city as the eye of the nations, the most precious pearl of all lands. Certainly the church of God, though despised of men, is the true joy and hope of the world.

On the sides of the north, the city of the great King. Either meaning that Jerusalem was in the northern extremity of Judah, or it may denote that part of the city which lay to the north of Mount Zion. It was the glory of Jerusalem to be God's city, the place of his regal dwelling, and it is the joy of the church that God is in her midst. The great God is the great King of the church, and for her sake he rules all the nations. The people among whom the Lord deigns to dwell are privileged above all others. The lines have fallen unto them in pleasant places, and they have a goodly heritage.

This God is our God for ever and ever: he will be our guide even unto death. *Psalm 48:14.*

This God is our God for ever and ever. A good reason for preserving a record of all that he has wrought. Israel will not change her God so as to wish to forget, nor will the Lord change so as to make the past mere history. He will be the covenant God of his people world without end. There is no other God, we wish for no other, we would have no other even if other there were. There are some who are so ready to comfort the wicked, that for the sake of ending their punishment they weaken the force of language, and make **for ever and ever** mean but a time. Nevertheless, despite their interpretations, we exult in the hope of an eternity of bliss, and to us *everlasting* and *for ever and ever* mean what they say.

He will be our guide even unto death. Throughout life, and to our dying couch, he will graciously conduct us, and even after death he will lead us to the living fountains of waters. We look to him for resurrection and eternal life. This consolation is clearly derivable from what has gone before. Hitherto our foes have been scattered, and our bulwarks have defied attack, for God has been in our midst, therefore all possible assaults in the future shall be equally futile. Farewell, fear. Come hither, gratitude and faith, and sing right joyously.

PSALM 49

Wherefore should I fear in the days of evil, when the iniquity of my heels shall compass me about? *Psalm 49:5.*

Wherefore should I fear in the days of evil? The man of God looks calmly forward to dark times when those evils which have dogged his heels shall gain a temporary advantage over him. Iniquitous men, here called in the abstract **iniquity,** lie in wait for the righteous, as serpents that aim at the heels of travellers. **The iniquity of our heels** is that evil which aims to trip us up or impede us. It was an old prophecy that the serpent should wound the heel of the woman's seed, and the enemy of our souls is diligent to fulfil that premonition. In some dreary part of our road it may be that evil will wax stronger and bolder, and gaining upon us will openly assail us. Those who followed at our heels like a pack of wolves, may perhaps overtake us, and **compass us about.**

What then? Shall we yield to cowardice? Shall we be a prey to their teeth? God forbid. Nay, we will not even fear, for what are these foes? What indeed, but mortal men who shall perish and pass away. There can be no real ground of alarm to the faithful. Their enemies are too insignificant to be worthy of one thrill of fear. Doth not the Lord say to us, I, *even I, am he that comforteth thee: who art thou, that thou shouldest be afraid of a man that shall die, and of the son of man which shall be made as grass?*

They that trust in their wealth, and boast themselves in the multitude of their riches; none of them can by any means redeem his brother, nor give to God a ransom for him. *Psalm 49:6–7.*

What if the good man's foes be among the great ones of the earth? He need not fear them. **They that trust in their wealth.** Poor fools, to be content with such a rotten confidence. When we set our rock in contrast with theirs, it would be folly to be afraid of them. Even though they are loud in their brags, we can afford to smile. What if they glory **and boast themselves in the multitude of their riches?** While we glory in our God we are not dismayed by their proud threatenings. Great strength, position, and estate, make wicked men very lofty in their own esteem, and tyrannical towards others; but the heir of heaven sees the small value of riches, and the helplessness of their owners in the hour of death.

None of them can by any means redeem his brother. With all their riches, the whole of them put together could not rescue a comrade from the chill grasp of death. They boast of what they will do with us. Let them see to themselves. Let them weigh their gold in the scales of death, and see how much they can buy therewith from the worm and the grave. The poor are their equals in this respect. Let them love their friend ever so dearly, they cannot **give to God a ransom for him.** A king's ransom would be of no avail. O ye boasters, think not to terrify us with your worthless wealth, go ye and intimidate death before ye threaten men in whom is immortality and life.

Be not thou afraid when one is made rich, when the glory of his house is increased; for when he dieth he shall carry nothing away: his glory shall not descend after him. *Psalm 49:16–17.*

The Psalmist becomes a preacher, and gives admonitory lessons which he has himself gathered from experience. **Be thou not afraid when one is made rich.** Let it not give thee any concern to see the godless prosper. Raise no questions as to divine justice. Suffer no foreboding to cloud thy mind. Temporal prosperity is too small a matter to be worth fretting about. Let the dogs have their bones, and the swine their draff. **When the glory of his house is increased.** Though the sinner and his family are in great esteem, and stand exceedingly high, never mind. All things will be righted in due time. Only those whose judgment is worthless will esteem men the more because their lands are broader. Those who are highly estimated for such unreasonable reasons will find their level ere long, when truth and righteousness come to the fore.

For when he dieth he shall carry nothing away. He has but a leasehold of his acres, and death ends his tenure. Through the river of death man must pass naked. Not a rag of all his raiment, not a coin of all his treasure, not a jot of all his honour, can the dying worldling carry with him. Why then fret ourselves about so fleeting a prosperity? **His glory shall not descend after him.** As he goes down, down, down for ever, none of his honours or possessions will follow him. Patents of nobility are invalid in the sepulchre. His worship, his honour, his lordship, and his grace, will alike find their titles ridiculous in the tomb. Hell knows no aristocracy.

PSALM 50

Gather my saints together unto me: those that have made a covenant with me by sacrifice. *Psalm 50:5.*

Gather my saints together unto me. Go, ye swift-winged messengers, and separate the precious from the vile. Gather out the wheat of the heavenly garner. Let the long-scattered but elect people, known by my separating grace to be my sanctified ones, be now assembled in one place. All are not **saints** who seem to be so—a severance must be made. Therefore let all who profess to be saints be gathered before my throne of judgment. Let them hear the word which will search and try the whole, that the false may be convicted and the true revealed.

Those that have made a covenant with me by sacrifice. This is the grand test, and yet some have dared to imitate it. The **covenant** was ratified by the slaying of victims, the cutting and dividing of offerings. This the righteous have done by accepting with true faith the great propitiatory **sacrifice,** and this the pretenders have done in merely outward form. Let them be gathered before the throne for trial, and testing, and as many as have really ratified the covenant by faith in the Lord Jesus shall be attested before all worlds as the objects of distinguishing grace while formalists shall learn that outward sacrifices are all in vain. Oh, solemn assize, how does my soul bow in awe at the prospect thereof!

Offer unto God thanksgiving; and pay thy vows unto the most High. *Psalm 50:14.*

Offer unto God thanksgiving. No longer look at your sacrifices as in themselves gifts pleasing to me, but present them as the tributes of your gratitude. It is then that I will accept them, but not while your souls have no love and no thankfulness to offer me. The sacrifices, as considered in themselves, are contemned. But the internal emotions of love consequent upon a remembrance of divine goodness, are commended as the substance, meaning, and soul of sacrifice. Even when the legal ceremonials were not abolished, this was true. When they came to an end, this truth was more than ever made manifest. Not for want of bullocks on the altar was Israel blamed, but for want of thankful adoration before the Lord. She excelled in the visible. But in the inward grace, which is the one thing needful, she sadly failed. Too many in these days are in the same condemnation.

And pay thy vows unto the most High. Let the sacrifice be really presented to the God who seeth the heart, **pay** to him the love you promised, the service you covenanted to render, the loyalty of heart you have vowed to maintain. O for grace to do this! O that we may be graciously enabled to love God, and live up to our profession! To be, indeed, the servants of the Lord, the lovers of Jesus, this is our main concern. What avails our baptism, to what end our gatherings at the Lord's table, to what purpose our solemn assemblies, if we have not the fear of the Lord, and vital godliness reigning within our bosoms?

Call upon me in the day of trouble: I will deliver thee, and thou shalt glorify me. *Psalm 50:15.*

Call upon me in the day of trouble. Herein is faith manifested, herein is love proved: for in the hour of peril we fly to those we love. It seems a small thing to pray to God when we are distressed, yet is it a more acceptable worship than the mere heartless presentation of bullocks and he-goats. This is a voice from the throne, and how full of mercy it is! It is very tempestuous round about Jehovah, and yet what soft drops of mercy's rain fall from the bosom of the storm! Who would not suffer such sacrifice? Troubled one, haste to present it now! Who shall say that Old Testament saints did not know the gospel? Its very spirit and essence breathe like frankincense all around this holy Psalm.

I will deliver thee. The reality of thy sacrifice of prayer shall be seen in its answer. Whether the smoke of burning bulls be sweet to me or no, certainly thy humble prayer shall be, and I will prove it so by my gracious reply to thy supplication. This promise is very large, and may refer both to temporal and eternal deliverances. Faith can turn it every way, like the sword of the cherubim. **And thou shalt glorify me.** Thy prayer will honour me, and thy grateful perception of my answering mercy will also glorify me. The goats and bullocks would prove a failure, but the true sacrifice never could. The calves of the stall might be a vain oblation, but not the calves of sincere lips.

Wash me throughly from mine iniquity, and cleanse me from my sin. *Psalm 51:2.*

Wash me throughly. It is not enough to blot out the sin. His person is defiled, and he fain would be purified. He would have God himself cleanse him, for none but he could do it effectually. The washing must be thorough. It must be repeated, therefore he cries, *Multiply to wash me.* The dye is in itself immovable, and I, the sinner, have lain long in it, till the crimson is ingrained. But, Lord, wash, and wash, and wash again, till the last stain is gone, and not a trace of my defilement is left. The hypocrite is content if his garments be washed. But the true suppliant cries, wash *me.* **Wash me throughly from mine iniquity.** It is viewed as one great pollution, polluting the entire nature, and as all his own; as if nothing were so much his own as his sin. The one sin against Bathsheba served to show David the whole mountain of his **iniquity,** of which that foul deed was but one falling stone.

And **cleanse me from my sin.** This is a more general expression; as if the Psalmist said, Lord, if washing will not do, try some other process; if water avails not, let fire, let anything be tried, so that I may but be purified. Rid me of my sin by some means, by any means, by every means, only do purify me completely, and leave no guilt upon my soul. It is not the punishment he cries out against, but the **sin.** The thief loves the plunder, though he fears the prison. Not so David. He is sick of sin as sin. His loudest outcries are against the evil of his transgression, and not against the painful consequences of it. When we deal seriously with our sin, God will deal gently with us. When we hate what the Lord hates, he will soon make an end of it, to our joy and peace.

Behold, thou desirest truth in the inward parts: and in the hidden part thou shalt make me to know wisdom. *Psalm 51:6.*

Behold. Here is the great matter of consideration. God desires not merely outward virtue, but inward purity, and the penitent's sense of sin is greatly deepened as with astonishment he discovers this truth, and how far he is from satisfying the divine demand. **Thou desirest truth in the inward parts.** Reality, sincerity, true holiness, heart-fidelity, these are the demands of God. He cares not for the pretence of purity. He looks to the mind, heart and soul. Always has the Holy One of Israel estimated men by their inner nature, and not by their outward professions. To him the inward is as visible as the outward, and he rightly judges that the essential character of an action lies in the motive of him who works it.

And in the hidden part thou shalt make me to know wisdom. The penitent feels that God is teaching him truth concerning his nature, which he had not before perceived. The love of the heart, the mystery of its fall, and the way of its purification—this hidden **wisdom** we must all attain. It is a great blessing to be able to believe that the Lord will make us to know it. No one can teach our innermost nature but the Lord, but he can instruct us to profit. The Holy Spirit can write the law on our heart, and that is the sum of practical wisdom. He can put the fear of the Lord within, and that is the beginning of wisdom. He can reveal Christ in us, and he is essential wisdom. Such poor, foolish, disarranged souls as ours, shall yet be ordered aright, and truth and wisdom shall reign within us.

Create in me a clean heart, O God; and renew a right spirit within me. *Psalm 51:10.*

Create. What! Has sin so destroyed us, that the Creator must be called in again? What ruin then doth evil work among mankind! **Create in me.** I, in outward fabric, still exist. But I am empty, desert, void. Come, then, and let thy power be seen in a new creation within my old fallen self. Thou didst make a man in the world at first. Lord, make a new man in me! **A clean heart.** In the seventh verse he asked to be **clean;** now he seeks a **heart** suitable to that cleanliness. But he does not say, Make my *old* heart clean. He is too experienced in the hopelessness of the old nature. He would have the old man buried as a dead thing, and a new creation brought in to fill its place. None but God can create either a new heart or a new earth. Salvation is a marvellous display of supreme power. The work *in* us as much as that *for* us is wholly of Omnipotence. The affections must be rectified first, or all our nature will go amiss. The heart is the rudder of the soul, and till the Lord take it in hand we steer in a false and foul way. O Lord, thou who didst once make me, be pleased to new-make me, and in my most secret parts renew me.

Renew a right spirit within me. It was there once, Lord. Put it there again. The law on my heart has become like an inscription hard to read. New write it, gracious Maker. Remove the evil as I have entreated thee. But, O replace it with good, lest into my swept, empty, and garnished heart, from which the devil has gone out for awhile, seven other spirits more wicked than the first should enter and dwell. The two sentences make a complete prayer. **Create** what is not there at all; **renew** that which is there, but in a sadly feeble state.

85

Deliver me from bloodguiltiness, O God, thou God of my salvation: and my tongue shall sing aloud of thy righteousness. *Psalm 51:14.*

Deliver me from bloodguiltiness. Honest penitents do not fetch a compass and confess their sins in an elegant periphrasis. They come to the point, call a spade a spade, and make a clean breast of all. What other course is rational in dealing with the Omniscient? **O God, thou God of my salvation.** He had not ventured to come so near before. It had been **O God** up till now. But here he cries **Thou God of my salvation.** Faith grows by the exercise of prayer. He confesses sin more plainly in this verse than before, and yet he deals with God more confidently. Growing upward and downward at the same time are perfectly consistent. None but the King can remit the death penalty. It is therefore a joy to faith that God is King, and that he is the author and finisher of our salvation.

And my tongue shall sing aloud of thy righteousness. One would rather have expected him to say, I will sing of thy mercy. But David can see the divine way of justification, that **righteousness** of God which Paul afterwards spoke of by which the ungodly are justified, and he vows to **sing,** yea, and to sing lustily of that righteous way of mercy. A great sinner pardoned makes a great singer. Sin has a loud voice, and so should our thankfulness have. We shall not sing our own praises if we be saved, but our theme will be *the Lord our righteousness,* in whose merits we stand righteously accepted.

The sacrifices of God are a broken spirit: a broken and a contrite heart, O God, thou wilt not despise. *Psalm 51:17.*

The sacrifices of God are a broken spirit. All **sacrifices** are presented to thee in one, by the man whose broken heart presents the Saviour's merit to thee. When the heart mourns for sin, thou art better pleased than when the bullock bleeds beneath the axe. **A broken spirit** is an expression implying deep sorrow, embittering the very life. It carries in it the idea of all but killing anguish in that region which is so vital as to be the very source of life. So excellent is a spirit humbled and mourning for sin, that it is not only a sacrifice, but it has a plurality of excellencies, and is pre-eminently God's **sacrifices.**

A broken and a contrite heart, O God, thou wilt not despise. A heart crushed is a fragrant heart. Men contemn those who are contemptible in their eyes. But the Lord seeth not as man seeth. He despises what men esteem, and values that which they despise. Never yet has God spurned a lowly, weeping penitent. Never will he, while God is love, and while Jesus is called the man who receiveth sinners. Bullocks and rams he desires not, but contrite hearts he seeks after. Yea, but one of them is better to him than all the varied offerings of the old Jewish sanctuary.

The righteous also shall see, and fear, and shall laugh at him: Lo, this is the man that made not God his strength; but trusted in the abundance of his riches, and strengthened himself in his wickedness. *Psalm 52:6–7.*

The righteous—the object of the tyrant's hatred—shall outlive his enmity, and **also shall see,** before his own face, the end of the ungodly oppressor. God permits Mordecai to see Haman hanging on the gallows. David had brought to him the tokens of Saul's death on Gilboa. **And fear.** Holy awe shall sober the mind of the good man. He shall reverently adore the God of providence. **And shall laugh at him.** If not with righteous joy, yet with solemn contempt. Schemes so far-reaching all baffled, plans so deep, so politic, all thwarted. Mephistopheles outwitted, the old serpent taken in his own subtlety. This is a goodly theme for that deep-seated laughter which is more akin to solemnity than merriment.

Lo. Look here, and read the epitaph of a mighty man, who lorded it proudly during his little hour, and set his heel upon the necks of the Lord's chosen. **This is the man that made not God his strength.** Behold the man! The great vainglorious man. He found a fortress, but not in God. He gloried in his might, but not in the Almighty. Where is he now? How has it fared with him in the hour of his need? Behold his ruin, and be instructed. **But trusted in the abundance of his riches, and strengthened himself in his wickedness.** The substance he had gathered, and the mischiefs he had wrought, were his boast and glory. Wealth and wickedness are dreadful companions; when combined they make a monster. When the devil is master of money bags, he is a devil indeed. Beelzebub and Mammon together heat the furnace seven times hotter for the child of God. But in the end they shall work out their own destruction. Wherever we see today a man great in sin and substance, we shall do well to anticipate his end, and view this verse as the divine *in memoriam*.

I will praise thee for ever, because thou hast done it: and I will wait on thy name; for it is good before thy saints. *Psalm 52:9.*

I will praise thee for ever. Like thy mercy shall my thankfulness be.

While others boast in their riches, I will boast in my God. When their glorying is silenced for ever in the tomb, my song shall continue to proclaim the lovingkindness of Jehovah. **Because thou hast done it.** Thou hast vindicated the righteous, and punished the wicked. God's memorable acts of providence, both to saints and sinners, deserve and must have our gratitude. David views his prayers as already answered, the promises of God as already fulfilled, and therefore at once lifts up the sacred Psalm.

And I will wait on thy name. God shall still be the Psalmist's hope. He will not in future look elsewhere. He whose **name** has been so gloriously made known in truth and righteousness, is justly chosen as our expectation for years to come. **For it is good before thy saints.** **Before,** or *among*, the **saints** David intended to wait, feeling it to be good both for him and them to look to the Lord alone, and wait for the manifestation of his character in due season. Men must not too much fluster us. Our strength is to sit still. Let the mighty ones boast, we will wait on the Lord. If their haste brings them present honour, our patience will have its turn by-and-by, and bring us the honour which excelleth.

PSALM 53

God looked down from heaven upon the children of men, to see if there were any that did understand, that did seek God. Every one of them is gone back: they are altogether become filthy; there is none that doeth good, no, not one. *Psalm 53:2–3.*

God looked down from heaven upon the children of men. He did so in ages past, and he has continued his steadfast gaze from his all-surveying observatory. **To see if there were any that did understand, that did seek God.** The Lord did not look for great grace, but only for sincerity and right desire, but these he found not. He saw all hearts in all men, and all motions of all hearts, but he saw neither a clear head nor a clean heart among them all. Where God's eyes see no favourable sign we may rest assured there is none. **Every one of them is gone back.** The whole mass of manhood, all of it, is gone back. The life of unregenerate manhood is in direct defiance of the law of God, not merely apart from it but opposed to it.

They are altogether become filthy. The whole lump is soured with an evil leaven, fouled with an all-pervading pollution, made rank with general putrefaction. Thus, in God's sight, our atheistic nature is not the pardonable thing that we think it to be. Errors as to God are not the mild diseases which some account them, they are abominable evils.

Fair is the world to blind eyes, but to the all-seeing Jehovah it is otherwise. **There is none that doeth good, no, not one.** How could there be, when the whole mass was leavened with so evil a leaven? The fallen race of man, left to its own energy, has not produced a single lover of God or doer of holiness, nor will it ever do so. Grace must interpose or not one specimen of humanity will be found to follow after the good and true. This is God's verdict after looking down upon the race. Who shall gainsay it?

There were they in great fear, where no fear was: for God hath scattered the bones of him that encampeth against thee: thou hast put them to shame, because God hath despised them. *Psalm 53:5.*

There were they in great fear, where no fear was. David sees the end of the ungodly and the ultimate triumph of the spiritual seed. The rebellious march in fury against the gracious. But suddenly they are seized with a causeless panic. The once fearless boasters tremble like the leaves of the aspen, frightened at their own shadows. In this sentence and this verse, this Psalm differs much from the fourteenth. It is evidently expressive of a higher state of realisation in the poet, he emphasises the truth by stronger expressions. Without cause the wicked are alarmed. He who denies God is at bottom a coward. In his infidelity he is like the boy in the churchyard who whistles to keep up his courage.

For God hath scattered the bones of him that encampeth against thee. When the wicked see the destruction of their fellows they may well quail. Mighty were the hosts which besieged Zion. But they were defeated. Their unburied carcasses proved the prowess of the God whose being they dared to deny. **Thou hast put them to shame, because God hath despised them.** God's people may well look with derision upon their enemies since they are the objects of divine contempt. They scoff at us. But we may, with far greater reason, laugh *them* to scorn, because the Lord our God considers them as less than nothing and vanity.

PSALM 54

Save me, O God, by thy name, and judge me by thy strength. Hear my prayer, O God; give ear to the words of my mouth. *Psalm 54:1-2.*

Save me, O God. Thou art my Saviour. All around me are my foes and their eager helpers. No shelter is permitted me. Every land rejects me and denies me rest. But thou, O God, wilt give me refuge, and deliver me from all my enemies. **By thy name,** by thy great and glorious nature. Employ all thine attributes for me. Let every one of the perfections which are blended in thy divine name work for me. Is not thine honour pledged for my defence? **And judge me by thy strength.** Render justice to me, for none else will or can. Thou canst give me efficient justice, and right my wrongs by thine omnipotence. We dare not appeal to God in a bad cause. But when we know that we can fearlessly carry our cause before his justice, we may well commit it to his power.

Hear my prayer, O God. This has ever been the defence of saints. As long as God hath an open ear we cannot be shut up in trouble. All other weapons may be useless, but all-prayer is evermore available. No enemy can spike this gun. **Give ear to the words of my mouth.** Vocal prayer helps the supplicant. We keep our minds more fully awake when we can use our tongues as well as our hearts. But what is prayer if God hear not? It is all one whether we babble nonsense or plead arguments if our God grant us not a hearing. When his case had become dangerous, David could not afford to pray out of mere custom. He must succeed in his pleadings, or become the prey of his adversary.

Behold, God is mine helper: the Lord is with them that uphold my soul. *Psalm 54:4.*

Behold, God is mine helper. David saw enemies everywhere. Now to his joy as he looks upon the band of his defenders he sees one whose aid is better than all the help of men. He is overwhelmed with joy at recognising his divine champion, and cries, **Behold.** Is not this a theme for pious exultation in all time, that the great God protects us, his own people? What matters the number or violence of our foes when *he* uplifts the shield of his omnipotence to guard us, and the sword of his power to aid us? Little care we for the defiance of the foe while we have the defence of God.

The Lord is with them that uphold my soul. The reigning Lord is in the camp of my defenders. Here was a greater champion than any of the valiant men who chose David for their captain. The Psalmist was very confident. He felt so thoroughly that his heart was on the Lord's side that he was sure God was on *his* side. He asked in the first verse for deliverance, and here he returns thanks for upholding. While we are seeking one mercy which we have not, we must not be unmindful of another which we have. It is a great mercy to have some friends left us, but a greater mercy still to see the Lord among them. Like so many cyphers our friends stand for nothing till the Lord sets himself as a great unit in the front of them.

I will freely sacrifice unto thee: I will praise thy name, O Lord; for it is good. *Psalm 54: 6.*

I will freely sacrifice unto thee. Spontaneously will I bring my free-will offerings. So certain is he of deliverance that he offers a vow by anticipation. His overflowing gratitude would load the altars of God with victims cheerfully presented. The more we receive, the more we ought to render. The spontaneousness of our gift is a great element in their acceptance. The Lord loveth a cheerful giver.

I will praise thy name, O Lord. As if no amount of sacrifice could express his joyful feelings, he resolves to be much in vocal thanksgiving. The name which he invoked in prayer (verse 1), he will now magnify in **praise.** Note how roundly he brings it out: *O Jehovah.* This is ever the grand **name** of the revealed God of Israel, a name which awakens the sublimest sentiments, and so nourishes the most acceptable praise. None can praise the Lord so well as those who have tried and proved the preciousness of his name in seasons of adversity. The Psalmist adds **for it is good.** Surely we may read this with a double nominative: God's *name* is **good,** and so is his *praise.* It is of great use to our souls to be much in praise. We are never so holy or so happy as when our adoration of God abounds. Praise is good in itself, good to us, and good to all around us.

Give ear to my prayer, O God; and hide not thyself from my supplication. Attend unto me, and hear me: I mourn in my complaint, and make a noise. *Psalm 55: 1–2.*

Give ear to my prayer, O God. How universally and constantly the saints resort to **prayer** in seasons of distress! From the Great Elder Brother down to the very least of the divine family, all of them delight in prayer. They run as naturally to the mercy-seat in time of trouble as chicks to the hen in the hour of danger. But note well that it is never the bare act of prayer which satisfies the godly. They crave an audience with heaven, and an answer from the throne. Nothing less will content them. **Hide not thyself from my supplication.** When a man saw his neighbour in distress, and deliberately passed him by, he was said to hide himself from him. The Psalmist begs that the Lord would not so treat him. In that dread hour when Jesus bore our sins upon the tree, his Father did hide himself. This was the most dreadful part of all the Son of David's agony.

Attend unto me, and hear me. This is the third time he prays the same prayer. He is in deep and bitter earnest. If his God do not hear, he feels that all is over with him. **I mourn in my complaint, and make a noise.** He sets loose his sorrows, pours them out in such language as suggests itself at the time, whether it be coherent or not. Our rambling thoughts when we are distracted with grief we may bring before him, and that too in utterances rather to be called **a noise** than language. He will attend so carefully that he will understand us. He will often fulfil desires which we ourselves could not have expressed in intelligible words. *Groanings that cannot be uttered* are often prayers which cannot be refused.

And I said, Oh that I had wings like a dove! for then would I fly away, and be at rest. Lo, then would I wander far off, and remain in the wilderness. *Psalm 55:6–7.*

And I said, Oh that I had wings like a dove! for then would I fly away and be at rest. His love of peace made him sigh for an escape from the scene of strife. We are all too apt to utter this vain desire, for vain it is. No wings of doves or eagles could bear us away from the sorrows of a trembling heart. Inward grief knows nothing of place. Moreover, it is cowardly to shun the battle which God would have us fight. We had better face the danger, for we have no armour for our backs. He had need of a swifter conveyance than doves' pinions who would outfly slander. He may be **at rest** who does not fly, but commends his case to his God. Even the dove of old found no rest till she returned to her ark. We amid all our sorrow may find rest in Jesus. We need not depart. All will be well if we trust in him. **Lo, then would I wander far off.** Yet when David was **far off,** he sighed to be once more near Jerusalem. Thus, in our ill estate we ever think the past to be better than the present. We shall be called to fly far enough away, and perchance we shall be loth to go. We need not indulge vain notions of premature escape from earth. **And remain in the wilderness.** He found it none such a dear abode when there, yet resolves now to make it his permanent abode. Our Lord, while free from all idle wishes, found much strength in solitude. It is better practically to use retirement than pathetically to sigh for it. Yet it is natural, when all men do us wrong, to wish to separate ourselves from their society. Nature, however, must yield to grace. We must endure the contradiction of sinners against ourselves, and not be weary and faint in our minds.

Evening, and morning, and at noon, will I pray, and cry aloud: and he shall hear my voice. *Psalm 55:17.*

Evening, and morning, and at noon, will I pray. Often, but none too often. Seasons of great need call for frequent seasons of devotion. The three periods chosen are most fitting. To begin, continue, and end the day with God is supreme wisdom. Where time has naturally set up a boundary, there let us set up an altar-stone. The Psalmist means that he will always pray. He will run a line of prayer right along the day and track the sun with his petitions. Day and night he saw his enemies busy (verse 10), and therefore he would meet their activity by continuous prayer.

And cry aloud. He would give a tongue to his complaint. He would be very earnest in his pleas with heaven. Some cry aloud who never say a word. It is the bell of the heart that rings loudest in heaven. Some read it, *I will muse and murmur.* Deep heart-thoughts should be attended with inarticulate, but vehement, utterances of grief. Blessed be God, moaning is translatable in heaven. A father's heart reads a child's heart. **And he shall hear my voice.** He is confident that he will prevail. He makes no question that he would be heard. He speaks as if already he were answered. When our window is opened towards heaven, the windows of heaven are open to us. Have but a pleading heart, and God will have a plenteous hand.

PSALM 56

What time I am afraid, I will trust in thee. *Psalm 56:3.*

What time I am afraid. David was no braggart. He does not claim never to be **afraid.** David's intelligence deprived him of the stupid heedlessness of ignorance. He saw the imminence of his peril, and was afraid. We are men, and therefore liable to overthrow. We are feeble, and therefore unable to prevent it. We are sinful men, and therefore deserving it. For all these reasons we are afraid. But the condition of the Psalmist's mind was complex. He feared—but that fear did not fill the whole area of his mind, for he adds **I will trust in thee.** It is possible, then, for *fear* and *faith* to occupy the mind at the same moment. We are strange beings, and our experience in the divine life is stranger still. We are often in a twilight, where light and darkness are both present, and it is hard to tell which predominates.

It is a blessed fear which drives us to **trust.** Unregenerate fear drives from God. Gracious fear drives to him. If I fear man, I have only to trust God, and I have the best antidote. To trust when there is no cause for fear, is but the name of faith. But to be reliant upon God when occasions for alarm are abundant and pressing, is the conquering faith of God's elect. Though the verse is in the form of a resolve, it became a fact in David's life. Let us make it so in ours. Whether the fear arise from without or within, from past, present, or future, from temporals, or spirituals, from men or devils, let us maintain faith, and we shall soon recover courage.

They gather themselves together, they hide themselves, they mark my steps, when they wait for my soul. *Psalm 56:6.*

They gather themselves together. Firebrands burn the fiercer for being pushed **together.** They are afraid to meet the good man till their numbers place terrible odds against him. Come out, ye cowards, man by man and fight the old hero! No, ye wait till ye are assembled like thieves in bands, and even then ye waylay the man. There is nothing brave about you. **They hide themselves.** In ambuscade they wait their opportunity. Men of malice are men of cowardice. He who dares not meet his man on the king's highway, writes himself down a villain. Constantly are the reputations of good men assailed with deep-laid schemes, and diabolical plots, in which the anonymous enemies stab in the dark.

They mark my steps, as hunters mark the trail of their game, and so track them. Malicious men are frequently very sharp-sighted to detect the failings, or supposed failings, of the righteous. Spies are not all in the pay of earthly governments. Some of them will have wages to take in red-hot coin from one who himself is more subtle than all the beasts of the field. **When they wait for my soul.** Nothing less than his life would content them. Only his present and eternal ruin could altogether glut them. The good man is no fool. He sees that he has enemies, and that they are many and crafty. He sees also his own danger. Then he shows his wisdom by spreading the whole case before the Lord, and putting himself under divine protection.

Thou tellest my wanderings: put thou my tears into thy bottle: are they not in thy book? *Psalm 56:8.*

Thou tellest my wanderings. Every step which the fugitive had taken when pursued by his enemies was not only observed but thought worthy of counting and recording. We perhaps are so confused after a long course of trouble, that we hardly know where we have or where we have not been. But the omniscient and considerate Father of our spirits remembers all in detail. He has counted them over as men count their gold, for even the trial of our faith is precious in his sight.

Put thou my tears into thy bottle. His sorrows were so many that there would need a great wine-skin to hold them all. There is no allusion to the little complimentary lachrymatories of fashionable and fanciful Romans. It is a robuster metaphor by far. Such floods of **tears** had David wept that a leathern **bottle** would scarce hold them. He trusts that the Lord will be so considerate of his tears as to store them up as men do the juice of the vine, and he hopes that the place of storage will be a special one—*thy* **bottle**, not *any* bottle. **Are they not in thy book?** Yes, they are recorded there. But let not only the record but the grief itself be present to thee. Look on my griefs as real things, for these move the heart more than a mere account, however exact. How condescending is the Lord! How exact his knowledge of us! How generous his estimations! How tender his regard!

In God will I praise his word: in the Lord will I praise his word. *Psalm 56:10.*

In God will I praise his word. Now comes the thanksgiving. He is a wretch who, having obtained help, forgets to return a grateful acknowledgement. The least we can do is to praise him from whom we receive such distinguished favours. Does David here mean *by God's grace* **will I praise** him? If so, he shows us that all our emotions towards God must be **in God,** produced by him and presented as such. Or does he mean that which in God is most the object of my praise is **his word,** and the faithfulness with which he keeps it? If so, we see how attached our hearts should be to the sure word of promise, and especially to *him* who is the Word incarnate.

The Lord is to be praised under every aspect, and in all his attributes and acts. But certain mercies more peculiarly draw out our admiration towards special portions of the great whole. That praise which is never special in its direction cannot be very thoughtful, and it is to be feared cannot be very acceptable. **In the Lord will I praise his word.** He delights to dwell on his praise, and therefore repeats his song. The change by which he brings in the glorious name of Jehovah is doubtless meant to indicate that under every aspect he delights in his God and in his word.

Thy vows are upon me, O God: I will render praises unto thee. For thou hast delivered my soul from death: wilt not thou deliver my feet from falling, that I may walk before God in the light of the living? *Psalm 56:12–13.*

Thy vows are upon me, O God. Vows made in his trouble he does not lightly forget. Nor should we. We voluntarily made them. Let us cheerfully keep them. All professed Christians are men under vows, but especially those who in hours of dire distress have re-dedicated themselves unto the Lord. **I will render praises unto thee.** With heart, and voice, and gift, we should cheerfully extol the God of our salvation. The practice of making solemn vows in times of trouble is to be commended—when it is followed by the far less common custom of fulfilling them after the trouble is over.

For thou hast delivered my soul from death. His enemies were defeated in their attempts upon his life, and therefore he vowed to devote his life to God. **Wilt not thou deliver my feet from falling?** One mercy is a plea for another. Indeed it may happen that the second is the necessary complement of the first. It little avails that we live, if we are made to fall in character by the thrusts of our enemies. As like not be, as live to be bereft of honour, and fallen prostrate before my enemies. **That I may walk before God in the light of the living,** enjoying the favour and presence of God, and finding the joy and brightness of life therein. Walking at liberty, in holy service, in sacred communion, in constant progress in holiness, enjoying the smile of heaven—this I seek after. Here is the loftiest reach of a good man's ambition: to dwell with God, to **walk** in righteousness before him, to rejoice in his presence, and **in the light** and glory which it yields.

PSALM 57

Be merciful unto me, O God, be merciful unto me: for my soul trusteth in thee: yea, in the shadow of thy wings will I make my refuge, until these calamities be overpast. *Psalm 57:1.*

Be merciful unto me, O God, be merciful unto me. Urgent need suggests the repetition of the cry, for thus intense urgency of desire is expressed. If he gives twice who gives quickly, so he who would receive quickly must ask twice. For mercy the Psalmist pleads at first, and he feels he cannot improve upon his plea, and therefore returns to it. God is the God of mercy, and the Father of mercies, it is most fit therefore that in distress we should seek mercy from him in whom it dwells. **For my soul trusteth in thee.** Faith urges her suit right well. How can the Lord be unmerciful to a trustful soul? Our faith does not deserve mercy, but it always wins it from the sovereign grace of God when it is sincere, as in this case where *the soul* of the man believed. *With the heart man believeth unto righteousness.*

Yea, in the shadow of thy wings will I make my refuge. Not in the cave alone would he hide, but in the cleft of the Rock of ages. As the little birds find ample shelter beneath the parental wing, even so would the fugitive place himself beneath the secure protection of the divine power. The emblem is delightfully familiar and suggestive. May we all experimentally know its meaning. When we cannot see the sunshine of God's face, it is blessed to cower down beneath **the shadow of his wings. Until these calamities be overpast.** Evil will pass away, and the eternal wings will abide over us till then. Blessed be God, our calamities are matters of time, but our safety is a matter of eternity. When we are under the divine shadow, the passing over of trouble cannot harm us. The hawk flies across the sky, but this is no evil to the chicks when they are safely nestling beneath the hen.

I will cry unto God most high; unto God that performeth all things for me. *Psalm 57:2.*

I will cry. He is quite safe. Yet he prays, for faith is never dumb. We pray because we believe. We exercise by faith the spirit of adoption whereby we cry. He says not, I do cry, or I have cried, but **I will cry.** Indeed, this resolution may stand with all of us until we pass through the gates of pearl. While we are here below we shall still have need to cry. **Unto God most high**—Prayers are for God only. The greatness and sublimity of his person and character suggest and encourage prayer. However high our enemies, our heavenly Friend is higher, for he is **most high,** and he can readily send from the height of his power the succour which we need.

Unto God that performeth all things for me. He has cogent reason for praying, for he sees God is in action. The believer waits and God works. The Lord has undertaken for us, and he will not draw back. He will go through with his covenant engagements. Our translators have very properly inserted the words **all things,** for there is a blank in the Hebrew, as if it were a *carte blanche,* and you might write therein that the Lord would finish anything and everything which he has begun. Whatsoever the Lord takes in hand he will accomplish. Hence past mercies are guarantees for the future, and admirable reasons for continuing to cry unto him.

He shall send from heaven, and save me from the reproach of him that would swallow me up. God shall send forth his mercy and his truth. *Psalm 57:3.*

He shall send from heaven. If there be no fit instruments on earth, **heaven** shall yield up its legions of angels for the succour of the saints. We may in times of great straits expect mercies of a remarkable kind.

97

Like the Israelites in the wilderness, we shall have our bread hot from heaven, new every morning. And for the overthrow of our enemies, God shall open his celestial batteries and put them to utter confusion. Wherever the battle is more fierce than ordinary, there shall come succours from headquarters, for the Commander-in-chief sees all.

And save me from the reproach of him that would swallow me up. He will be in time, not only to rescue his servants from being swallowed up, but even from being reproached. Not only shall they escape the flames, but not even the smell of fire shall pass upon them. O dog of hell, I am not only *delivered from* thy bite, but even from thy bark. Our foes shall not have the power to sneer at us. Their cruel jests and taunting gibes shall be ended by the message from heaven, which shall for ever save us. **God shall send forth his mercy and his truth.** He asked for **mercy,** and **truth** came with it. Thus evermore doth God give us more than we ask or think. His attributes, like angels on the wing, are ever ready to come to the rescue of his chosen.

PSALM 58

Do ye indeed speak righteousness, O congregation? do ye judge uprightly, O ye sons of men? *Psalm 58:1.*

Do ye indeed speak righteousness, O congregation? The enemies of David were a numerous and united band. Because they so unanimously condemned the persecuted one, they were apt to take it for granted that their verdict was a right one. *What everybody says must be true* is a lying proverb based upon the presumption which comes of large combinations. Have we not all agreed to hound the man to the death, and who dare hint that so many great ones can be mistaken? Yet the persecuted one lays the axe at the root by requiring his judges to answer the question whether or not they were acting according to justice. It were well if men would sometimes pause, and candidly consider this. Some of those who surrounded Saul were rather passive than active persecutors. They held their tongues when the object of royal hate was slandered. In the original this first sentence appears to be addressed to them, and they are asked to justify their silence. Silence gives consent. He who refrains from defending the right is himself an accomplice in the wrong.

Do ye judge uprightly, O ye sons of men? Ye too are only men, though dressed in a little brief authority. Your office for men, and your relation to men, both bind you to rectitude. But have ye remembered this? Have ye not put aside all truth when ye have condemned the godly, and united in seeking the overthrow of the innocent? Yet in doing this be not too sure of success, for ye are only the **sons of men,** and there is a God who can and will reverse your verdicts.

PSALM 59

The God of my mercy shall prevent me: God shall let me see my desire upon mine enemies. *Psalm 59:10.*

The God of my mercy shall prevent me. God who is the giver and fountain of all the undeserved goodness I have received, will go before me and lead my way as I march onward. He will meet me in my time of need. Not alone shall I have to confront my foes. He whose goodness I have long tried and proved will gently clear my way, and be my faithful protector. How frequently have we met with preventing mercy—the supply prepared before the need occurred, the refuge built before the danger arose. Far ahead into the future the foreseeing grace of heaven has projected itself, and forestalled every difficulty.

God shall let me see my desire upon mine enemies. Observe that the words **my desire** are not in the original. From the Hebrew we are taught that David expected to see his enemies without fear. God will enable his servant to gaze steadily upon the foe without trepidation. He shall be calm, and self-possessed, in the hour of peril. Ere long he shall look down on the same foes discomfited, overthrown, destroyed. When Jehovah leads the way victory follows at his heels. See God, and you need not fear to see your enemies. Thus the hunted David, besieged in his own house by traitors, looks only to God, and exults over his enemies.

I will sing of thy power; yea, I will sing aloud of thy mercy in the morning: for thou hast been my defence and refuge in the day of my trouble. *Psalm 59:16.*

I will sing of thy power. The wicked howl, but I sing and will sing. Their power is weakness, but thine is omnipotence. I see them vanquished and thy power victorious, and for ever and ever will I sing of thee. **Yea, I will sing aloud of thy mercy in the morning.** When those lovers of darkness find their game is up, and their midnight howlings die away, then will I lift up my voice on high and praise the lovingkindness of God without fear of being disturbed. What a blessed **morning** will soon break for the righteous, and what a song will be theirs! Sons of the morning, ye may sigh tonight, but joy will come on the wings of the rising sun. Tune your harps even now, for the signal to commence the eternal music will soon be given. The morning cometh and your sun shall go no more down for ever.

For thou hast been my defence. The song is for God alone, and it is one which none can sing but those who have experienced the loving-kindness of their God. Looking back upon a past all full of mercy, the saints will bless the Lord with their whole hearts, and triumph in him as the high place of their security. **And refuge in the day of my trouble.** The greater our present trials the louder will our future songs be, and the more intense our joyful gratitude. Had we no **day of trouble,** where were our season of retrospective thanksgiving?

PSALM 60

Thou hast showed thy people hard things: thou hast made us to drink the wine of astonishment. *Psalm 60:3.*

Thou hast showed thy people hard things. Hardships had been heaped upon them, and the Psalmist traces these rigorous providences to their fountainhead. Nothing had happened by chance, but all had come by divine design and with a purpose. Yet for all that things had gone hard with Israel. The Psalmist claims that they were still the Lord's own people, though in the first verse he had said, *Thou hast cast us off.* The language of complaint is usually confused, and faith in time of trouble ere long contradicts the desponding statements of the flesh.

Thou hast made us to drink the wine of astonishment. Our afflictions have made us like men drunken with some potent and bitter wine. We are in amazement, confusion, delirium. Our steps reel, and we stagger as those about to fall. The great physician gives his patients potent potions to purge out their abounding and deep-seated diseases. Astonishing evils bring with them astonishing results. The grapes of the vineyard of sin produce a wine which fills the most hardened with anguish when justice compels them to quaff the cup. There is a fire-water of anguish of soul which even to the righteous makes a cup of trembling, which causes them to be exceeding sorrowful almost unto death. When grief becomes so habitual as to be our drink, and to take the place of our joys, becoming our only wine, then are we in an evil case indeed.

Thou hast given a banner to them that fear thee, that it may be displayed because of the truth. *Psalm 60:4.*

Thou hast given a banner to them that fear thee. Their afflictions had led them to exhibit holy fear, and then being fitted for the Lord's favour, he gave them **a banner,** which would be both a rallying point for their hosts, a proof that he had sent them to fight, and a guarantee of victory. The bravest men are usually entrusted with the ensign, and it is certain that those who most fear God have less fear of man than any others. The Lord has given us the standard of the gospel. Let us live to uphold it, and if needful die to defend it. Our right to contend for God, and our reason for expecting success, are found in the fact that the faith has been once committed to the saints, and that by the Lord himself.

That it may be displayed because of the truth. Banners are for the breeze, the sun, the battle. Israel might well come forth boldly, for a sacred standard was borne aloft before them. To publish the gospel is a sacred duty. To be ashamed of it a deadly sin. The truth of God was involved in the triumph of David's armies. He had promised them victory. So in the proclamation of the gospel we need feel no hesitancy, for as surely as God is true he will give success to his own word. For the truth's sake, and because the true God is on our side, let us in these modern days of warfare emulate the warriors of Israel, and unfurl our banners to the breeze with confident joy. Dark signs of present or coming ill must not dishearten us. If the Lord had meant to destroy us, he would not have given us the gospel. The very fact that he has revealed himself in Christ Jesus involves the certainty of victory.

That thy beloved may be delivered; save with thy right hand, and hear me. *Psalm 60:5.*

That thy beloved may be delivered. David was the Lord's **beloved.** His name signifies *dear,* or *beloved,* and there was in Israel a remnant according to the election of grace, who were the beloved of the Lord. For their sakes the Lord wrought great marvels, and he had an eye to them in all his mighty acts. God's beloved are the inner seed, for whose sake he preserves the entire nation, which acts as a husk to the vital part. This is the main design of providence, **That thy beloved may be delivered.** If it were not for their sakes, he would neither give a banner nor send victory to it.

Save with thy right hand, and hear me. Save at once, before the prayer is over. The case is desperate unless there be immediate salvation. Tarry not, O Lord, till I have done pleading. Save first and hear afterwards. Urgent distress puts men upon pressing and bold petitions such as this. We may by faith ask for and expect that our extremity will be God's opportunity. Special and memorable deliverances will be wrought out when dire calamities appear to be imminent. Here is one suppliant for many, even as in the case of our Lord's intercession for his saints. He, the Lord's David, pleads for the rest of the beloved, beloved and accepted in him the Chief Beloved. He seeks salvation as though it were for himself. But his eye is ever upon all those who are one with him in the Father's love. When divine interposition is necessary for the rescue of the elect it must occur, for the first and greatest necessity of providence is the honour of God, and the salvation of his chosen. This is the centre of the immutable decree, the inmost thought of the unchangeable Jehovah.

Through God we shall do valiantly: for he it is that shall tread down our enemies. *Psalm 60:12.*

Through God we shall do valiantly. From God all power proceeds, and all we do well is done by divine operation. But still we, as soldiers of the great king, are to fight, and to fight valiantly too. Divine working is not an argument for human inaction. Rather is it the best excitement for courageous effort. Helped in the past, we shall also be helped in the future, and being assured of this we resolve to play the man.

For he it is that shall tread down our enemies. From him shall the might proceed, to him shall the honour be given. Like straw on the thrashing-floor beneath the feet of the oxen shall we tread upon our abject foes, but it shall rather be *his* foot which presses them down than ours. *His* hand shall go out against them so as to put them down and keep them in subjection. In the case of Christians there is much encouragement for a resolve similar to that of the first clause. **We shall do valiantly.** We will not be ashamed of our colours, afraid of our foes, or fearful of our cause. The Lord is with us, omnipotence sustains us, and we will not hesitate, we dare not be cowards. O that our King, the true David, were come to claim the earth, for the kingdom is the Lord's, and he is the governor among the nations.

PSALM 61

Lead me to the rock that is higher than I. *Psalm 61:2.*

I see thee to be my refuge, sure and strong. But alas! I am confused, and cannot find thee. I am weak, and cannot climb thee. Thou art so steadfast, guide me. Thou art so high, uplift me. There is a mine of meaning in this brief prayer. Our experience leads us to understand this verse right well. The time was with us when we were in such amazement of soul by reason of sin, that although we knew the Lord Jesus to be a sure salvation for sinners, yet we could not come at him, by reason of our many doubts and forebodings. A Saviour would have been of no use to us if the Holy Spirit had not gently led us to him, and enabled us to rest upon him. To this day we often feel that we not only want a **rock,** but to be led to it. With this in view we treat very leniently the half-unbelieving prayers of awakened souls. In their bewildered state we cannot expect from them all at once a fully believing cry. A seeking soul should at once believe in Jesus. But it is legitimate for a man to ask to be led to Jesus. The Holy Spirit is able to effect such a leading. He can do it even though the heart be on the borders of despair.

How infinitely **higher** than we are is the salvation of God. We are low and grovelling, but it towers like some tall cliff far above us. This is its glory, and is our delight when we have once climbed into the rock, and claimed an interest in it. But while we are as yet trembling seekers, the glory and sublimity of salvation appal us. We feel that we are too unworthy even to be partakers of it. Hence we are led to cry for grace upon grace, and to see how dependent we are for everything, not only for the Saviour, but for the power to believe on him.

I will abide in thy tabernacle for ever: I will trust in the covert of thy wings. *Psalm 61:4.*

I will abide in thy tabernacle for ever. Let me once get back to thy courts, and nothing shall again expel me from them. Even now in my banishment my heart is there; and ever will I continue to worship thee in spirit wherever my lot may be cast. Perhaps by the word **tabernacle** is here meant the dwelling-place of God. If so, the sense is, *I will dwell with the Lord,* enjoying his sacred hospitality and sure protection. He who communes with God is always at home. The divine omnipresence surrounds such a one consciously. His faith sees all around him the palace of the King, in which he walks with exulting security and overflowing delight. Happy are the indoor servants who go not out from his presence. Hewers of wood and drawers of water in the tents of Jehovah are more to be envied than the princes who riot in the pavilions of kings. The best of all is that our residence with God is not for a limited period of time, but for ages. Yea, for ages, for time and for eternity. This is our highest and most heavenly privilege. **I will abide in thy tabernacle for ever.**

I will trust in the covert of thy wings. Often does our sweet singer use this figure. Far better is it to repeat one apt and instructive image, than for the sake of novelty to ransack creation for poor, strained metaphors. The chicks beneath the hen—how safe, how comfortable, how happy! How warm the parent's bosom! How soft the cherishing feathers! Divine condescension allows us to appropriate the picture to ourselves, and how blessedly instructive and consoling it is! O for more **trust**. It cannot be too implicit. Such a **covert** invites us to the most unbroken repose.

Thou, O God, hast heard my vows : thou hast given me the heritage of those that fear thy name. *Psalm 61:5.*

Thou, O God, hast heard my vows. **Vows** may rightly be joined with prayers when they are lawful, well considered, and truly for God's glory. It is great mercy on God's part to take any notice of the vows and promises of such faithless and deceitful creatures as we are. What we promise him is his due already, and yet he designs to accept our vows as if we were not so much his servants as his free suitors who could give or withhold at pleasure.

Thou hast given me the heritage of those that fear thy name. We are made heirs, joint-heirs with all the saints, partakers of the same portion. With this we ought to be delighted. If we suffer, it is the heritage of the saints. If we are persecuted, are in poverty, or in temptation all this is contained in the title-deeds of the **heritage** of the chosen. Those we are to sup with we may well be content to dine with. We have the same inheritance as the First-born himself. What better is conceivable? Saints are described as **those that fear** the **name** of God. They are reverent worshippers. They stand in awe of the Lord's authority. They are afraid of offending him. They feel their own nothingness in the sight of the Infinite One. To share with such men, to be treated by God with the same favour as he metes out to them, is matter for endless thanksgiving. All the privileges of all the saints are also the privilege of each one.

PSALM 62

Truly my soul waiteth upon God : from him cometh my salvation. *Psalm 62:1.*

Truly, or *verily,* or *only.* The last is probably the most prominent sense here. That faith alone is true which rests on God alone. That confidence which relies but partly on the Lord is vain confidence. **My soul waiteth upon God.** My inmost self draws near in reverent obedience to God. I am no hypocrite or mere posture maker. To *wait* upon God, and for God, is the habitual position of faith. To wait on him *truly* is sincerity. To wait on him *only* is spiritual chastity. The original is *only* *to God is my soul silence.* The presence of God alone could awe his heart into quietude, submission, rest, and acquiescence. But when that was felt, not a rebellious word or thought broke the peaceful silence. No eloquence in the world is half so full of meaning as the patient silence of a child of God. It is an eminent work of grace to bring down the will and subdue the affections. The whole mind lies before the Lord like the sea beneath the wind. It is ready to be moved by every breath of his mouth. Yet it is free from all inward and self-caused emotion, as also from all power to be moved by anything other than the divine will. We should be wax to the Lord, but adamant to every other force.

From him cometh my salvation. Faith can hear the footsteps of coming **salvation** because she has learned to be silent. Our salvation in no measure or degree comes to us from any inferior source. Let us, therefore, look alone to the true fountain, and avoid the detestable crime of ascribing to the creature what belongs alone to the Creator. If to wait on God be worship, to wait on the creature is idolatry.

He only is my rock and my salvation; he is my defence; I shall not be greatly moved. *Psalm 62:2.*

He only is my rock and my salvation. Sometimes a metaphor may be more full of meaning and more suggestive than literal speech. Hence the use of the figure of a *rock*, the very mention of which would awaken grateful memories in the Psalmist's mind. David had often lain concealed in rocky caverns, and here he compares his God to such a secure refuge. Indeed, he declares him to be his only real protection, all-sufficient in himself and never failing. At the same time, as if to show us that what he wrote was not mere poetic sentiment, but blessed reality, the literal word **salvation** follows the figurative expression. That our God is our refuge is no fiction. Nothing in the word is more a matter of fact.

He is my defence, my height, my lofty rampart, my high-fort. Here we have another and bolder image. The tried believer not only abides in God as in a cavernous rock. He dwells in him as a warrior in some bravely defiant tower or lordly castle. **I shall not be greatly moved.** His personal weakness might cause him to be somewhat moved. But his faith would come in to prevent any very great disturbance: not much would he be tossed about. **Moved,** but not *removed*. Moved like a ship at anchor which swings with the tide, but is not swept away by the tempest. When a man knows assuredly that the Lord is his salvation, he cannot be very much cast down. It would need more than all the devils in hell greatly to alarm a heart which knows God to be its salvation.

My soul, wait thou only upon God; for my expectation is from him. *Psalm 62:5.*

My soul, wait thou only upon God. When we have already practised a virtue, it is yet needful that we bind ourselves to a continuance in it. The soul is apt to be dragged away from its anchorage, or is readily tempted to add a second confidence to the one sole and sure ground of reliance. We must, therefore, stir ourselves up to maintain the holy position which we were at first able to assume. Be still silent, O my soul! Submit thyself completely, trust immovably, wait patiently. Let none of thy enemies' imaginings, consultings, flatteries, or maledictions cause thee to break the King's peace. Be like the sheep before her shearers, and like thy Lord, conquer by the passive resistance of victorious patience. Thou canst only achieve this as thou shalt be inwardly persuaded of God's presence, and as thou waitest solely and alone on him. Unmingled faith is undismayed. Faith with a single eye sees herself secure. But if her eye be darkened by two confidences, she is blind and useless.

For my expectation is from him. We expect from God because we believe in him. **Expectation** is the child of prayer and faith, and is owned of the Lord as an acceptable grace. We should desire nothing but what it would be right for God to give. Then our expectation would be all from God. Concerning truly good things we should not look to second causes, but to the Lord alone, and so again our expectation would be all from him. The vain expectations of worldly men come not. They promise, but there is no performance. Our expectations are on the way, and in due season will arrive to satisfy our hopes. Happy is the man who feels that all he has, all he wants, and all he expects are to be found in his God.

Trust in him at all times; ye people, pour out your heart before him: God is a refuge for us. *Psalm 62:8.*

Trust in him at all times. Faith is an abiding duty, a perpetual privilege. We should **trust** when we can see, as well as when we are utterly in the dark. Adversity is a fit season for faith. But prosperity is not less so. God **at all times** deserves our confidence. We at all times need to place our confidence in him. A day without trust in God is a day of wrath, even if it be a day of mirth. Lean ever, ye saints, on him, on whom the world leans. **Ye people, pour out your heart before him.** Ye to whom his love is revealed, reveal yourselves to him. His heart is set on you. Lay bare your hearts to him. Turn the vessel of your soul upside down in his secret presence, and let your inmost thoughts, desires, sorrows, and sins be poured out like water. Hide nothing from him, for you *can* hide nothing. To the Lord unburden your soul. Let him be your only father-confessor, for he only can absolve you when he has heard your confession.

To keep our griefs to ourselves is to hoard up wretchedness. The stream will swell and rage if you dam it up. Give it a clear course, and it leaps along and creates no alarm. Sympathy we need, and if we unload our hearts at Jesus' feet, we shall obtain a sympathy as practical as it is sincere, as consolatory as it is ennobling. **God is a refuge for us.** Whatever he may be to others, his own people have a peculiar heritage in him. **For us** he is undoubtedly **a refuge.** Here then is the best of reasons for resorting to him whenever sorrows weigh upon our bosoms. Prayer is peculiarly the duty of those to whom the Lord has specially revealed himself as their defence.

PSALM 63

Because thy lovingkindness is better than life, my lips shall praise thee. *Psalm 63:3.*

Because thy lovingkindness is better than life. Life is dear, but God's love is dearer. To dwell with God is **better than life** at its best: life at ease, in a palace, in health, in honour, in wealth, in pleasure. Yea, a thousand lives are not equal to the eternal life which abides in Jehovah's smile. In him we truly live, and move, and have our being. The withdrawal of the light of his countenance is as the shadow of death to us. Hence we cannot but long after the Lord's gracious appearing. Life is to many men a doubtful good. **Lovingkindness** is an unquestioned boon. Life is but transient; mercy is everlasting. Life is shared in by the lowest animals; but the lovingkindness of the Lord is the peculiar portion of the chosen.

My lips shall praise thee. Openly, so that thy glory shall be made known, I will tell of thy goodness. Even when our heart is rather desiring than enjoying, we should still continue to magnify the Most High, for his love is truly precious. We may not personally, for the time being, happen to be rejoicing in it. We ought not to make our praises of God to depend upon our own personal and present reception of benefits. This would be mere selfishness. Even publicans and sinners have a good word for those whose hands are enriching them with gifts. It is the true believer only who will bless the Lord when he takes away his gifts or hides his face.

I remember thee upon my bed, and meditate on thee in the night watches. *Psalm 63:6.*

I remember thee upon my bed. Lying awake, the good man betook himself to meditation, and then began to sing. He had a feast in the night, and a song in the night. He turned his bedchamber into an oratory. He consecrated his pillow. His praise anticipated the place of which it is written, *There is no night there.* Perhaps the wilderness helped to keep him awake. If so, all the ages are debtors to it for this delightful hymn. If day's cares tempt us to forget God, it is well that night's quiet should lead us to remember him. We see best in the dark if we there see God best.

And meditate on thee in the night watches. Keeping up sacred worship in my heart as the priests and Levites celebrated it in the sanctuary. Perhaps David had formerly united with those *who by night stand in the house of the Lord.* Now as he could not be with them in person, he remembers the hours as they pass, and unites with the choristers in spirit, blessing Jehovah as they did. It may be, moreover, that the king heard the voices of the sentries as they relieved guard, and each time he returned with renewed solemnity to his meditations upon his God. Night is congenial, in its silence and darkness, to a soul which would forget the world, and rise into a higher sphere. Absorption in the most hallowed of all themes makes watches, which else would be weary, glide away all too rapidly. It causes the lonely and hard couch to yield the most delightful repose—repose more restful than even sleep itself. We read of beds of ivory. But beds of piety are better far. Some revel in the night. But they are not a tithe so happy as those who meditate in God.

The king shall rejoice in God; every one that sweareth by him shall glory: but the mouth of them that speak lies shall be stopped. *Psalm 63:11.*

The king shall rejoice in God. Usurpers shall fade, but he shall flourish, and his prosperity shall be publicly acknowledged as the gift of God. The Lord's anointed shall not fail to offer his joyful thanksgiving. His well-established throne shall own the superior lordship of the King of kings. His rejoicing shall be alone in God. **Every one that sweareth by him shall glory.** His faithful followers shall have occasion for triumph. They shall never need to blush for the oath of their allegiance. Or, **sweareth by** *him* may signify adherence to *God,* and worship paid to him. The heathen swore by their gods, and the Israelites called Jehovah to witness to his asseveration. Those, therefore, who owned the Lord as their God should have reason to **glory** when he proved himself the defender of the king's righteous cause, and the destroyer of traitors.

But the mouth of them that speak lies shall be stopped. And the sooner the better. If shame will not do it, nor fear, nor reason, then let them **be stopped** with the sexton's shovel-full of earth. A liar is a human devil. He is the curse of men, and accursed of God, who has comprehensively said, *All liars shall have their part in the lake which burneth with fire and brimstone.* See the difference between the mouth that praises God, and the mouth that forges **lies**: the first shall never be stopped, but shall sing on for ever; the second shall be made speechless at the bar of God.

PSALM 64

Hear my voice, O God, in my prayer: preserve my life from fear of the enemy. Hide me from the secret counsel of the wicked; from the insurrection of the workers of iniquity. *Psalm 64:1–2.*

Hear my voice, O God, in my prayer. It often helps devotion if we are able to use the voice and speak audibly. But even mental prayer has a voice with God which he will **hear.** *Why criest thou unto me?* Prayers which are unheard on earth may be among the best heard in heaven. It is our duty to note how constantly David turns to **prayer.** It is his battleaxe and weapon of war. He uses it under every pressure, whether of inward sin or outward wrath, foreign invasion or domestic rebellion. We shall act wisely if we make prayer to God our first and best trusted resource in every hour of need. **Preserve my life from fear of the enemy.** From harm and dread of harm protect me. Or it may be read as an expression of his assurance that it would be so: *from fear of the foe thou wilt preserve me.* With all our sacrifices of prayer we should offer the salt of faith.

Hide me from the secret counsel of the wicked. From their hidden snares hide me. Circumvent their counsels. Let their secrets be met by thy secret providence, their counsels of malice by thy counsels of love. **From the insurrection of the workers of iniquity.** When their secret counsels break forth into clamorous tumults, be thou still my preserver. When they think evil, let thy divine thoughts defeat them. When they do evil, let thy powerful justice overthrow them. In both cases, let me be out of reach of their cruel hand, and even out of sight of their evil eye. It is a good thing to conquer malicious foes, but a better thing still to be screened from all conflict with them, by being hidden from the strife.

They encourage themselves in an evil matter: they commune of laying snares privily; they say, Who shall see them? *Psalm 64:5.*

They encourage themselves in an evil matter. Good men are frequently discouraged, and not unfrequently discourage one another. But the children of darkness are wise in their generation and keep their spirits up, and each one has a cheering word to say to his fellow villain. Anything by which they can strengthen each other's hands in their one common design they resort to. Their hearts are thoroughly in their black work. **They commune of laying snares privily.** Laying their heads together they count and recount their various devices, so as to come at some new and masterly device. They know the benefit of co-operation, and are not sparing in it. They pour their experience into one common fund. They teach each other fresh methods.

They say, Who shall see them? So sedulously do they mask their attacks, that they defy discovery. Their pitfalls are too well hidden, and themselves too carefully concealed to be found out. *So they think.* But they forget the all-seeing eye, and the all-discovering hand, which are ever hard by them. Great plots are usually laid bare. There is usually a breakdown somewhere or other. Among the conspirators themselves truth finds an ally, or the stones of the field cry out against them. Therefore, fear not, ye tremblers. The Lord is at your right hand, and ye shall not be hurt of the enemy.

PSALM 65

Praise waiteth for thee, O God, in Sion: and unto thee shall the vow be performed. *Psalm 65:1.*

Praise waiteth for thee, O God, in Sion. The praises of the saints wait for a signal from the divine Lord, and when he shows his face they burst forth at once. **Praise waiteth** like a servant or courtier in the royal halls—gratitude is humble and obedient. Praise attends the Lord's pleasure, and continues to bless him, whether he shows tokens of present favour or no. She is not soon wearied, but all through the night she sings on in sure hope that the morning cometh. The passage may be rendered **praise** *is silent* **for thee.** It is calm, peaceful, and ready to adore thee in quietness. Or, it may mean, *in solemn silence we worship thee*, because our praise cannot be uttered. Accept, therefore, our silence as praise. Certainly, when the soul is most filled with adoring awe, she is least content with her own expressions, and feels most deeply how inadequate are all mortal songs to proclaim the divine goodness. Yet, vocal music is not to be neglected, for this sacred hymn was meant to be sung. It is well, before singing, to have the soul placed in a waiting attitude, and to be humbly conscious that our best praise is but silence compared with Jehovah's glory.

And unto thee shall the vow be performed. We are not to forget our vows, or to redeem them to be seen of men—*unto God* alone must they be performed, with a single eye to his acceptance. Vows of service, of donation, of praise, or whatever they may be, are no trifles. In the day of grateful praise they should, without fail, be fulfilled to the utmost of our power.

O thou that hearest prayer, unto thee shall all flesh come. *Psalm 65:2.*

O thou that hearest prayer. This is thy name, thy nature, thy glory. God not only has heard, but is now hearing prayer, and always must hear prayer, since he is an immutable being, and never changes in his attributes. What a delightful title for the God and Father of our Lord Jesus Christ! Every right and sincere prayer is as surely heard as it is offered. Here the Psalmist brings in the personal pronoun **thou.** Notice how often *thou*, *thee*, and *thy*, occur in this hymn. David evidently believed in a personal God, and did not adore a mere idea or abstraction.

Unto thee shall all flesh come. This shall encourage men of all nations to become suppliants to the one and only God, who proves his Deity by answering those who seek his face. **Flesh** they are, and therefore weak. Frail and sinful, they need to pray. Thou art such a God as they need, for thou art touched with compassion, and dost condescend to hear the cries of poor flesh and blood. Many come to thee now in humble faith, and are filled with good. But more shall be drawn to thee by the attractiveness of thy love, and at length the whole earth shall bow at thy feet. To **come** to God is the life of true religion. We come weeping in conversion, hoping in supplication, rejoicing in praise, and delighting in service. False gods must in due time lose their deluded votaries, for man when enlightened will not be longer befooled. But each one who tries the true God is encouraged by his own success to persuade others also. So the kingdom of God comes to men, and men come to it.

Blessed is the man whom thou choosest, and causest to approach unto thee, that he may dwell in thy courts. *Psalm 65:4.*

Blessed is the man whom thou choosest, and causest to approach unto thee. First, we are chosen of God, according to the good pleasure of his will, and this alone is blessedness. Then, since we cannot and will not come to God of ourselves, he works graciously in us, and attracts us powerfully. He subdues our unwillingness, and removes our inability by the almighty workings of his transforming grace. This also is no slight blessedness. Furthermore, we, by his divine drawings, are made nigh by the blood of his Son, and brought near by his Spirit, into intimate fellowship. So we have access with boldness, and are no longer as those who are afar off by wicked works. Here also is unrivalled blessedness. To crown all, we do not come nigh in peril of dire destruction, as Nadab and Abihu did, but we approach as chosen and accepted ones, to become dwellers in the divine household. This is heaped-up blessedness, vast beyond conception.

But dwelling in the house we are treated as sons, for the servant abideth not in the house for ever, but the son abideth ever. Behold what manner of love and blessedness the Father has bestowed upon us that we may dwell in his house, and go no more out for ever. Happy men who dwell at home with God. May both writer and reader be such men. **That he may dwell in thy courts.** Acceptance leads to abiding. God does not make a temporary choice, or give and take. His gifts and calling are without repentance. He who is once admitted to God's courts shall inhabit them for ever.

PSALM 66

All the earth shall worship thee, and shall sing unto thee; they shall sing to thy name. *Psalm 66:4.*

All the earth shall worship thee, and shall sing unto thee. All men must even now prostrate themselves before thee. But a time will come when they shall do this cheerfully. To the worship of fear shall be added the singing of love. What a change shall have taken place when singing shall displace sighing, and music shall thrust out misery!

They shall sing to thy name. The nature and works of God will be the theme of earth's universal song. He himself shall be the object of the joyful adoration of our emancipated race. Acceptable worship not only praises God as the mysterious Lord. It is rendered fragrant by some measure of knowledge of his name or character. God would not be worshipped as an unknown God, nor have it said of his people, *Ye worship ye know not what.* May the knowledge of the Lord soon cover the earth, that so the universality of intelligent worship may be possible. Such a consummation was evidently expected by the writer of this Psalm. Indeed, throughout all Old Testament writings, there are intimations of the future general spread of the worship of God. It was an instance of wilful ignorance and bigotry when the Jews raged against the preaching of the gospel to the Gentiles. Perverted Judaism may be exclusive, but the religion of Moses, and David, and Isaiah was not so.

We went through fire and through water: but thou broughtest us out into a wealthy place. *Psalm 66:12.*

We went through fire and through water. Trials many and varied were endured by Israel in Egypt, and are still the portion of the saints. The fires of the brick-kilns and the waters of the Nile did their worst to destroy the chosen race. But Israel went through both ordeals unharmed, and ever thus the church of God has outlived, and will outlive, all the artifices and cruelties of man. Fire and water are pitiless and devouring, but a divine fiat stays their fury.

But thou broughtest us out into a wealthy place. A blessed issue to a mournful story. Canaan was indeed a broad and royal domain for the once enslaved tribes. God, who took them into Egypt, also brought them into the land which flowed with milk and honey. Egypt was in his purposes *en route* to Canaan. The way to heaven is *via* tribulation. How **wealthy** is the place of every believer, and how doubly does he feel it to be so in contrast with his former slavery! What songs shall suffice to set forth our joy and gratitude for such a glorious deliverance and such a bountiful heritage! More awaits us. The depth of our griefs bears no proportion to the height of our bliss. Instead of the net, liberty. Instead of a burden, a crown on our heads. **Fire** shall no more try us, for we shall stand in glory on the sea of glass mingled with fire. **Water** shall not harm us, for there shall be no more sea. O the splendour of this brilliant conclusion to a gloomy history! Glory be unto him who saw in the apparent evil the true way to the real good. With patience we will endure the present gloom, for the morning cometh. Over the hills faith sees the daybreak, in whose light we shall enter into the **wealthy place.**

Come and hear, all ye that fear God, and I will declare what he hath done for my soul. *Psalm 66:16.*

Come and hear. Before, they were bidden to **come and** *see.* Hearing is faith's seeing. Mercy comes to us by way of ear-gate. *Hear, and your soul shall live.* They saw how terrible God was, but they heard how gracious he was. **All ye that fear God.** These are a fit audience when a good man is about to relate his experience. It is well to select our hearers when inward soul matters are our theme. It is forbidden us to throw pearls before swine. It is wise to speak of personal spiritual matters where they can be understood.

And I will declare what he hath done for my soul. I will count and recount the mercies of God to me, to **my soul,** my best part, my most real self. Testimonies ought to be borne by all experienced

Christians, in order that the younger and feebler sort may be encouraged by the recital to put their trust in the Lord. To declare man's doings is needless. They are too trivial. Besides, there are trumpeters enough of man's trumpery deeds. But to **declare** the gracious acts of God is instructive, consoling, inspiriting, and beneficial in many respects. Let each man speak for himself, for a personal witness is the surest and most forcible. Second-hand experience lacks the flavour of first-hand interest. Let no mock modesty restrain the grateful believer from speaking of himself, or rather of God's dealings to himself, for it is justly due to God. Neither let him shun the individual use of the first person, which is most correct in detailing the Lord's ways of love. We must not be egotists, but we must be egotists when we bear witness for the Lord.

If I regard iniquity in my heart, the Lord will not hear me: But verily God hath heard me; he hath attended to the voice of my prayer. *Psalm 66:18-19.*

If I regard iniquity in my heart. If, having seen it to be there, I continue to gaze upon it without aversion; if I cherish it, have a side glance of love towards it, excuse it, and palliate it: **The Lord will not hear me.** How can he? Can I desire him to connive at my sin, and accept me while I wilfully cling to any evil way? Nothing hinders prayer like **iniquity** harboured in the breast. As with Cain, so with us: *sin lieth at the door*, and blocks the passage. If thou listen to the devil, God will not listen to thee. If thou refusest to hear God's commands, he will surely refuse to hear thy prayers. An imperfect petition God will hear for Christ's sake, but not one which is wilfully mis-written by a traitor's hand.

But verily God hath heard me. Sure sign this that the petitioner was no secret lover of sin. The answer to his prayer was a fresh assurance that his heart was sincere before the Lord. See how sure the Psalmist is that he has been heard. It is with him no hope, surmise, or fancy, but he seals it with a **verily.** Facts are blessed things when they reveal both God's heart as loving and our own heart as sincere. **He hath attended to the voice of my prayer.** He gave his mind to consider my cries, interpreted them, accepted them, and replied to them; and therein proved his grace and also my uprightness of heart. Love of sin is a plague spot, a condemning mark, a killing sign. But those prayers, which evidently live and prevail with God, most clearly arise from a heart which is free from dalliance with evil. Let the reader see to it, that his inmost soul be rid of all alliance with iniquity, all toleration of secret lust, or hidden wrong.

God be merciful unto us, and bless us. *Psalm 67:1.*

God be merciful unto us. The Psalmist begins at the beginning with a cry for *mercy*. Forgiveness of sin is always the first link in the chain of mercies experienced by us. Mercy is a foundation attribute in our salvation. The best saints and the worst sinners may unite in this petition. It is addressed to the God of mercy, by those who feel their need of mercy, and it implies the death of all legal hopes or claims of merit. Next, he begs for a blessing: **bless us**—a very comprehensive and far-reaching prayer. When we bless God we do but little, for *our* blessings are but words. But when God blesses he enriches us indeed, for his blessings are gifts and deeds. But his blessing alone is not all his people crave. They desire a personal consciousness of his favour, and pray for a smile from his face. These three petitions include all that we need here or hereafter.

This verse may be regarded as the prayer of Israel, and spiritually of the Christian church. The largest charity is shown in this Psalm, but it begins at home. The whole church, each church, and each little company, may rightly pray: **Bless** *us*. It would, however, be very wrong to let our charity end where it begins, as some do. Our love must make long marches. Our prayers must have a wide sweep. We must embrace the whole world in our intercessions.

O let the nations be glad and sing for joy: for thou shalt judge the people righteously, and govern the nations upon earth. *Psalm 67:4.*

O let the nations be glad and sing for joy, or, *they shall joy and triumph.* **Nations** never will be glad till they follow the leadership of the great Shepherd. They may shift their modes of government from monarchies to republics, and from republics to communes. But they will retain their wretchedness till they bow before the Lord of all. What a sweet word is that to **sing for joy!** Some sing for form, others for show, some as a duty, others as an amusement. But to sing from the heart, because overflowing joy must find a vent—this is to sing indeed. Whole nations will do this when Jesus reigns over them in the power of his grace. We have heard hundreds and even thousands sing in chorus. But what will it be to hear whole nations lifting up their voices, as the noise of many waters and like great thunders? When shall the age of song begin? When shall groans and murmurs be exchanged for holy hymns and joyful melodies?

For thou shalt judge the people righteously. Wrong on the part of governors is a fruitful source of national woe. But where the Lord rules, rectitude is supreme. He doeth ill to none. His laws are righteousness itself. He rights all wrongs and releases all who are oppressed. Justice on the throne is a fit cause for national exultation. **And govern the nations upon earth.** He will lead them as a shepherd his flock. Through his grace they shall willingly follow. Then will there be peace, plenty, and prosperity. It is great condescension on God's part to become the Shepherd of nations, and to govern them for their good. It is a fearful crime when a people who know the salvation of God, apostatise and say to the Lord, *Depart from us.*

Then shall the earth yield her increase; and God, even our own God, shall bless us. *Psalm 67:6.*

Then shall the earth yield her increase. Sin first laid a curse on the soil, and grace alone can remove it. We read that the Lord turneth *a fruitful land into barrenness* for the wickedness of them that dwell therein. Observation confirms the truth of the divine threatening. But even under the law it was promised that *the Lord God shall make thee plenteous in every work of thine hand, in the fruit of thy cattle, and in the fruit of thy land for good.* There is certainly an intimate relation between moral and physical evil, and between spiritual and physical good. The Hebrew is in the past tense. The prophet-bard, hearing the nations praise the Lord, speaks of the bounteous harvest as already given in consequence. On the supposition that all the people praise Jehovah, **the earth** has yielded **her increase.** The future in the English appears to be the clearest rendering of the Hebrew.

And God, even our own God, shall bless us. He will make earth's increase to be a real blessing. Men shall see in his gifts the hand of that same God whom Israel of old adored, and Israel, especially, shall rejoice in the blessing, and exult in her own God. We never love God aright till we know him to be ours, and the more we love him the more do we long to be fully assured that he is ours. What dearer name can we give to him than *mine own God.* The spouse in the song has no sweeter canticle than *my beloved is mine and I am his.* Every believing Jew must feel a holy joy at the thought that the nations shall all be blessed by Abraham's God. But every Gentile believer also rejoices that the whole world shall yet worship the God and Father of our Lord and Saviour Jesus Christ, who is our Father and our God.

PSALM 68

Let God arise, let his enemies be scattered : let them also that hate him flee before him. *Psalm 68:1.*

Let God arise. In some such words Moses spake when the cloud moved onward, and the ark was carried forward. The ark would have been a poor leader if the Lord had not been present with the symbol. Before we move, we should always desire to see the Lord lead the way. The words suppose the Lord to have been passive for awhile, suffering his enemies to rage, but restraining his power. Israel beseeches him to **arise,** as elsewhere to *awake, gird on his sword,* and other similar expressions. We, also, may thus importunately cry unto the Lord, that he would be pleased to make bare his arm, and plead his own cause. **Let his enemies be scattered.** Our glorious Captain of the vanguard clears the way readily, however many may seek to obstruct it. He has but to arise, and they flee. He has easily overthrown his foes in days of yore, and will do so all through the ages to come. Sin, death, and hell know the terror of his arm. Their ranks are broken at his approach. Our enemies are *his* enemies, and in this is our confidence of victory.

Let them also that hate him flee before him. To hate the infinitely good God is infamous, and the worst punishment is not too severe. Hatred of God is impotent. His proudest foes can do him no injury. Alarmed beyond measure, they shall **flee** before it comes to blows. Long before the army of Israel can come into the fray, the haters of God shall flee **before him** who is the champion of his chosen. He comes; he sees; he conquers. How fitting a prayer is this for the commencement of a revival! How it suggests the true mode of conducting one: the Lord leads the way; his people follow; the enemies flee.

A father of the fatherless, and a judge of the widows, is God in his holy habitation. *Psalm 68:5.*

A father of the fatherless, and a judge of the widows, is God in his holy habitation. In the wilderness the people were like an orphan nation, but God was more than a father to them. As the generation which came out of Egypt gradually died away, there were many widows and fatherless ones in the camp. But they suffered no want or wrong. The righteous laws and the just administrators whom God had appointed looked well to the interests of the needy. The tabernacle was the Palace of Justice; the ark was the seat of the great King. This was great cause for joy to Israel, that they were ruled by one who would not suffer the poor and needy to be oppressed.

To this day and for ever, God is, and will be, the peculiar guardian of the defenceless. He is the President of Orphanages, the Protector of Widows. He is so glorious that he rides on the heavens, but so compassionate that he remembers the poor of the earth. How zealously ought his church to cherish those who are here marked out as Jehovah's especial charge. Does he not here in effect say, *Feed my lambs?* Blessed duty, it shall be our privilege to make this one of our life's dearest objects. The reader is warned against misquoting this verse. It is generally altered into '*the husband* of the widow'. But Scripture had better be left as God gave it.

God setteth the solitary in families: he bringeth out those which are bound with chains: but the rebellious dwell in a dry land. *Psalm 68:6.*

God setteth the solitary in families. The people had been sundered and scattered over Egypt. Family ties had been disregarded, and affections crushed. But when the people escaped from Pharaoh they came together again, and all the fond associations of household life were restored. This was a great joy. **He bringeth out those which are bound with chains.** He who did this of old continues his gracious work. The solitary heart, convinced of sin and made to pine alone, is admitted into the family of the First-born. The fettered spirit is set free, and its prison broken down, when sin is forgiven. For all this, God is to be greatly extolled, for he hath done it, and magnified the glory of his grace.

But the rebellious dwell in a dry land. Israel did not find the desert dry, for the smitten rock gave forth its streams. But even in Canaan itself men were consumed with famine, because they cast off their allegiance to their covenant God. Even where God is revealed on the mercy-seat, some men persist in rebellion. Such need not wonder if they find no peace, no comfort, no joy, even where all these abound. Justice is the rule of the Lord's kingdom. Hence there is no provision for the unjust to indulge their evil lustings. A perfect earth, and even heaven itself, would be **a dry land** to those who can only drink of the waters of sin. Of the most soul-satisfying of sacred ordinances these witless rebels cry, *What a weariness it is!* Under the most soul-sustaining ministry, they complain of *the foolishness of preaching.* When a man has a **rebellious** heart, he must of necessity find all around him a dry land.

Thou, O God, didst send a plentiful rain, whereby thou didst confirm thine inheritance, when it was weary. *Psalm 68:9.*

Thou, O God, didst send a plentiful rain. The march of God was not signalised solely by displays of terror. Goodness and bounty were also made conspicuous. Such **rain** as never fell before dropped on the desert sand. Bread from heaven and winged fowls fell all around the host. Good gifts were poured upon them. Rivers leaped forth from rocks. The earth shook with fear, and in reply, the Lord, as from a cornucopia, shook out blessings upon it: so the original may be rendered.

Whereby thou didst confirm thine inheritance, when it was weary. As at the end of each stage, when they halted, **weary** with the march, they found such showers of good things awaiting them that they were speedily refreshed. Their foot did not swell all those forty years. When they were exhausted, God was not. When they were weary, he was not. They were his chosen heritage. Therefore, although for their good he allowed them to be weary, yet he watchfully tended them and tenderly considered their distresses. In like manner, to this day, the elect of God in this wilderness state are apt to become tired and faint. But their ever-loving Jehovah comes in with timely succours, cheers the faint, strengthens the weak, and refreshes the hungry. So that once again, when the silver trumpets sound, the church militant advances with bold and firm step towards *the rest which remaineth*. By this faithfulness, the faith of God's people is confirmed, and their hearts stablished. If fatigue and want made them waver, the timely supply of grace stays them again upon the eternal foundation.

The chariots of God are twenty thousand, even thousands of angels: the Lord is among them, as in Sinai, in the holy place. *Psalm 68:17.*

The chariots of God are twenty thousand. The Lord of Hosts could summon more forces into the field than all the petty lords who boasted in their armies. His horses of fire and **chariots** of fire would be more than a match for their fiery steeds and flashing cars. The original is grandly expressive: *the war-chariots of Elohim are myriads, a thousand thousands*. The marginal reading of our Bibles, *even many thousands*, is far more correct than the rendering, **even thousands of angels.** It is not easy to see where our venerable translators found these **angels,** for they are not in the text. However, as it is a blessing to entertain them unawares, we are glad to meet with them in English, even though the Hebrew knows them not; and the more so because it cannot be doubted that they constitute a right noble squadron of the myriad hosts of God. We read in Deut. 33:2 of the Lord's coming *with ten thousands of saints*, or *holy ones*, and in Heb. 12:22 we find upon Mount Zion *an innumerable company of angels*, so that our worthy translators putting the texts together, inferred the angels. The clause is so truthfully explanatory that we have no fault to find with it.

The Lord is among them, as in Sinai, in the holy place, or, *it is a*

Sinai in holiness. God is in Zion as the Commander-in-chief of his countless hosts, and where he is, there is holiness. The throne of grace on Zion is as holy as the throne of justice on Sinai. How joyful was it to a pious Hebrew to know that God was as truly with his people in the tabernacle and temple as amid the terrors of the Mount of Horeb. It is even more heart-cheering to us to be assured that the Lord abides in his church. All power is ours when God is ours.

Blessed be the Lord, who daily loadeth us with benefits, even the God of our salvation. *Psalm 68:19.*

Blessed be the Lord. At the mention of the presence of God among men the singers utter an earnest acclamation suggested by reverential love, and return blessings to him who so plentifully blesses his people. **Who daily loadeth us with benefits.** Our version contains a great and precious truth, though probably not the doctrine intended here. God's benefits are not few nor light. They are *loads.* Neither are they intermittent, but they come **daily.** Nor are they confined to one or two favourites, for all Israel can say, He **loadeth** *us* **with benefits.**

If he himself burdens us with sorrow, he gives strength sufficient to sustain it. If others endeavour to oppress us, there is no cause for fear, for the Lord will come to the rescue of his people. Happy nation, to be subdued by a King whose yoke is easy, and who secures his people from all fear of foreign burdens which their foes might try to force upon them. **Even the God of our salvation.** A name most full of glory to him, and consolation to us. No matter how strong the enemy, we shall be delivered out of his hands. God himself, as King, undertakes to save his people from all harm. What a glorious stanza this is! It is dark only because of its excessive light. A world of meaning is condensed into a few words. His yoke is easy, and his burden is light. Therefore blessed be the Saviour's name for evermore. All hail! thou thrice blessed Prince of Peace! All thy saved ones adore thee, and call thee blessed.

PSALM 69

I sink in deep mire, where there is no standing: I am come into deep waters, where the floods overflow me. *Psalm 69:2.*

I sink in deep mire. In water one might swim. But in mud and mire all struggling is hopeless. The **mire** sucks down its victim. **Where there is no standing.** Everything gave way under the Sufferer. He could not get foothold for support—this is a worse fate than drowning.

Here our Lord pictures the close, clinging nature of his heart's woes. *He began to be sorrowful, and very heavy.* Sin is as mire for its filthiness. The holy soul of the Saviour must have loathed even that connection with it which was necessary for its expiation. His pure and sensitive nature seemed to sink in it, for it was not his element. He was not like us born and acclimatised to this great dismal swamp. Let our hearts feel the emotions, both of contrition and gratitude, as we see in this simile the deep humiliation of our Lord.

I am come into deep waters, where the floods overflow me. The sorrow gathers even greater force. He is as one cast into the sea. The waters go over his head. His sorrows were first within, then around, and now above him. Our Lord was no faint-hearted sentimentalist. His were real woes, and though he bore them heroically, yet were they terrible even to him. His sufferings were unlike all others in degree. The waters were such as soaked into the soul. The mire was the mire of the abyss itself, and the **floods** were deep and overflowing. To us the promise is, *the rivers shall not overflow thee.* But no such word of consolation was vouchsafed to him. My soul, thy Well-beloved endured all this for thee. Many waters could not quench his love. He stemmed the torrent of almighty wrath, that we might for ever rest in Jehovah's love.

I am weary of my crying: my throat is dried: mine eyes fail while I wait for my God. *Psalm 69:3.*

I am weary of my crying. Not of it, but by it, with it. He had prayed till he sweat great drops of blood, and well might physical weariness intervene. **My throat is dried,** parched, and inflamed. Long pleading with awful fervour had scorched his throat as with flames of fire. Few, very few, of his saints follow their Lord in prayer as far as this. We are, it is to be feared, more likely to be hoarse with talking frivolities to men than by pleading with God. Yet our sinful nature demands more prayer than his perfect humanity might seem to need. His prayers should shame us into fervour. Our Lord's supplications were salted with fire. They were hot with agony. Hence they weakened his system, and made him *a weary man and full of woes.*

Mine eyes fail while I wait for my God. He wanted in his direst distress nothing more than his **God.** That would be all in all to him. Many of us know what watching and waiting mean. We know something of the failing eye when hope is long deferred. But in all this Jesus bears the palm. No eyes ever failed as his did or for so deep a cause. No painter can ever depict those eyes. Their pencils fail in every feature of his all fair but all marred countenance. But most of all do they come short when they venture to portray those eyes which were fountains of tears. He knew how both to pray and to watch, and he would have us learn the like. There are times when we should pray till the throat is dry, and watch till the eyes grow dim. Only thus can we have fellowship with him in his sufferings. What! can we not watch with him one hour? Does the flesh shrink back? O cruel flesh to be so tender of thyself, and so ungenerous to thy Lord!

Let not them that wait on thee, O Lord God of hosts, be ashamed for my sake: let not those that seek thee be confounded for my sake, O God of Israel. *Psalm 69:6.*

Let not them that wait on thee, O Lord God of hosts, be ashamed for my sake. If he were deserted, others who were walking in the same path of faith would be discouraged and disappointed. Unbelievers are ready enough to catch at anything which may turn humble faith into ridicule. Therefore, O God of all the armies of Israel, let not my case cause the enemy to blaspheme—such is the spirit of this verse. Our blessed Lord ever had a tender concern for his people, and would not have his own oppression of spirit become a source of discouragement to them. **Let not those that seek thee be confounded for my sake, O God of Israel.** He appealed to the **Lord of hosts** by his power to help him, and now to the **God of Israel** by his covenant faithfulness to come to the rescue. If the captain of the host fail, how will it fare with the rank and file? If David flee, what will his followers do? If the king of believers shall find his faith unrewarded, how will the feeble ones hold on their way?

Our Lord's behaviour during his sharpest agonies is no cause of shame to us. He wept, for he was man. But he murmured not, for he was sinless man. He cried, *My Father, if it be possible, let this cup pass from me*; for he was human. But he added, *Nevertheless, not as I will, but as thou wilt*, for his humanity was without taint of rebellion. In the depths of tribulation no repining word escaped him, for there was no repining in his heart. The Lord of martyrs witnessed a good confession. He was strengthened in the hour of peril, and came off more than a conqueror. We also shall do, if we hold fast our confidence even to the end.

The zeal of thine house hath eaten me up; and the reproaches of them that reproached thee are fallen upon me. *Psalm 69:9.*

The zeal of thine house hath eaten me up. His burning ardour, like the flame of a candle, fed on his strength and consumed it. His heart, like a sharp sword, cut through the scabbard. Some men are eaten up with lechery, others with covetousness, and a third class with pride. But the master-passion with our great leader was the glory of God, jealousy for his name, and love to the divine family. **Zeal** for God is so little understood by men of the world, that it always draws down opposition upon those who are inspired with it. They are sure to be accused of sinister motives, or of hypocrisy, or of being out of their senses. When zeal eats us up, ungodly men seek to eat us up too. This was pre-eminently the case with our Lord, because his holy jealousy was pre-eminent. With more than a seraph's fire he glowed, and consumed himself with his fervour.

And the reproaches of them that reproached thee have fallen upon me. Those who habitually blasphemed God now curse me instead. I have become the butt for arrows intended for the Lord himself. Thus, the Great Mediator was, in this respect, a substitute for God as well as for man. He bore **the reproaches** aimed at the one, as well as the sins committed by the other.

Reproach hath broken my heart; and I am full of heaviness: and I looked for some to take pity, but there was none; and for comforters, but I found none. *Psalm 69:20.*

Reproach hath broken my heart. There is no hammer like it. Our Lord died of a broken heart, and **reproach** had done the deed. Intense mental suffering arises from slander. In the case of the sensitive nature of the immaculate Son of Man, it sufficed to lacerate the heart till it broke. *Then burst his mighty heart.* **And I am full of heaviness.** Calumny and insult bowed him to the dust. He was sick at heart. The heaviness of our Lord in the garden is expressed by many and forcible words in the four gospels. Each term goes to show that the agony was beyond measure great. He was filled with misery, like a vessel which is full to the brim.

And I looked for some to take pity, but there was none. *Deserted in his utmost need by those his former bounty fed.* Not one to say him a kindly word, or drop a sympathetic tear. Amongst ten thousand foes there was not one who was touched by the spectacle of his misery; not one with a heart capable of humane feeling towards him. **And for comforters, but I found none.** His dearest ones had sought their own safety, and left their Lord alone. A sick man needs comforters, and a persecuted man needs sympathy. But our blessed Surety found neither on that dark and doleful night when the powers of darkness had their hour. A spirit like that of our Lord feels acutely desertion by beloved and trusted friends, and yearns for real sympathy.

Let all those that seek thee rejoice and be glad in thee: and let such as love thy salvation say continually, Let God be magnified. But I am poor and needy: make haste unto me, O God: thou art my help and my deliverer; O Lord, make no tarrying. *Psalm 70:4–5.*

Let all those that seek thee rejoice and be glad in thee. All true worshippers, though as yet in the humble ranks of seekers, shall have cause for joy. Even though the seeking commence in darkness, it shall bring light with it. And let such as love thy salvation say continually, Let God be magnified. Those who have tasted divine grace, and are, therefore, wedded to it, are a somewhat more advanced race. They shall not only feel joy, but shall with holy constancy and perseverance tell abroad their joy, and call upon men to glorify God.

But I am poor and needy. Just the same plea as in the preceding Psalm. It seems to be a favourite argument with tried saints. Evidently our poverty is our wealth, even as our weakness is our strength. May we learn well this riddle. Make haste unto me, O God. This is written instead of *yet the Lord thinketh upon me*, in Psalm 40. There is a reason for the change, since the key note of the Psalm frequently dictates its close. Psalm 40 sings of God's thoughts, and, therefore, ends therewith. But the peculiar note of Psalm 70 is Make haste, and, therefore, so it concludes. Thou art my help and my deliverer. My help in trouble, my deliverer out of it. O Lord, make no tarrying. Here is the name of *Jehovah* instead of *my God*. We are warranted in using all the various names of God. Each has its own beauty and majesty. We must reverence each by its holy use as well as by abstaining from taking it in vain.

Be thou my strong habitation, whereunto I may continually resort: thou hast given commandment to save me; for thou art my rock and my fortress. *Psalm 71:3.*

Be thou my strong habitation. Here we see a weak man, but he is in a strong habitation. His security rests upon the tower in which he hides, and is not placed in jeopardy through his personal feebleness. Whereunto I may continually resort. There is a secret door, by which friends of the great Lord can enter at all hours of the day or night, as often as ever they please. There is never an hour when it is unlawful to pray. Believers find their God to be their habitation, strong and accessible. This is for them a sufficient remedy for all the ills of their mortal life. **Thou hast given commandment to save me.** Nature is charged to be tender with God's servants. Providence is ordered to work their good. The forces of the invisible world are ordained as their guardians. No stones of the field can throw us down, while angels bear us up in their hands. Neither can the beasts of the field devour us, while David's God delivers us from their ferocity, or Daniel's God puts them in awe of us.

For thou art my rock and my fortress. In God we have all the security that nature which furnishes the **rock,** and art which builds the **fortress,** could supply. Immutability may be set forth by the rock, and omnipotence by the fortress. Happy is he who can use the personal pronoun *my*—not only once, but as many times as the many aspects of the Lord may render desirable. Is he a strong habitation? I will call him *my* **strong habitation,** and he shall be *my* rock, *my* fortress, *my* God (verse 4), *my* trust (verse 5), *my* praise (verse 6). All mine shall be his, all his shall be mine.

Cast me not off in the time of old age; forsake me not when my strength faileth. For mine enemies speak against me; and they that lay wait for my soul take counsel together. *Psalm 71:9-10.*

Cast me not off in the time of old age. David was not tired of his Master. His only fear was lest his Master should be tired of him. The Amalekite in the Bible history left his Egyptian servant to famish when he grew old and sick. But not so the Lord of saints. Even to hoar hairs he bears and carries us. Old age robs us of personal beauty, and deprives us of strength for active service. But it does not lower us in the love and favour of God. The pensioners of heaven are satisfied with good things. **Forsake me not when my strength faileth.** Bear with me, and endure my infirmities. To be forsaken of God is the worst of all conceivable ills. If the believer can be but clear of that grievous fear, he is happy. No saintly heart need be under any apprehension upon this point.

For mine enemies speak against me. The text most probably means that David's enemies had said that God would forsake him. Therefore, he is the more earnest that the Lord's faithful dealings may give them the lie. **And they that lay wait for my soul take counsel together.** The Psalmist had enemies, and these were most malicious. Seeking his utter destruction, they were very persevering, and stayed long upon the watch. To this they added cunning, for they lay in ambush to surprise him, and take him at a disadvantage. All this they did with the utmost unanimity and deliberation, neither spoiling their design by want of prudence, nor marring its accomplishment by a lack of unity. The Lord our God is our only and all-sufficient resort from every form of persecution.

I will go in the strength of the Lord God: I will make mention of thy righteousness, even of thine only. *Psalm 71:16.*

I will go in the strength of the Lord God. Our translators give us a good sense, but not the sense in this place, which is: *I will come with the mighty deeds of the Lord Jehovah.* He would enter into those deeds by admiring study. Then, wherever he went, he would continue to rehearse them. He should ever be a welcome guest who can tell us of the mighty acts of the Lord, and help us to put our trust in him. The Authorised Version may be used by us as a resolve in all our exertions and endeavours. In our own strength we must fall. But, when we hear the voice which saith, *Go in this thy might,* we may advance without fear. Though hell itself were in the way, the believer would pursue the path of duty, crying: **I will go in the strength of the Lord God.**

I will make mention of thy righteousness, even of thine only. Man's righteousness is not fit to be mentioned—filthy rags are best hidden. Neither is there any righteousness under heaven, or in heaven, comparable to the divine. God's righteousness, in Christ Jesus, fills the believer's soul, and he counts all other things but dross and dung *that he may win Christ, and be found in him, not having his own righteousness which is of the law, but the righteousness which is of God by faith.* What would be the use of speaking upon any other righteousness to a dying man? And all are dying men. Let those who will cry up man's natural innocence, the dignity of the race, the purity of philosophers, the loveliness of untutored savages, the power of sacraments, and the infallibility of pontiffs. This is the true believer's immovable resolve: **I will make mention of thy righteousness, even of thine only.**

When I am old and greyheaded, O God, forsake me not; until I have showed thy strength unto this generation, and thy power to every one that is to come. *Psalm 71:18.*

When I am old and greyheaded, O God, forsake me not. There is something touching in the sight of hair whitened with the snows of many a winter. The old and faithful soldier receives consideration from his king. The venerable servant is beloved by his master. When our infirmities multiply, we may, with confidence, expect enlarged privileges in the world of grace, to make up for our narrowing range in the field of nature. Nothing shall make God forsake those who have not forsaken him. Our fear is lest he should do so. But his promise kisses that fear into silence.

Until I have showed thy strength unto this generation. He desired to continue his testimony and complete it. He had respect to the young men and little children about him. Knowing the vast import- ance of training them in the fear of God, he longed to make them all acquainted with the power of God to support his people, that they also might be led to walk by faith. He had leaned on the almighty arm, and could speak experimentally of its all-sufficiency, and longed to do so ere life came to a close. **And thy power to every one that is to come.** He would leave a record for unborn ages to read. He thought the Lord's power to be so worthy of praise, that he would make the ages ring with it till time should be no more. For this cause believers live. They should take care to labour zealously for the accomplishment of this their most proper and necessary work. Blessed are they who begin in youth to proclaim the name of the Lord, and cease not until their last hour brings their last word for their divine Master.

I will also praise thee with the psaltery, even thy truth, O my God: unto thee will I sing with the harp, O thou Holy One of Israel. My lips shall greatly rejoice when I sing unto thee; and my soul, which thou hast redeemed. *Psalm 71:22–23.*

I will also praise thee with the psaltery. Love so amazing calls for sweetest praise. David would give his best music, both vocal and instrumental, to the best of Masters. His harp should not be silent, nor his voice. **Even thy truth, O my God.** This is ever a most enchanting attribute—viz., the **truth** or faithfulness of our covenant God. On this we rest, and from it we draw streams of richest consolation. His promises are sure, his love unalterable, his veracity indisputable. What saint will not praise him as he remembers this? **Unto thee will I sing with the harp, O thou Holy One of Israel.** Here is a new name, and, as it were, a new song. The **Holy One of Israel** is at once a lofty and an endearing name, full of teaching. Let us resolve, by all means within our power, to honour him.

My lips shall greatly rejoice when I sing unto thee. It shall be no weariness to me to praise thee. It shall be a delightful recreation, a solace, a joy. The essence of song lies in the holy joy of the singer. **And my soul, which thou hast redeemed.** Soul-singing is the soul of singing. Till men are redeemed, they are like instruments out of tune. But when once the precious blood has set them at liberty, then are they fitted to magnify the Lord who bought them. Our being bought with a price is a more than sufficient reason for our dedicating ourselves to the earnest worship of God our Saviour.

Give the king thy judgments, O God, and thy righteousness unto the king's son. He shall judge thy people with righteousness, and thy poor with judgment. *Psalm 72:1–2.*

Give the king thy judgments, O God. The right to reign was transmitted by descent from David to Solomon, but not by that means alone. Israel was a theocracy, and the kings were but the viceroys of the greater King. Hence the prayer that the new king might be enthroned by divine right, and then endowed with divine wisdom. **And thy righteousness unto the king's son.** Solomon was both king and king's son. So also is our Lord. He has power and authority in himself, and also royal dignity given him of his Father. He is the righteous king. In a word, he is *the Lord our righteousness.*

He shall judge thy people with righteousness. What a consolation to feel that none can suffer wrong in Christ's kingdom. He sits upon the great white throne, unspotted by a single deed of injustice, or even mistake of judgment. Reputations are safe enough with him. **And thy poor with judgment.** True wisdom is manifest in all the decisions of Zion's King. We do not always understand his doings. But they are always right. Partiality has been too often shown to rich and great men. But the King of the last and best of monarchies deals out even-handed justice, to the delight of the poor and despised. Here we have the **poor** mentioned side by side with the king. The sovereignty of God is a delightful theme to the poor in spirit. They love to see the Lord exalted, and have no quarrel with him for exercising the prerogatives of his crown. A deep sense of spiritual need prepares the heart loyally to worship the Redeemer King.

He shall come down like rain upon the mown grass: as showers that water the earth. *Psalm 72:6.*

He shall come down like rain upon the mown grass. Blessings upon his gentle sway! Those great conquerors who have been the scourges of mankind have fallen like the fiery hail of Sodom, transforming fruitful lands into deserts. But he with mild, benignant influence softly refreshes the weary and wounded among men, and makes them spring up into newness of life. Pastures **mown** with the scythe, or shorn by the teeth of cattle, present, as it were, so many bleeding stems of grass. But when the **rain** falls it is balm to all these wounds, and it renews the verdure and beauty of the field: fit image of the visits and benedictions of *the consolation of Israel.* My soul, how well it is for thee to be brought low, and to be even as the meadows eaten bare and trodden down by cattle. Then to thee shall the Lord have respect. He shall remember thy misery, and with his own most precious love restore thee to more than thy former glory.

As showers that water the earth. Each crystal drop of rain tells of heavenly mercy which forgets not the parched plains. Jesus is all grace. All that he does is love, and his presence among men is joy. We need to preach him more, for no shower can so refresh the nations. Philosophic preaching mocks men as with a dust shower. But the gospel meets the case of fallen humanity, and happiness flourishes beneath its genial power. Come down, O Lord, upon my soul, and my heart shall blossom with thy praise!

He shall deliver the needy when he crieth; the poor also, and him that hath no helper. He shall spare the poor and needy, and shall save the souls of the needy. *Psalm 72:12–13.*

He shall deliver the needy. Here is an excellent reason for man's submission to the Lord Christ. Who would not fear so good a Prince, who makes the needy his peculiar care, and pledges himself to be their deliverer in times of need? **When he crieth.** A child's cry touches a father's heart, and our King is the Father of his people. If we can do no more than cry, it will bring omnipotence to our aid. A cry is the native language of a spiritually needy soul. It has done with fine phrases and long orations, and it takes to sobs and moans. It grasps the most potent of all weapons, for heaven always yields to such artillery. **The poor also, and him that hath no helper.** The proverb says, *God helps those that help themselves.* But it is yet more true that Jesus helps those who cannot help themselves, nor find help in others. All helpless ones are under the especial care of Zion's compassionate King. Let them hasten to put themselves in fellowship with him. Let them look to him, for he is looking for them.

He shall spare the poor and needy. His pity shall be manifested to them. He will not allow their trials to overwhelm them. His rod of correction shall fall lightly. He will be sparing of his rebukes, and not sparing in his consolations. **And shall save the souls of the needy.** His is the dominion of souls, a spiritual and not a worldly empire. The needy, that is to say, the consciously unworthy and weak, shall find that he will give them his salvation. We ought to be anxious to be among these needy ones whom the Great King so highly favours.

He shall live, and to him shall be given of the gold of Sheba: prayer also shall be made for him continually; and daily shall he be praised. *Psalm 72:15.*

He shall live. O King! live for ever! He was slain, but is risen and ever liveth. **And to him shall be given of the gold of Sheba.** These are coronation gifts of the richest kind, cheerfully presented at his throne. How gladly would we give him all that we have and are, and count the tribute far too small. We may rejoice that Christ's cause will not stand still for want of funds. The silver and the gold are his, and if they are not to be found at home, far-off lands shall hasten to make up the deficit. Would to God we had more faith and more generosity.

Prayer also shall be made for him continually. May all blessings be upon his head! All his people desire that his cause may prosper. Therefore do they hourly cry, *Thy kingdom come.* **Prayer** *for* Jesus is a very sweet idea, and one which should be for evermore lovingly carried out. The church is Christ's body, and the truth is his sceptre. Therefore we pray for him when we plead for these. The verse may, however, be read as *through him*, for it is by Christ as our Mediator that prayer enters heaven and prevails. *Continue in prayer* is the standing precept of Messiah's reign, and it implies that the Lord will continue to bless. **And daily shall he be praised.** As he will perpetually show himself to be worthy of honour, so shall he be incessantly praised.

There shall be an handful of corn in the earth upon the top of the mountains; the fruit thereof shall shake like Lebanon: and they of the city shall flourish like grass of the earth. *Psalm 72:16.*

There shall be an handful of corn in the earth upon the top of the mountains. From small beginnings great results shall spring. A mere handful in a place naturally ungenial shall produce a matchless harvest. What a blessing that there is **a handful.** Except the Lord of hosts had left unto us a very small remnant we should have been as Sodom, and we should have been like unto Gomorrah. But now the faithful are a living seed, and shall multiply in the land.

The fruit thereof shall shake like Lebanon. The harvest shall be so great that the wind shall rustle through it, and sound like the cedars upon **Lebanon.** God's church is no mean thing. Its beginnings are small, but its increase is of the most astonishing kind. As Lebanon is conspicuous and celebrated, so shall the church be. **And they of the city shall flourish like grass of the earth.** Another figure. Christ's subjects shall be as plentiful as blades of grass, and shall as suddenly appear as eastern verdure after a heavy shower. We need not fear for the cause of truth in the land. It is in good hands, where the pleasure of the Lord is sure to prosper. *Fear not, little flock, it is your Father's good pleasure to give you the kingdom.* When shall these words, which open up such a vista of delight, be fulfilled in the midst of the earth?

Truly God is good to Israel, even to such as are of a clean heart. *Psalm 73:1.*

Truly, or, more correctly, *only,* **God is good to Israel.** He is only **good,** nothing else but good to his own covenanted ones. He cannot act unjustly or unkindly to them. His goodness to them is beyond dispute, and without mixture. **Even to such as are of a clean heart.** These are the true Israel, not the ceremonially **clean** but the really so— those who are clean in the inward parts, pure in the vital mainspring of action. To such he is, and must be, goodness itself. The writer does not doubt this, but lays it down as his firm conviction. It is well to make sure of what we do know, for this will be good anchor-hold for us when we are molested by those mysterious storms which arise from things which we do not understand.

Whatever may or may not be the truth about mysterious and inscrutable things, there are certainties somewhere. Experience has placed some tangible facts within our grasp. Let us, then, cling to these. They will prevent our being carried away by those hurricanes of infidelity which still come from the wilderness, and, like whirlwinds, smite the four corners of our house and threaten to overthrow it. O my God, however perplexed I may be, let me never think ill of thee. If I cannot understand thee, let me never cease to believe in thee. It must be so. It cannot be otherwise. Thou art good to those whom thou hast made good. Where thou hast renewed the heart thou wilt not leave it to its enemies.

As for me, my feet were almost gone; my steps had well nigh slipped. For I was envious at the foolish, when I saw the prosperity of the wicked. *Psalm 73:2–3.*

The Lord is good to his saints. **As for me,** am I one of them? Can I expect to share his grace? Yes, I do share it; but I have acted an unworthy part, very unlike one who is truly pure in heart. **My feet were almost gone.** Errors of heart and head soon affect the conduct. When men doubt the righteousness of God, their own integrity begins to waver. **My steps had well nigh slipped.** The Psalmist could make no progress in the good road. His feet ran away from under him like those of a man on a sheet of ice. He was weakened for all practical action, and in great danger of actual sin, and so of a disgraceful fall. How ought we to watch the inner man, since it has so forcible an effect upon the outward character. The confession in this case is, **as it** should be, very plain and explicit.

For I was envious at the foolish. The foolish is the generic title of all the wicked. They are beyond all other fools, and he must be a fool who envies fools. It is a pitiful thing that an heir of heaven should have to confess *I was envious*, but worse still that he should have to put it, *I was envious at the foolish*. Yet this acknowledgement is, we fear, due from most of us. **When I saw the prosperity of the wicked.** His eye was fixed too much on one thing. He saw their present, and forgot their future; saw their outward display, and overlooked their soul's discomfort. Who envies the bullock his fat when he recollects the shambles? Yet some poor afflicted saint has been sorely tempted to grudge the ungodly sinner his temporary plenty. All things considered, Dives had more cause to envy Lazarus than Lazarus to be envious of Dives.

They are not in trouble as other men; neither are they plagued like other men. *Psalm 73:5.*

They are not in trouble as other men. The prosperous wicked escape the killing toils which afflict the mass of mankind. Their bread comes to them without care, their wine without stint. They have no need to enquire, *Whence shall we get bread for our children, or raiment for our little ones?* Ordinary domestic and personal troubles do not appear to molest them.

Neither are they plagued like other men. Fierce trials do not arise to assail them. They smart not under the divine rod. While many saints are both poor and afflicted, the prosperous sinner is neither. He is worse than other men, and yet he is better off. He ploughs least, and yet has the most fodder. He deserves the hottest hell, and yet has the warmest nest. All this is clear to the eye of faith, which unriddles the riddle. But to the bleared eye of sense it seems an enigma indeed. They are to have nothing hereafter, let them have what they can here. They, after all, only possess what is of secondary value, and their possessing it is meant to teach us to set little store by transient things. If earthly good were of much value, the Lord would not give so large a measure of it to those who have least of his love.

It is good for me to draw near to God: I have put my trust in the Lord God, that I may declare all thy works. *Psalm 73:28.*

It is good for me to draw near to God. Had he done so at first, he would not have been immersed in such affliction. When he did so, he escaped from his dilemma. If he continued to do so, he would not fall into the same evil again. The greater our nearness to God, the less we

132

are affected by the attractions and distractions of earth. Access into the most holy place is a great privilege, and a cure for a multitude of ills. It is good for all saints. It is good for me in particular. It is always good and always will be good for me to approach the greatest good, the source of all good, even God himself.

I have put my trust in the Lord God. He dwells upon the glorious name of the Lord Jehovah, and avows it as the basis of his faith. Faith is wisdom. It is the key of enigmas, the clue of mazes, and the pole star of pathless seas. Trust and you will know. **That I may declare all thy works.** He who believes shall understand, and so be able to teach. The Psalmist hesitated to utter his evil surmisings, but he has no diffidence in publishing abroad a good matter. God's ways are the more admired the more they are known. He who is ready to believe the goodness of God shall always see fresh goodness to believe in. He who is willing to declare the works of God shall never be silent for lack of wonders to declare.

PSALM 74

O God, why hast thou cast us off for ever? why doth thine anger smoke against the sheep of thy pasture? *Psalm 74:1.*

O God, why hast thou cast us off for ever? Sin is usually at the bottom of all the hidings of the Lord's face. Let us ask the Lord to reveal the special form of it to us, that we may repent of it, overcome it, and henceforth forsake it. When a church is in a forsaken condition it must not sit still in apathy, but turn to the hand which smiteth it, and humbly enquire the reason why. At the same time, the enquiry of the text is a faulty one, for it implies two mistakes. There are two questions, which only admit of negative replies. *Hath God cast away his people?* (Rom. 11:1); and the other, *Will the Lord cast off for ever* (Psalm 77:7). God is never weary of his people so as to abhor them. Even when his anger is turned against them, it is but for a small moment, and with a view to their eternal good. Grief in its distraction asks strange questions and surmises impossible terrors. It is a wonder of grace that the Lord has not long ago put us away as men lay aside cast-off garments. But he hateth putting away, and will still be patient with his chosen.

Why doth thine anger smoke against the sheep of thy pasture? They are thine. They are the objects of thy care. They are poor, silly, and defenceless things. Pity them, forgive them, and come to their rescue. They are but **sheep.** Do not continue to be wroth with them. It is meet to pray the Lord to remove every sign of his wrath, for it is to those who are truly the Lord's sheep a most painful thing to be the objects of his displeasure. To vex the Holy Spirit is no mean sin. Yet how frequently are we guilty of it. Hence it is no marvel that we are often under a cloud.

Remember thy congregation, which thou hast purchased of old; the rod of thine inheritance, which thou hast redeemed; this mount Zion, wherein thou hast dwelt. *Psalm 74:2.*

Remember thy congregation, which thou hast purchased of old. What a mighty plea is redemption! The church is no new purchase of the Lord. From before the world's foundation the chosen were regarded as redeemed by the Lamb slain. Shall ancient love die out, and the eternal purpose become frustrate? The Lord would have his people remember the Paschal Lamb, the bloodstained lintel, and the overthrow of Egypt. Will he forget all this himself? Let us put him in remembrance. Let us plead together. Can he desert his blood-bought and forsake his redeemed? Impossible. The woes of Calvary, and the covenant of which they are the seal, are the security of the saints.

The rod of thine inheritance, which thou hast redeemed. So sweet a plea deserved to be repeated and enlarged upon. The Lord's portion is his people—will he lose his inheritance? His church is his kingdom, over which he stretches the rod of sovereignty. Will he allow his possessions to be torn from him? God's property in us is a fact full of comfort. No man will willingly lose his inheritance, and no prince will relinquish his dominions. Therefore we believe that the King of kings will hold his own, and maintain his rights against all comers. **This mount Zion, wherein thou hast dwelt.** The Lord's having made Zion the especial centre of his worship, and place of his manifestation, is yet another plea for the preservation of Jerusalem. Shall the sacred temple of Jehovah be desecrated by heathen, and the throne of the Great King be defiled by his enemies? Has the Spirit of God dwelt in our hearts, and will he leave them to become a haunt for the devil?

We see not our signs: there is no more any prophet: neither is there among us any that knoweth how long. *Psalm 74:9.*

We see not our signs. Alas, poor Israel! No Urim and Thummim blazed on the High Priest's bosom, and no Shekinah shone from between the cherubim. The smoke of sacrifice and cloud of incense no more arose from the holy hill. Solemn feasts were suspended, and even circumcision, the covenant sign, was forbidden by the tyrant. We, too, as believers, know what it is to lose our evidence and grope in darkness. Too often do our churches also miss the tokens of the Redeemer's presence, and their lamps remain untrimmed. Sad plaint of a people under a cloud! **There is no more any prophet.** Prophecy was suspended. No inspiring psalm or consoling promise fell from bard or seer. It is ill with the people of God when the voice of the preacher of the gospel fails, and a famine of the word of life falls on the people. God-sent ministers are as needful to the saints as their daily bread. It is a great sorrow when a congregation is destitute of a faithful pastor. It is to be feared, that with all the ministers now existing, there is yet a dearth of men whose hearts and tongues are touched with the celestial fire.

Neither is there among us any that knoweth how long. If someone could foretell an end, the evil might be borne with a degree of patience. But when none can see a termination, or foretell an escape, the misery has a hopeless appearance, and is overwhelming. Blessed be God, he has not left his church in these days to be so deplorably destitute of cheering words. Let us pray that he never may. Contempt of the word is very common, and may well provoke the Lord to withdraw it from us. May his longsuffering endure the strain, and his mercy afford us still the word of life.

Why withdrawest thou thy hand, even thy right hand? pluck it out of thy bosom. *Psalm 74:11.*

Why withdrawest thou thy hand, even thy right hand? Wherefore this inaction, this indifference for thine own honour and thy people's safety? How bold is the suppliant! Does he err? Nay, verily, we who are so chill, and distant, and listless in prayer are the erring ones. The kingdom of heaven suffereth violence, and he who learns the art shall surely prevail with God by its means. It is fit that we should enquire why the work of grace goes on so slowly, and the enemy has so much power over men. The enquiry may suggest practical reflections of unbounded value.

Pluck it out of thy bosom. A bold simile, but dying men must venture for their lives. When God seems to fold his arms we must not fold ours, but rather renew our entreaties that he would again put his hand to the work. O for more agony in prayer among professing Christians. Then should we see miracles of grace. We have here before us a model of pleading, a very rapture of prayer. It is humble, but very bold, eager, fervent, and effectual. The heart of God is always moved by such entreaties. When we bring forth our strong reasons, then will he bring forth his choice mercies.

The day is thine, the night also is thine: thou hast prepared the light and the sun. Thou hast set all the borders of the earth: thou hast made summer and winter. *Psalm 74:16–17*.

The day is thine, the night also is thine. Thou art not restricted by times and seasons. Our prosperity comes from thee, and our adversity is ordained by thee. Thou rulest in the darkness, and one glance of thine eye kindles it into day. Lord, be not slack to keep thy word, but rise for the help of thy people. **Thou hast prepared the light and the sun.** Both light and the light-bearer are of thee. Our help and the instrument of it, are both in thy hand. There is no limit to thy power. Be pleased to display it and make thy people glad. Let thy sacred preparations of mercy ripen. Say, *Let there be light*, and light shall at once dispel our gloom.

Thou hast set all the borders of the earth. Observe, again, how everything is ascribed to the divine agency by the use of the pronoun **thou**. Not a word about natural laws, and original forces, but the Lord is seen as working all. It will be well when our *ologies* are tinctured with *theology*, and the Creator is seen at work amid his universe. The argument of our text is, that he who bounds the sea can restrain his foes; and he who guards the borders of the dry land can also protect his chosen. **Thou hast made summer and winter.** Return, then, good Lord, to us the bright summer days of joy. We know that all our changes come of thee, We have already felt the rigours of thy **winter**. Grant us now the genial glow of thy **summer** smile. The God of nature is the God of grace. We may argue from the revolving seasons that sorrow is not meant to rule the year. The flowers of hope will blossom, and ruddy fruits of joy will ripen yet.

Have respect unto the covenant: for the dark places of the earth are full of the habitations of cruelty. O let not the oppressed return ashamed: let the poor and needy praise thy name. *Psalm 74:20–21*.

Have respect unto the covenant. Here is the master-key. Heaven's gate must open to this. God is not a man that he should lie. His covenant he will not break, nor alter the thing that hath gone forth out of his lips. The Lord had promised to bless the seed of Abraham, and make them a blessing. Here they plead that ancient word, even as we also may plead the covenant made with the Lord Jesus for all believers. What a grand word it is! Reader, do you know how to cry, *Have respect unto thy covenant*? **For the dark places of the earth are full of the habitations of cruelty.** Darkness is the fit hour for beasts of prey, and ignorance the natural dwelling-place of cruelty. All the world is in a measure dark, and hence everywhere there are cruel enemies of the Lord's people. Has not the Lord declared that the whole earth shall be filled with his glory? How can this be if he always permits cruelty to riot in dark places? Surely, he must arise, and end the days of wrong, the era of oppression. This verse is a most telling missionary prayer.

O let not the oppressed return ashamed. Though broken and crushed, they come to thee with confidence. Suffer them not to be disappointed, for then they will be ashamed of their hope. **Let the poor and needy praise thy name.** By thy speedy answer to their cries, make their hearts glad. They will render to thee their gladdest songs. It is not the way of the Lord to allow any of those who trust in him to be put to shame. His word is, *He shall call upon me, and I will deliver him, and he shall glorify me.*

PSALM 75

Unto thee, O God, do we give thanks, unto thee do we give thanks: for that thy name is near thy wondrous works declare. *Psalm 75:1.*

Unto thee, O God, do we give thanks. Not to ourselves for we were helpless, but to Elohim who heard our cry, and replied to the taunt of our foes. Never let us neglect thanksgiving, or we may fear that another time our prayers will remain unanswered. As the smiling flowers gratefully reflect in their lovely colours the various constituents of the solar ray, so should gratitude spring up in our hearts after the smiles of God's providence. **Unto thee do we give thanks.** We should praise God again and again. Stinted gratitude is ingratitude. For infinite goodness there should be measureless thanks. Faith promises redoubled praise for greatly needed and signal deliverances.

For that thy name is near thy wondrous works declare. God is at hand to answer and do wonders—adore we then the present Deity. We sing not of a hidden God, who sleeps and leaves the church to her fate, but of one who ever in our darkest days is most near, a very present help in trouble: *Near is his name.* Baal is on a journey, but Jehovah dwells in his church. Glory be unto the Lord, whose perpetual deeds of grace and majesty are the sure tokens of his being with us always, even unto the end of the world.

Promotion cometh neither from the east, nor from the west, nor from the south. But God is the judge: he putteth down one, and setteth up another. *Psalm 75:6–7.*

Promotion cometh neither from the east, nor from the west, nor from the south. There is a God, and a providence. Things happen not by chance. Though deliverance be hopeless from all points of the compass, yet God can work it for his people. Though judgment come neither from the rising or the setting of the sun, nor from the wilderness of mountains, yet come it will, for the Lord reigneth. Men forget that all things are ordained in heaven. They see but the human force, and the carnal passion. But the unseen Lord is more real far than these. He is at work behind and within the cloud. The foolish dream that he is not, but he is near even now, and on the way to bring in his hand that cup of spiced wine of vengeance, one draught of which shall stagger all his foes.

But God is the judge. Even now he is actually judging. His seat is not vacant. His authority is not abdicated. The Lord reigneth evermore. **He putteth down one, and setteth up another.** Empires rise and fall at his bidding. A dungeon here, and there a throne, his will assigns. Assyria yields to Babylon, and Babylon to the Medes. Kings are but puppets in his hand. They serve his purpose when they rise and when they fall. God only is. All power belongs to him. All else is shadow, coming and going, unsubstantial, misty, dream-like.

PSALM 76

In Judah is God known: his name is great in Israel. In Salem also is his tabernacle, and his dwelling place in Zion. *Psalm 76:1-2.*

In Judah is God known. If unknown in all the world beside, he has so revealed himself to his people by his deeds of grace, that he is no unknown God to them. **His name is great in Israel.** To be known, in the Lord's case, is to be honoured. Those who know **his name** admire the greatness of it. Although Judah and Israel were unhappily divided politically, yet the godly of both nations were agreed concerning Jehovah their God. Truly whatever schisms may mar the visible church, the saints always appear as one in magnifying the Lord their God. Dark is the outer world. But within the favoured circle Jehovah is revealed, and is the adoration of all who behold him. The world knows him not, and therefore blasphemes him. But his church is full of ardour to proclaim his fame unto the ends of the earth.

In Salem also is his tabernacle. In the peaceful city he dwells, and the peace is perpetuated, because there his sacred tent is pitched. The church of God is the place where the Lord abides, and he is to her the Lord and giver of peace. **And his dwelling place in Zion.** Upon the chosen hill was the palace of Israel's Lord. It is the glory of the church that the Redeemer inhabits her by his Holy Spirit. Vain are the assaults of the enemy, for they attack not us alone, but the Lord himself. Immanuel, God with us, finds a home among his people. Who then shall work us ill?

At thy rebuke, O God of Jacob, both the chariot and horse are cast into a dead sleep. *Psalm 76:6.*

At thy rebuke. A word accomplished all. There was no need of a single blow. **O God of Jacob.** God of thy wrestling people, who again like their father supplant their enemy. God of the covenant and the promise, thou hast in this gracious character fought for thine elect nation. **Both the chariot and horse are cast into a dead sleep.** They will neither neigh nor rattle again. Still are the trampings of the horses and the crash of the cars. The cavalry no more creates its din. The Israelites always had a special fear of horses and scythed chariots. Therefore, the sudden stillness of the entire force of the enemy in this department is made the theme of special rejoicing. The horses were stretched on the ground, and the chariots stood still, as if the whole camp had fallen asleep.

Thus can the Lord send a judicial sleep over the enemies of the church, a premonition of the second death. This he can do when they are in the zenith of power; and, as they imagine, in the very act of blotting out the remembrance of his people. The world's Rabshakehs can write terrible letters. But the Lord answers not with pen and ink, but with rebukes, which bear death in every syllable.

Thou didst cause judgment to be heard from heaven; the earth feared, and was still. When God arose to judgment, to save all the meek of the earth. *Psalm 76:8–9.*

Thou didst cause judgment to be heard from heaven. Man will not hear God's voice if he can help it. But God takes care to cause it to be heard. The echoes of that judgment executed on the haughty Assyrian are heard still, and will ring on adown all the ages, to the praise of divine justice. **The earth feared, and was still.** All nations trembled at the tidings, and sat in humbled awe. Repose followed the former turmoils of war, when the oppressor's power was broken, and God was reverenced for having given quiet to the peoples. How readily can Jehovah command an audience! It may be that in the latter days he will, by some such miracles of power in the realms of grace, constrain all earth's inhabitants to attend to the gospel, and submit to the reign of his all-glorious Son. So be it, good Lord.

When God arose to judgment. Men were hushed when he ascended the judgment-seat and actively carried out the decrees of justice. When God is still the people are in tumult. When he arises they are still as a stone. **To save all the meek of the earth.** The Ruler of men has a special eye towards the poor and despised. He makes it his first point to right all their wrongs. *Blessed are the meek, for they shall inherit the earth.* They have little enough of it now, but their avenger is strong and he will surely save them. He who saves his people is the same God who overthrew their enemies. He is as omnipotent to save as to destroy. Glory be unto his name.

PSALM 77

I cried unto God with my voice, even unto God with my voice; and he gave ear unto me. *Psalm 77:1.*

I cried unto God with my voice. This Psalm has much sadness in it. But we may be sure it will end well, for it begins with prayer, and prayer never has an ill issue. The Psalmist did not run to man but to the Lord, and to him he went, not with studied, stately, stilted words, but with a cry, the natural, unaffected, unfeigned expression of pain. He used his **voice** also, for though vocal utterance is not necessary to the life of prayer, it often seems forced upon us by the energy of our desires. Sometimes the soul feels compelled to use the voice, for thus it finds a freer vent for its agony. It is a comfort to hear the alarm-bell ringing when the house is invaded by thieves.

Even unto God with my voice. He returned to his pleading. If once sufficed not, he cried again. He needed an answer, he expected one, he was eager to have it soon, therefore he cried again and again, and with his voice too, for the sound helped his earnestness. **And he gave ear unto me.** Importunity prevailed. The gate opened to the steady knock. It shall be so with us in our hour of trial, the God of grace will hear us in due season.

In the day of my trouble I sought the Lord: my sore ran in the night, and ceased not: my soul refused to be comforted. *Psalm 77:2.*

In the day of my trouble I sought the Lord. All day long his distress drove him to his God, so that when night came he continued still in the same search. God had hidden his face from his servant, therefore the first care of the troubled saint was to seek his Lord again. Diseases and tribulations are easily enough endured when God is found of us.

But without him they crush us to the earth. **My sore ran in the night, and ceased not.** As by day so by night his trouble was on him and his prayer continued. Some of us know what it is, both physically and spiritually, to be compelled to use these words. No respite has been afforded us by the silence of the night. Our bed has been a rack to us. Our body has been in torment, and our spirit in anguish. It appears that this sentence is wrongly translated, and should be, *my hand was stretched out all night.* This shows that his prayer ceased not, but with uplifted hand he continued to seek succour of his God.

My soul refused to be comforted. He refused some comforts as too weak for his case, others as untrue, others as unhallowed. But chiefly because of distraction, he declined even those grounds of consolation which ought to have been effectual with him. As a sick man turns away even from the most nourishing food, so did he. It is impossible to comfort those who refuse to be comforted. You may bring them to the waters of the promise. But who shall make them drink if they will not do so? Many a daughter of despondency has pushed aside the cup of gladness, and many a son of sorrow has hugged his chains. There are times when we are suspicious of good news, and are not to be persuaded into peace, though the happy truth should be as plain before us as the King's highway.

Will the Lord cast off for ever? And will he be favourable no more? Is his mercy clean gone for ever? Doth his promise fail for evermore? Hath God forgotten to be gracious? Hath he in anger shut up his tender mercies? *Psalm 77:7–9.*

Will the Lord cast off for ever? The Psalmist painfully knew that the Lord might leave his people for a season. But his fear was that the time might be prolonged and have no close. Eagerly, therefore, he asked, will the Lord utterly and finally reject those who are his own, and suffer them to be his everlasting cast-offs? This he was persuaded could not be. No instance in the years of ancient times led him to fear that such could be the case. **And will he be favourable no more?** Favourable he had been. Would that goodwill never again show itself? Was the sun set never to rise again? Would spring never follow the long and dreary winter? The questions are suggested by fear. But they are also the cure of fear. It is a blessed thing to have grace enough to look such questions in the face, for their answer is self-evident and eminently fitted to cheer the heart.

Is his mercy clean gone for ever? If he has no love for his elect, has he not still his **mercy** left? Has he no pity for the sorrowful? **Doth his promise fail for evermore?** Shall it be said that from one generation to another the Lord's word has fallen to the ground? **Hath God forgotten to be gracious?** Has El, the Mighty One, become great in everything but grace? Does he know how to afflict, but not how to uphold? Can he forget anything? Above all, can he forget to exercise that attribute which lies nearest to his essence, for he is love? **Hath he in anger shut up his tender mercies?** Are the pipes of goodness choked up so that love can no more flow through them? Unbelief raises questions and we will meet it with questions. Strip it naked, and mistrust is a monstrous piece of folly.

I said, This is my infirmity: but I will remember the years of the right hand of the most High. I will remember the works of the Lord: surely I will remember thy wonders of old. *Psalm 77:10–11.*

I said, This is my infirmity. The Psalmist has won the day, and surveys the field with a cooler mind. He confesses that unbelief is an **infirmity,** a weakness, a folly, a sin. He may also be understood to mean *this is my appointed sorrow.* I will bear it without complaint. When we perceive that our affliction is meted out by the Lord, and is the ordained portion of our cup, we become reconciled to it, and no longer rebel against the inevitable. Why should we not be content if it be the Lord's will?

But I will remember the years of the right hand of the most High. Here a good deal is supplied by our translators. They make the sense to be that the Psalmist would console himself by remembering the goodness of God to himself and others in times gone by. But the original seems to consist only of the words, **the years of the right hand of the most High,** and to express the idea that his long continued affliction, reaching through several years, was allotted to him by the Sovereign Lord of all. 'Tis well when a consideration of the divine goodness and greatness silences all complaining, and creates a childlike acquiescence. **I will remember the works of the Lord.** Fly back, my soul, away from present turmoils, for he is the same and is ready even now to defend his servants as in the days of yore. **Surely I will remember thy wonders of old.** Whatever else may glide into oblivion, the marvellous works of the Lord in the ancient days must not be suffered to be forgotten. Memory is a fit handmaid for faith. When faith has its seven years of famine, memory like Joseph in Egypt opens her granaries.

I will meditate also of all thy work, and talk of thy doings. Thy way, O God, is in the sanctuary: who is so great a God as our God? *Psalm 77:12–13.*

ıd gems of spiritual truth, cap-
into the depths and bring them
ut the inner sense is beyond all
er and hidden meaning, which
ceive.

and our fathers have told us.
ners laid the instructed believer
e truth to the next generation.
and we know personally what
turn to hand it on. Blessed be
estimony of written revelation.
gation to instruct our children
her, with such a gracious help,
ʹ ᵔ things of God. The more of
ₐ ıd Sabbath-school teachers
emʹmothers' tears and fathers'
ʒuʹ
ʹ

children, showing to the
Lord, and his strength, and
ne. *Psalm 78:4.*

ıildren. Our negligent silence
ner's offspring of the precious
leed if we did so. **Showing to**
f the Lord. We will look for-
our to provide for their godly
of God to maintain, in fullest
ʹigious education of the young.
of the future, and as we sow
n are to be taught to magnify
ıed as to his wonderful doings
know **his strength, and his**

best things. Grammar is poor
ith grace. Every satchel should
secular knowledge alone; 'tis
rch must not deal so with her
y Timothy, and see to it that
ʹres. Fathers should repeat not
ff the martyrs and reformers,
ʹrd with themselves both in
ʹs and pleasant evenings have

children had at their parents' k
story of old. Reader, if you have
duty.

PSALM 79

O God, the heathen are cor
temple have they defiled; t
Psalm 79:1.

O God, the heathen are come
amazement at sacrilegious intr
horror. The stranger pollutes t
Canaan is thy land, but thy fo
have they defiled. Into the
forced their way, and there be
holy land, the holy house, and
uncircumcised. It is an awful t
church and numbered with her
the wheat, and the poisoned g

They have laid Jerusalem
they have come to destroying,
completeness. Jerusalem, the
abode of her God, was totally
to see the foe in our own house
God. They strike hardest who
up the agony. He was a suppli
strong points of his case. We
with as much care as if our su
earthly courts use all their powe
state our case with earnestness

Let the sighing of the prise
the greatness of thy power p
to die. *Psalm 79:11.*

Let the sighing of the prisor
cannot sing, and dare not sho
into thine ear, and secure for
able for the afflicted in a great
will know how to adapt them
in reference to others.

According to the greatne

that are appointed to die. Faith grows while it prays. The appeal to the Lord's tender mercy is here supplemented by another addressed to the divine power. The petitioner rises from a request for those who are brought low, to a prayer for those who are on the verge of death, set apart as victims for the slaughter. How consoling is it to desponding believers to reflect that God can preserve even those who bear the sentence of death in themselves. Men and devils may consign us to perdition, while sickness drags us to the grave, and sorrow sinks us in the dust. But there is One who can keep our soul alive, ay, and bring it up again from the depths of despair. A lamb shall live between the lion's jaws if the Lord wills it. Even in the charnel, life shall vanquish death if God be near.

PSALM 80

Give ear, O Shepherd of Israel, thou that leadest Joseph like a flock; thou that dwellest between the cherubims, shine forth. *Psalm 80:1.*

Give ear, O Shepherd of Israel. Hear thou the bleatings of thy suffering flock. The name is full of tenderness. Good old Jacob delighted to think of God as the **Shepherd of Israel,** and this verse may refer to his dying expression: *From thence is the Shepherd, the stone of Israel.* We may be quite sure that he who deigns to be a shepherd to his people will not turn a deaf ear to their complaints. **Thou that leadest Joseph like a flock.** The people are called here by the name of that renowned son who became a second father to the tribes, and kept them alive in Egypt. Possibly they were known to the Egyptians under the name of *the family of Joseph.* If so, it seems most natural to call them by that name in this place. The term may, however, refer to the ten tribes of which Manasseh was the acknowledged head. The Lord had of old in the wilderness led, guided, shepherded all the tribes; and, therefore, the appeal is made to him. The Lord's doings in the past are strong grounds for appeal and expectation as to the present and the future.

Thou that dwellest between the cherubims, shine forth. The Lord's especial presence was revealed upon the mercy-seat **between the cherubims.** In all our pleadings we should come to the Lord by this way. Only upon the mercy-seat will God reveal his grace, and only there can we hope to commune with him. Let us ever plead the name of Jesus, who is our true mercy-seat, to whom we may come boldly, and through whom we may look for a display of the glory of the Lord on our behalf. Our greatest dread is the withdrawal of the Lord's presence, and our brightest hope is the prospect of his return. In the darkest times of Israel, the light of her Shepherd's countenance is all she needs.

Turn us again, O God, and cause thy face to shine; and we shall be saved. *Psalm 80:3.*

Turn us again, O God. It is not so much said, *turn our captivity,* but **turn *us*.** All will come right, if we are right. The best turn is not that of circumstances but of character. When the Lord turns his people, he will soon turn their condition. It needs the Lord himself to do this, for conversion is as divine a work as creation. Those who have been once turned unto God, if they at any time backslide, as much need the Lord to turn them again as to turn them at the first. The word may be read, *restore us.* Verily, it is a choice mercy that *he restoreth my soul.*

And cause thy face to shine. Be favourable to us, smile upon us. This was the high priest's blessing upon Israel. What the Lord has already given us by our High-priest and Mediator we may right confidently ask of him. **And we shall be saved.** All that is wanted for salvation is the Lord's favour. No matter how fierce the foe, or dire the captivity, the shining face of God ensures both victory and liberty. This verse is a very useful prayer. Since we too often turn aside, let us often with our lips and heart cry, **Turn us again, O God, and cause thy face to shine; and we shall be saved.**

Let thy hand be upon the man of thy right hand, upon the son of man whom thou madest strong for thyself. So will not we go back from thee: quicken us, and we will call upon thy name. *Psalm 80:17–18.*

Let thy hand be upon the man of thy right hand. Let thy power rest on thy true Benjamin, *son of thy right hand.* Give a commission to some chosen man by whom thou wilt deliver. Honour him, save us, and glorify thyself. There is no doubt here an outlook to the Messiah, for whom believing Jews had learned to look as the Saviour in time of trouble. **Upon the son of man whom thou madest strong for thyself.** Send forth thy power with him whom thou shalt strengthen to accomplish thy purposes of grace. It pleases God to work for the sons of men by sons of men. *By man came death, by man came also the resurrection from the dead.* It is by the man Christ Jesus that fallen Israel is yet to rise, and indeed through him, who deigns to call himself **the Son of Man,** the world is to be delivered from the dominion of Satan and the curse of sin. O Lord, fulfil thy promise to **the man of thy**

right hand, who participates in thy glory, and give him to see the pleasure of the Lord prospering in his hand.

So will not we go back from thee. Under the leadership of one whom God had chosen the nation would be kept faithful, grace would work gratitude, and so cement them to their allegiance. It is in Christ that we abide faithful. Because he lives we live also. There is no hope of our perseverance apart from him. **Quicken us, and we will call upon thy name.** If the Lord gives life out of death, his praise is sure to follow. The Lord Jesus is such a leader, that in him is life, and the life is the light of men. He is our life. When he visits our souls anew we shall be revivified, and our praise shall ascend unto the name of the Triune God.

PSALM 81

Sing aloud unto God our strength: make a joyful noise unto the God of Jacob. *Psalm 81:1.*

Sing in tune and measure, so that the public praise may be in harmony. Sing with joyful notes, and sounds melodious. **Aloud.** The heartiest praise is due to our good Lord. His acts of love to us speak more loudly than any of our words of gratitude can do. No dullness should ever stupefy our psalmody, or half-heartedness cause it to limp along. **Sing aloud,** ye debtors to sovereign grace. Your hearts are profoundly grateful. Let your voices express your thankfulness. **Unto God our strength.** The Lord was the **strength** of his people in delivering them out of Egypt with a high hand, and also in sustaining them in the wilderness, placing them in Canaan, preserving them from their foes, and giving them victory. To whom do men give honour, but to those upon whom they rely. Therefore let us sing aloud unto our God, who is our strength and our song.

Make a joyful noise unto the God of Jacob. The God of the nation, the God of their father Jacob, was extolled in gladsome music by the Israelitish people. Let no Christian be silent, or slack in praise, for this God is our God. It is to be regretted that the niceties of modern singing frighten our congregations from joining lustily in the hymns. For our part we delight in full bursts of praise, and had rather discover the ruggedness of a want of musical training than miss the heartiness of universal congregational song. The gentility which lisps the tune in well-bred whispers, or leaves the singing altogether to the choir, is very like a mockery of worship. Jehovah can only be adored with the heart. That music is the best for his service which gives the heart most play.

Thou calledst in trouble, and I delivered thee; I answered thee in the secret place of thunder: I proved thee at the waters of Meribah. *Psalm 81: 7.*

Thou calledst in trouble, and I delivered thee. God heard his people's cries in Egypt, and at the Red Sea. This ought to have bound them to him. Since God does not forsake us in our need, we ought never to forsake him at any time. When our hearts wander from God, our answered prayers cry *shame* upon us. **I answered thee in the secret place of thunder.** Out of the cloud the Lord sent forth tempest upon the foes of his chosen. That cloud was his secret pavilion, within it he hung up his weapons of war, his javelins of lightning, his trumpet of thunder. Forth from that pavilion he came and overthrew the foe that his own elect might be secure.

I proved thee at the waters of Meribah. They had proved him and found him faithful. He afterwards proved them in return. Precious things are tested, therefore Israel's loyalty to her King was put to trial. Alas, it failed lamentably. The God who was adored one day for his goodness was reviled the next, when the people for a moment felt the pangs of hunger and thirst. The story of Israel is only our own history in another shape. God has heard us, delivered us, liberated us, and too often our unbelief makes the wretched return of mistrust, murmuring, and rebellion. Great is our sin. Great is the mercy of our God. Let us reflect upon both, and pause awhile.

PSALM 82

I have said, Ye are gods; and all of you are children of the most High. But ye shall die like men, and fall like one of the princes. *Psalm 82: 6–7.*

I have said, ye are gods. The greatest honour was thus put upon Israel's judges. They were delegated **gods,** clothed for a while with a little of that authority by which the Lord judges among the sons of men. **And all of you are children of the most High.** This was their *ex-officio* character, not their moral or spiritual relationship. There must be some government among men, and as angels are not sent to dispense it, God allows men to rule over men. Magistrates would have no right to condemn the guilty if God had not sanctioned the establishment of government, the administration of law, and the execution of sentences. Here the Spirit speaks most honourably of these offices, even when it censures the officers. It thereby teaches us to render honour to whom honour is due, honour to the office, even if we award censure to the office-bearer.

But ye shall die like men. What sarcasm it seems! Great as the office made the men, they were still but men, and must die. Every judge must leave the bench to stand at the bar, and on the way must put off the ermine to put on the shroud. **And fall like one of the princes.** Who were usually the first to die. Battle, sedition, and luxury, made greater havoc among the great than among any others. Even as princes have been cut off by sudden and violent deaths, so should the judges be who forget to do justice. Men usually respect the office of a judge, and do not conspire to slay him, as they do to kill princes and kings. But injustice withdraws this protection, and puts the unjust magistrate in personal danger. How quickly death unrobes the great. No places are too high for Death's arrows. He brings down his birds from the tallest trees. It is time that all men considered this.

PSALM 83

Keep not thou silence, O God: hold not thy peace, and be not still, O God. For, lo, thine enemies make a tumult: and they that hate thee have lifted up the head. *Psalm 83:1-2.*

Keep not thou silence, O God. Man is clamorous. Be not thou speechless. He rails and reviles. Wilt not thou reply? One word of thine can deliver thy people. Therefore, O Lord, break thy quiet and let thy voice be heard. **Hold not thy peace, and be not still, O God.** Here the appeal is to *El*, the Mighty One. He is entreated to act and speak, because his nation suffers and is in great jeopardy. Now entirely the Psalmist looks to God. He asks not for a leader bold and brave, or for any form of human force, but casts his burden upon the Lord, being well assured that his eternal power and Godhead could meet every difficulty of the case.

For, lo, thine enemies make a tumult. They are by no means sparing of their words. They are like a hungry pack of dogs, all giving tongue at once. So sure are they of devouring thy people that they already shout over the feast. **And they that hate thee have lifted up the head.** Confident of conquest, they carry themselves proudly and exalt themselves as if their anticipated victories were already obtained. These enemies of Israel were also God's enemies, and are here described as such by way of adding intensity to the argument of the intercession. The adversaries of the church are usually a noisy and a boastful crew. Their pride is a brass which always sounds, a cymbal which is ever tinkling.

They have taken crafty counsel against thy people, and consulted against thy hidden ones. They have said, Come, and let us cut

them off from being a nation; that the name of Israel may be no more in remembrance. *Psalm 83:3-4.*

They have taken crafty counsel against thy people. Whatever we may do, our enemies use their wits and lay their heads together. In united conclave they discourse upon the demands and plans of the campaign, using much treachery and serpentine cunning in arranging their schemes. Malice is cold-blooded enough to plot with deliberation. Pride, though it be never wise, is often allied with craft. **And consulted against thy hidden ones.** Hidden away from all harm are the Lord's chosen. Their enemies think not so, but hope to smite them. They might as well attempt to destroy the angels before the throne of God.

They have said, Come, and let us cut them off from being a nation. Easier said than done. Yet it shows how thorough-going are the foes of the church. Theirs was the policy of extermination. They laid the axe at the root of the matter. **That the name of Israel may be no more in remembrance.** They would blot them out of history as well as out of existence. Evil is intolerant of good. If Israel would let Edom alone yet Edom cannot be quiet, but seeks like its ancestor to kill the chosen of the Lord. Men would be glad to cast the church out of the world because it rebukes them, and is thus a standing menace to their sinful peace.

PSALM 84

My soul longeth, yea, even fainteth for the courts of the Lord: my heart and my flesh crieth out for the living God. *Psalm 84:2.*

My soul longeth. It pines to meet with the saints in the Lord's house. The desire was deep and insatiable. The very soul of the man was yearning for his God. **Yea, even fainteth;** as though it could not long hold out, but was exhausted with delay. He had a holy lovesickness upon him, and was wasted with an inward consumption because he was debarred the worship of the Lord in the appointed place. **For the courts of the Lord.** To stand once again in those areas which were dedicated to holy adoration was the soul-longing of the Psalmist. True subjects love the courts of their king.

My heart and my flesh crieth out for the living God. It was God himself that he pined for, the only living and true God. His whole nature entered into his longing. Even the clay-cold flesh grew warm through the intense action of his fervent spirit. Seldom, indeed, does the flesh incline in the right direction. But in the matter of Sabbath services our weary body sometimes comes to the assistance of our longing heart, for it desires the physical rest as much as the soul desires the spiritual repose. The Psalmist declared that he could not remain silent in his desires, but began to cry out for God and his house. He wept, he sighed, he pleaded for the privilege. Some need to be whipped to church, while here is David crying for it. He needed no clatter of bells from the belfry to ring him in, he carried his bell in his own bosom. Holy appetite is a better call to worship than a full chime.

Yea, the sparrow hath found an house, and the swallow a nest for herself, where she may lay her young, even thine altars, O Lord of hosts, my King, and my God. *Psalm 84:3.*

Yea, the sparrow hath found an house. He envied the sparrows which lived around the house of God, and picked up the stray crumbs in the courts thereof. He only wished that he, too, could frequent the solemn assemblies and bear away a little of the heavenly food. **And the swallow a nest for herself, where she may lay her young.** He envied also the swallows whose nests were built under the eaves of the priests' houses, who there found a place for their young, as well as for themselves. We rejoice not only in our personal religious opportunities, but in the great blessing of taking our children with us to the sanctuary. The church of God is a house for us and a nest for our little ones.

Even thine altars, O Lord of hosts. To the very altars these free birds drew near. None could restrain them nor would have wished to do so, and David wished to come and go as freely as they did. Mark how he repeats the blessed name of Jehovah of Hosts. He found in it a sweetness which helped him to bear his inward hunger. Probably David himself was with the host, and, therefore, he dwelt with emphasis upon the title which taught him that the Lord was in the tented field as well as within the holy curtains. **My King and my God.** Here he utters his loyalty from afar. If he may not tread the courts, yet he loves the King. If an exile, he is not a rebel. When we cannot occupy a seat in God's house, he shall have a seat in our memories and a throne in our hearts. The double *my* is very precious. He lays hold upon his God with both his hands, as one resolved not to let him go till the favour requested be at length accorded.

Blessed are they that dwell in thy house: they will be still praising thee. *Psalm 84:4.*

Blessed are they that dwell in thy house. Those he esteems to be highly favoured who are constantly engaged in divine worship. To come and go is refreshing. But to abide in the place of prayer must be heaven below. To be the guests of God, enjoying the hospitalities of heaven, set apart for holy work, screened from a noisy world, and familiar with sacred things—why this is surely the choicest heritage a son of man can possess.

They will be still praising thee. So near to God, their very life must be adoration. Surely their hearts and tongues never cease from magnifying the Lord. We fear David here drew rather a picture of what should be than of what is. Those occupied daily with the offices needful for public worship are not always among the most devout. On the contrary, *the nearer the church, the further from God*. Yet in a spiritual sense this is most true, for those children of God who in spirit abide ever in his house, are also ever full of the praises of God. Communion is the mother of adoration. They fail to praise the Lord who wander far from him. But those who dwell in him are always magnifying him.

A day in thy courts is better than a thousand. I had rather be a doorkeeper in the house of my God, than to dwell in the tents of wickedness. *Psalm 84:10.*

A day in thy courts is better than a thousand. Of course the Psalmist means a thousand days spent elsewhere. Under the most favourable circumstances in which earth's pleasures can be enjoyed, they are not comparable by so much as one in a thousand to the delights of the service of God. To feel his love, to rejoice in the person of the anointed Saviour, to survey the promises and feel the power of the Holy Ghost in applying precious truth to the soul, is a joy which worldlings cannot understand, but which true believers are ravished with. Even a glimpse at the love of God is better than ages spent in the pleasures of sense.

I had rather be a doorkeeper in the house of my God, than to dwell in the tents of wickedness. The lowest station in connection with the Lord's house is better than the highest position among the godless. Only to wait at his threshold and peep within, so as to see Jesus, is bliss. To bear burdens and open doors for the Lord is more honour than to reign among the wicked. Every man has his choice, and this is ours. God's worst is better than the devil's best. God's doorstep is a happier rest than downy couches within the pavilions of royal sinners, though we might lie there for a lifetime of luxury. Note how he calls the tabernacle **the house of** *my* **God.** There's where the sweetness lies. If Jehovah be our God, his house, his altars, his doorstep, all become precious to us. We know by experience that where Jesus is within, the outside of the house is better than the noblest chambers where the Son of God is not to be found.

The Lord God is a sun and shield: the Lord will give grace and glory: no good thing will he withhold from them that walk uprightly. *Psalm 84:11.*

The Lord God is a sun and shield. Heavenly pilgrims are not left uncomforted or unprotected. The pilgrim nation found both **sun and shield** in that fiery cloudy pillar which was the symbol of Jehovah's presence. The Christian still finds both light and shelter in the Lord his God. A **sun** for happy days and a **shield** for dangerous ones. A light to show the way and a shield to ward off its perils. Blessed are they who journey with such a convoy. The sunny and the shady side of life are alike happy to them. **The Lord will give grace and glory.** Both in due time, both as needed, both to the full, both with absolute certainty. The Lord has both **grace and glory** in infinite abundance. Jesus is the fullness of both. As his chosen people, we shall receive both as a free gift from the God of our salvation. What more can the Lord give, or we receive, or desire?

No good thing will he withhold from them that walk uprightly. Grace makes us **walk uprightly** and this secures every covenant blessing to us. What a wide promise! Some apparent good may be withheld, but no real good, no, not one. *All things are yours, and ye are Christ's and Christ is God's.* God has all good. There is no good apart from him. There is no good which he either needs to keep back or will on any account refuse us, if we are but ready to receive it. We must be upright and neither lean to this or that form of evil. And this uprightness must be practical. We must *walk* in truth and holiness. Then shall we be heirs of all things, and as we come of age all things shall be in our actual possession. Meanwhile, according to our capacity for receiving shall be the measure of the divine bestowal. This is true, not of a favoured few, but of all the saints for evermore.

PSALM 85

Lord, thou hast been favourable unto thy land. *Psalm 85:1.*

Lord, thou hast been favourable unto thy land. The self-existent, all-sufficient Jehovah is addressed. By that name he revealed himself to Moses when his people were in bondage. By that name he is here pleaded with. It is wise to dwell upon that view of the divine character which arouses the sweetest memories of his love. Sweeter still is that dear name of *Our Father*, with which Christians have learned to commence their prayers. The Psalmist speaks of Canaan as the Lord's land, for he chose it for his people, conveyed it to them by covenant, conquered it by his power, and dwelt in it in mercy. It was meet therefore that he should smile upon a land so peculiarly his own. It is most wise to plead the Lord's union of interest with ourselves, to lash our little boat as it were close to his great barque, and experience a sacred community in the tossings of the storm. It is *our* land that is devastated. But O Jehovah, it is also *thy* land. The Psalmist dwells upon the Lord's favour to the chosen land, which he had showed in a thousand ways.

God's past doings are prophetic of what he will do. Hence the encouraging argument—**Thou has been favourable unto thy land,** therefore deal graciously with it again. Many a time had foes been baffled, pestilence stayed, famine averted, and deliverance vouchsafed, because of the Lord's favour. That same favourable regard is therefore again invoked. With an immutable God this is powerful reasoning. It is because he changes not that we are not consumed, and know we never shall be if he has once been favourable to us. From this example of prayer let us learn how to order our cause before God.

Turn us, O God of our salvation, and cause thine anger toward us to cease. *Psalm 85:4.*

Turn us, O God of our salvation. This was the main business. Could the erring tribes be rendered penitent, all would be well. It is not that *God* needs turning from his anger so much as that *we* need turning from our sin. Here is the hinge of the whole matter. Our trials frequently arise out of our sins. They will not go till the sins go. We need to be turned from our sins, but only God can **turn us.** God the Saviour must put his hand to the work. It is indeed a main part of our salvation. Conversion is the dawn of salvation. To turn a heart to God is as difficult as to make the world revolve upon its axis. Yet when a man learns to pray for conversion there is hope for him. He who turns to prayer is beginning to turn from sin. It is a very blessed sight to see a whole people turn unto their God. May the Lord so send forth his converting grace on our land that we may live to see the people flocking to the loving worship of God as the doves to their cotes.

And cause thine anger toward us to cease. Make an end of it. Let it no longer burn. When sinners cease to rebel, the Lord ceases to be angry with them. When they return to him he returns to them. Yea, he is first in the reconciliation and turns them when otherwise they would never turn of themselves. May all those who are now enduring the hidings of Jehovah's face seek with deep earnestness to be turned anew unto the Lord, for so shall all their despondencies come to an end.

Wilt thou not revive us again: that thy people may rejoice in thee? *Psalm 85:6.*

156

Wilt thou not revive us again? Hope here grows almost confident. She feels sure that the Lord will return in all his power to save. We are dead or dying, faint and feeble. God alone can **revive** us. He has in other times refreshed his people. He is still the same. He will repeat his love. Will he not? Why should he not? We appeal to him—**Wilt thou not? That thy people may rejoice in thee.** Thou lovest to see thy children happy with that best of happiness which centres in thyself. Therefore revive us, for revival will bring us the utmost joy.

The words before us teach us that gratitude has an eye to the giver, even beyond the gift—**thy people may rejoice** *in thee*. Those who were revived would rejoice not only in the new life but in the Lord who was the author of it. Joy in the Lord is the ripest fruit of grace. All revivals and renewals lead up to it. By our possession of it we may estimate our spiritual condition. It is a sure gauge of inward prosperity. A genuine revival without joy in the Lord is as impossible as spring without flowers, or dawn without light. If, either in our own souls or in the hearts of others, we see declension, it becomes us to be much in the use of this prayer. If on the other hand we are enjoying visitations of the Spirit and bedewings of grace, let us abound in holy joy and make it our constant delight to joy in God.

Truth shall spring out of the earth; and righteousness shall look down from heaven. *Psalm 85:11.*

Truth shall spring out of the earth. Promises which lie unfulfilled, like buried seeds, shall spring up and yield harvests of joy. Men renewed by grace shall learn to be true to one another and their God, and abhor the falsehood which they loved before. **And righteousness shall look down from heaven,** as if it threw up the windows and leaned out to gaze upon a penitent people, whom it could not have looked upon before without an indignation which would have been fatal to them. This is a delicious scene. Earth yielding flowers of truth, and heaven shining with stars of holiness. The spheres echoing to each other, or being mirrors of each other's beauties. *Earth carpeted with truth and canopied with righteousness* shall be a nether heaven. When God looks down in grace, man sends his heart upward in obedience.

The person of our adorable Lord Jesus Christ explains this verse most sweetly. In him truth is found in our humanity, and his deity brings divine righteousness among us. His Spirit's work even now creates a hallowed harmony between his church below, and the sovereign righteousness above. In the latter day, earth shall be universally adorned with every precious virtue, and heaven shall hold intimate intercourse with it.

Bow down thine ear, O Lord, hear me: for I am poor and needy.
Psalm 86:1.

Bow down thine ear, O Lord, hear me. In condescension to my littleness, and in pity to my weakness, **bow down thine ear, O Lord.** When our prayers are lowly by reason of our humility, or feeble by reason of our sickness, or without wing by reason of our despondency, the Lord will bow down to them, the infinitely exalted Jehovah will have respect unto them. Faith, when she has the loftiest name of God on her tongue, and calls him Jehovah, yet dares to ask from him the most tender and condescending acts of love. Great as he is he loves his children to be bold with him.

For I am poor and needy—doubly a son of poverty, because, first, **poor** and without supply for my needs, and next, **needy,** and so full of wants though unable to supply them. Our distress is a forcible reason for our being heard by the Lord God, merciful, and gracious, for misery is ever the master argument with mercy. Such reasoning as this would never be adopted by a proud man. Of all despicable sinners those are the worst who use the language of spiritual poverty while they think themselves to be rich and increased in goods.

Preserve my soul; for I am holy: O thou my God, save thy servant that trusteth in thee. *Psalm 86:2.*

Preserve my soul. Let my life be safe from my enemies, and my spiritual nature be secure from their temptations. He feels himself unsafe except he be covered by the divine protection. **For I am holy.** I am set apart for holy uses. Therefore do not let thine enemies commit a sacrilege by injuring or defiling me. I am clear of the crimes laid to my charge, and in that sense innocent. Therefore, I beseech thee, do not allow me to suffer from unjust charges. I am inoffensive, meek, and gentle towards others. Therefore deal mercifully with me as I have dealt with my fellow-men. It is not self-righteous in good men to plead their innocence as a reason for escaping from the results of sins wrongfully ascribed to them. The humblest saint is not a fool, and he is well aware of the matters wherein he is clear. To plead guilty to offences we have never committed is as great a lie as the denial of our real faults.

O thou my God, save thy servant that trusteth in thee. Lest any man should suppose that David trusted in his own holiness, he immediately declared his trust in the Lord. He begged to be saved as one who was not holy in the sense of being perfect, but was even yet in need of the very elements of salvation. How sweet is that title, **my God,**

when joined to the other, **servant**. How sweet is the hope that on this ground we shall be saved. Our God is not like the Amalekitish master who left his poor sick servant to perish. Note how David's poor **I am** (or rather the *I* repeated without the *am*) appeals to the great I AM with that sacred boldness engendered by the necessity which breaks through stone walls, aided by the faith which removes mountains.

Thou art great, and doest wondrous things: thou art God alone. *Psalm 86:10.*

Thou art great. He had earlier said, *Thou art good.* It is a grand thing when greatness and goodness are united. Happy is it for us that they both exist in the Lord to an equal degree. To be great and not good might lead to tyranny in the King. For him to be good and not great might involve countless calamities upon his subjects from foreign foes. Either alternative would be terrible. Let the two be blended, and we have a monarch in whom the nation may rest and rejoice. **And doest wondrous things.** Being good, he is said to be ready to forgive. Being great, he works wonders. We may blend the two, for there is no wonder so wonderful as the pardon of our transgressions. All that God does or makes has wonder in it. He breathes, and the wind is mystery. He speaks, and the thunder astounds us. Even the commonest daisy is a marvel, and a pebble enshrines wisdom.

Note that the verb **doest** is in the present. The Lord *is doing* wondrous things. They are transpiring before our eyes. Where are they? Look upon the bursting buds of spring or the maturing fruits of autumn, gaze on the sky or skim the sea, mark the results of providence and the victories of grace. **Thou art God alone.** Alone wast thou God before thy creatures were. Alone in godhead still art thou now that thou hast given life to throngs of beings. Alone for ever shalt thou be, for none can ever rival thee. Our God is not to be worshipped as one among many good and true beings, but as God alone. His gospel is not to be preached as one of several saving systems, but as the one sole way of salvation. Lies can face each other beneath one common dome. But in the temple of truth the worship is one and indivisible.

Teach me thy way, O Lord; I will walk in thy truth: unite my heart to fear thy name. *Psalm 86:11.*

Teach me thy way, O Lord. Instruct me thus at all times. Let me live in thy school. But **teach** me now especially since I am in trouble and perplexity. Be pleased to show me the **way** which thy wisdom and mercy have prepared for my escape. Behold I lay aside all wilfulness, and only desire to be informed as to thy holy and gracious mind. Not *my* way give me, but *thy* way teach me. **I will walk in thy truth.** When taught I will practise what I know. Truth shall not be a mere doctrine or sentiment to me, but a matter of daily life. The true servant of God regulates his walk by his master's will. Providence has a way for us, and it is our wisdom to keep in it. We must not be as the bullock which needs to be driven and urged forward because it likes not the road, but be as men who voluntarily go where their trusted friend and helper appoints their path.

Unite my heart to fear thy name. Having taught me one way, give me one heart to walk therein. Too often I feel a heart and a heart, two natures contending, two principles struggling for sovereignty. Our minds are apt to be divided between a variety of objects, like trickling streamlets which waste their force in a hundred runnels. Our great desire should be to have all our life-floods poured into one channel and to have that channel directed towards the Lord alone. A man of divided heart is weak. God who created the bands of our nature can draw them together, tighten, strengthen, and fasten them. So braced and inwardly knit by his uniting grace, we shall be powerful for good. But not otherwise. To fear God is both the beginning, the growth, and the maturity of wisdom. Therefore should we be undividedly given up to it, heart, and soul.

O God, the proud are risen against me, and the assemblies of violent men have sought after my soul; and have not set thee before them. But thou, O Lord, art a God full of compassion, and gracious, longsuffering, and plenteous in mercy and truth. *Psalm 86:14–15.*

O God, the proud are risen against me. They could not let God's poor servant alone. None hate good men so fiercely as do the high-minded and domineering. **And the assemblies of violent men have sought after my soul.** Unitedly oppressors sought the good man's life. They hunted in packs, with keen scent, and eager foot. In persecuting times many a saint has used these words. **And have not set thee before them.** They would not have molested the servant if they had cared one whit for the master. Those who fear not God are not afraid to commit violent and cruel acts.

But thou, O Lord. What a contrast! We get away from the hectorings and blusterings of proud but puny men to the glory and goodness of the Lord. **Art a God full of compassion, and gracious, longsuffering, and plenteous in mercy and truth.** A truly glorious doxology, in which there is not one redundant word. It is mainly transcribed from Exodus 34:6. Here is **compassion** for the weak and sorrowing, grace for the undeserving, **longsuffering** for the provoking, **mercy** for the guilty, and **truth** for the tried. God's love assumes many forms, and is lovely in them all. Into whatsoever state we may be cast, there is a peculiar hue in the light of love which will harmonise with our condition. Are we sorrowful? We find the Lord full of compassion. Are we contending with temptation? His grace comes to our aid. Do we err? He is patient with us. Have we sinned? He is plenteous in mercy. Are we resting on his promises? He will fulfil them with abundant truth.

PSALM 87

The Lord loveth the gates of Zion more than all the dwellings of Jacob. *Psalm 87:2.*

The Lord loveth the gates of Zion more than all the dwellings of Jacob. The **gates** are put for the city itself. The love of God is greatest to his own elect nation, descended from his servant **Jacob.** Yet the central seat of his worship is dearer still. No other supposable comparison could have so fully displayed the favour which Jehovah bore to Jerusalem. He loves Jacob best and Zion better than the best.

At this hour the mystical teaching of these words is plain. God delights in the prayers and praises of Christian families and individuals. But he has a special eye to the assemblies of the faithful. He has a special delight in their devotions in their church capacity. The great festivals, when the crowds surrounded the temple gates, were fair in the Lord's eyes, and even such is the general assembly and church of the first-born, whose names are written in heaven. This should lead each separate believer to identify himself with the church of God. Where the Lord reveals his love the most, there should each believer most delight to be found. Our own dwellings are very dear to us, but we must not prefer them to the assemblies of the saints.

Of Zion it shall be said, This and that man was born in her: and the highest himself shall establish her. *Psalm 87:5.*

Of Zion it shall be said, This and that man was born in her. One by one, as individuals, the citizens of the New Jerusalem shall be counted, and their names publicly declared. Man by man will the Lord reckon them, for they are each one precious in his sight. The individual shall not be lost in the mass. What a patent of nobility is it, for a man to have it certified that he **was born in Zion.** The twice-born are a royal priesthood, the true aristocracy, the imperial race of men. The original, by using the noblest word for man, intimates that many remarkable men will be born in the church. Indeed every man who is renewed in the image of Christ is an eminent personage. There are some, who, even to the dim eyes of the world, shine forth with a lustre of character which cannot but be admitted to be unusual and admirable. The church has illustrious names of prophets, apostles, martyrs, confessors, reformers, missionaries and the like, which bear comparison with the grandest names honoured by the world, nay, in many respects far excel them. Zion has no reason to be ashamed of her sons, nor her sons of her. *Wisdom is justified of her children.*

And the highest himself shall establish her—the only establishment worth having. When the numbers of the faithful are increased by the new birth, the Lord proves himself to be the upbuilder of the church. The Lord alone deserves to wear the title of Defender of the Faith. He is the sole and sufficient Patron and Protector of the true church. There is no fear for the Lord's heritage. His own arm is sufficient to maintain his rights. The Highest is higher than all those who are against us, and the good old cause shall triumph over all.

As well the singers as the players on instruments shall be there: all my springs are in thee. *Psalm 87:7.*

In vision the Psalmist sees the citizens of Zion rejoicing at some sacred festival, and marching in triumphant procession with vocal and instrumental music. **As well the singers as the players on instruments shall be there.** Where God is there must be joy, and where the church is increased by numerous conversions the joy becomes exuberant and finds out ways of displaying itself. Singers and dancers, Psalmists and pipers, united their efforts and made a joyful procession to the temple, inspired by draughts from the sacred source of all good, of which they each one sing **All my springs are in thee.** Did the poet mean that henceforth he would find all his joys in Zion? Or that to the Lord he would look for all inspiration, comfort, strength, joy, life and everything? The last is the truer doctrine. Churches have not such all-sufficiency within them that we can afford to look to them for all. But the Lord who founded the church is the eternal source of all our supplies. Looking to him we shall never flag or fail.

How truly does all our experience lead us to look to the Lord by faith, and say **all my** *fresh* **springs are in thee.** The springs of my faith and all my graces; the springs of my life and all my pleasures; the springs of my activity and all its right doings; the springs of my hope, and all its heavenly anticipations, all lie **in thee,** my Lord. Without thy

162

Spirit I should be as a dry well, a mocking cistern, destitute of power to bless myself or others. O Lord, I am assured that I belong to the regenerate whose life is in thee, for I feel that I cannot live without thee. Therefore, with all thy joyful people will I sing thy praises.

O Lord God of my salvation, I have cried day and night before thee. *Psalm 88:1.*

O Lord God of my salvation. This is a hopeful title by which to address the Lord. The writer has salvation, he is sure of that, and God is the sole author of it. While a man can see God as his Saviour, it is not altogether midnight with him. It is one of the characteristics of true faith that she turns to Jehovah, the saving God, when all other confidences have proved liars unto her. **I have cried day and night before thee.** His distress had not blown out the sparks of his prayer, but quickened them into a greater ardency, till they burned perpetually like a furnace at full blast. His prayer was personal—whoever had not prayed, he had done so. It was intensely earnest, so that it was correctly described as a cry, such as children utter to move the pity of their parents. It was unceasing, neither the business of the day nor the weariness of the night had silenced it. Surely such entreaties could not be in vain.

It is a good thing that sickness will not let us rest if we spend our restlessness in prayer. **Day and night** are both suitable to prayer. It is no work of darkness. Therefore let us go with Daniel and pray when men can see us. Yet, since supplication needs no light, let us accompany Jacob and wrestle at Jabbok till the day breaketh. Evil is transformed to good when it drives us to prayer. One expression of the text is worthy of special note: **before thee** is a remarkable intimation that the Psalmist's cries had an aim and a direction towards the Lord, and were not the mere clamours of nature, but the groanings of a gracious heart towards Jehovah, the God of salvation. Of what use are arrows shot into the air? The archer's business is to look well at the mark he drives at. Prayers must be directed to heaven with earnest care.

I will sing of the mercies of the Lord for ever: with my mouth will I make known thy faithfulness to all generations. *Psalm 89:1.*

I will sing of the mercies of the Lord for ever. Whether others sing or not, believers must never give over. In them should be constancy of praise, since God's love to them cannot by any possibility have changed, however providence may seem to frown. The Lord's goodness is the source of all our joy; and as it cannot be dried up, so the stream ought never to fail to flow, or cease to flash in sparkling crystal of song. We have not one, but many **mercies** to rejoice in, and should therefore multiply the expressions of our thankfulness. It is *Jehovah* who deigns to deal out to us our daily benefits, and he is the all-sufficient and immutable God. Therefore our rejoicing in him must never suffer diminution. Even time itself must not bound our praises—they must leap into eternity. He blesses us with eternal mercies—let us sing unto him **for ever.**

With my mouth will I make known thy faithfulness to all generations. The utterances of the present will instruct future generations. What the Psalmist sung is now a text-book for Christians, and will be so as long as this dispensation shall last. He first spoke with his mouth that which he recorded with his pen. The mouth has a warmer manner than the pen, but the pen's speech lives longest, and is heard farther and wider. **Faithfulness** is the mercy of God's mercies—the brightest jewel in the crown of goodness. Unchangeable love and immutable promises demand everlasting songs. In times of trouble it is the divine faithfulness which the soul hangs upon. It will also be always desirable to make it known, for men are too apt to forget it, or to doubt it, when hard times press upon them. We cannot too much multiply testimonies to the Lord's faithful mercy. If our own generation should not need them others will. Sceptics are so ready to repeat old doubts and invent new ones that believers should be equally prompt to bring forth evidences both old and new.

Who in the heaven can be compared unto the Lord? who among the sons of the mighty can be likened unto the Lord? *Psalm 89:6.*

Who in the heaven can be compared unto the Lord? Therefore all heaven worships him, seeing none can equal him. **Who among the sons of the mighty can be likened unto the Lord?** Therefore the assemblies of the saints on earth adore him, seeing none can rival him. Until we can find one equally worthy to be praised, we will give unto the Lord alone all the homage of our praise. Neither among the sons of the morning nor the sons of the mighty can any peer be found for Jehovah, yea none that can be mentioned in the same day. Therefore he is rightly praised. Since the Lord Jesus, both as God and as man, is far above all craetures, he also is to be devoutly worshipped. How full

of poetic fire is this verse! How bold is the challenge! How triumphant
the holy boasting!

The sweet singer dwells upon the name of Jehovah with evident
exultation. To him the God of Israel is God indeed and God alone. He
closely follows the language long before rehearsed by Miriam, when
she sang, *Who is like unto thee, O Jehovah, among the gods? Who is like thee?*
His thoughts are evidently flying back to the days of Moses and the
marvels of the Red Sea, when God was gloriously known by his in-
communicable name. There is a ring of timbrels in the double question,
and a sound as of the twinkling feet of rejoicing maidens. Have we no
poets now? Is there not a man among us who can compose hymns
flaming with this spirit? O, Spirit of the living God, be thou the
inspirer of some master minds among us!

**Blessed is the people that know the joyful sound: they shall
walk, O Lord, in the light of thy countenance.** *Psalm 89:15.*

Blessed is the people that know the joyful sound. He is a blessed
God of whom the Psalmist has been singing. Therefore they are a
blessed people who partake of his bounty, and know how to exult in
his favour. Praise is a peculiarly **joyful sound,** and **blessed** are those
who are familiar with its strains. The covenant promises have also a
sound beyond measure precious. They are highly favoured who understand their meaning and recognise their own personal interest in them.
There may also be a reference here to the blowing of trumpets and
other gladsome noises which attended the worship of Jehovah, who,
unlike the gods of the heathen was not adored by the shrieks of wretched
victims, or the yells and outcries of terror-stricken crowds, but by the
joyful shouts of his happy people.

They shall walk, O Lord, in the light of thy countenance. For
them it is joy enough that Jehovah is favourable to them. All day long
this contents them and enables them with vigour to pursue their
pilgrimage. Only a covenant God could look with favour upon men.
Those who have known him in that relationship learn to rejoice in
him, yea, to **walk** with him in fellowship, and to continue in communion with him. If we give God our ear and hear the joyful sound,
he will show us his face and make us glad. While the sun shines, men
walk without stumbling as to their feet. When the Lord smiles on us,
we live without grief as to our souls.

**Thou art the glory of their strength: and in thy favour our horn
shall be exalted.** *Psalm 89:17.*

Thou art the glory of their strength. Surely in the Lord Jehovah have we both righteousness and strength. He is our beauty and glory when we are strong in him, as well as our comfort and sustenance when we tremble because of conscious weakness in ourselves. No man whom the Lord makes strong may dare to glory in himself, he must ascribe all honour to the Lord alone. We have neither strength nor beauty apart from him.

And in thy favour our horn shall be exalted. By the use of the word **our** the Psalmist identifies himself with the blessed people, and this indicates how much sweeter it is to sing in the first person than concerning others. May we have grace to claim a place among those in covenant with God, in Christ Jesus, for then a sense of divine favour will make us also bold and joyous. A creature full of strength and courage lifts up its horn, and so also does a believer become potent, valiant, and daring. The **horn** was an eastern ornament, worn by men and women, and by the uplifting of this the wearer showed himself to be in good spirits, and in a confident frame of mind. We wear no such outward vanities, but our inward soul is adorned and made bravely triumphant when the favour of God is felt by us. Worldly men need outward prosperity to make them lift up their heads. But the saints find more than enough encouragement in the secret love of God.

My covenant will I not break, nor alter the thing that is gone out of my lips. *Psalm 89:34.*

My covenant will I not break. It is his own **covenant.** He devised it, drew up the draft of it, and voluntarily entered into it. He therefore thinks much of it. It is not a man's covenant, but the Lord claims it as his own. It is an evil thing among men for one to be a covenant-breaker, and such an opprobrious epithet shall never be applicable to the Most High. **Nor alter the thing that is gone out of my lips.** Alterations and afterthoughts belong to short-sighted beings who meet with unexpected events which operate upon them to change their minds. But the Lord who sees everything from the beginning has no such reason for shifting his ground. He is besides immutable in his nature and designs, and cannot change in heart, and therefore not in promise.

A word once given is sacred. Once let a promise pass our lips and honesty forbids that we should recall it—unless indeed the thing promised be impossible, or wicked, neither of which can happen with the promises of God. How consoling it is to see the Lord thus resolute. He, in the words before us, virtually reasserts his covenant and rehearses his engagements. This he does at such length, and with such reiteration, that it is evident he takes pleasure in that most ancient and solemn contract. If it were conceivable that he had repented of it, he would not be found dwelling upon it, and repeating it with renewed emphasis.

Remember, Lord, the reproach of thy servants; how I do bear in my bosom the reproach of all the mighty people. *Psalm 89:50.*

Remember, Lord, the reproach of thy servants. By reason of their great troubles they were made a mock of by ungodly men, and hence the Lord's pity is entreated. Will a father stand by and see his children insulted? The Psalmist entreats the Lord to compassionate the wretchedness brought upon his servants by the taunts of their adversaries, who jested at them on account of their sufferings. **How I do bear in my bosom the reproach of all the mighty people.** The Psalmist himself laid the scorn of the great and the proud to heart. He felt as if all the reproaches which vexed his nation were centred in himself, and therefore in sacred sympathy with the people he poured out his heart. We ought to weep with those that weep. Reproach brought upon the saints and their cause ought to burden us. If we can hear Christ blasphemed, and see his servants insulted, and remain unmoved, we have not the true Israelite's spirit. Our grief at the griefs of the Lord's people may be pleaded in prayer, and it will be acceptable argument.

There is one interpretation of this verse which must not be passed over. The original is, *Remember my bearing in my bosom all the many nations.* This may be understood as a pleading of the church that the Lord would remember her because she was yet to be the mother of many nations, according to the prophecy of Ps. 87. She was, as it were, ready to give birth to nations. But how could they be born if she herself died in the meanwhile? The church is the hope of the world. Should she expire, the nations would never come to the birth of regeneration, but must abide in death.

PSALM 90

A thousand years in thy sight are but as yesterday when it is past, and as a watch in the night. *Psalm 90:4.*

A thousand years in thy sight are but as yesterday when it is past. A thousand years! This is a long stretch of time. How much may be crowded into it—the rise and fall of empires, the glory and obliteration of dynasties, the beginning and the end of elaborate systems of human philosophy, and countless events, all important to household and individual, which elude the pens of historians. Yet this period, which might even be called the limit of modern history, and is in human language almost identical with an indefinite length of time, is to the Lord as nothing, even as time already gone. A moment yet to come is longer than **yesterday when it is past,** for that no longer exists at all, yet such is a chiliad to the Eternal. In comparison with eternity, the most lengthened reaches of time are mere points. There is, in fact, no possible comparison between them.

And as a watch in the night, a time which is no sooner come than gone. There is scarce time enough in a thousand years for the angels to change watches. When their millennium of service is almost over, it seems as though the watch were newly set. We are dreaming through the long night of time. But God is ever keeping watch, and a thousand years are as nothing to him. A host of days and nights must be combined to make up a thousand years to us. But to God that space of time does not make up a whole night, but only a brief portion of it. If a thousand years be to God as a single night-watch, what must be the life-time of the Eternal!

The days of our years are threescore years and ten; and if by reason of strength they be fourscore years, yet is their strength labour and sorrow; for it is soon cut off, and we fly away. *Psalm 90:10.*

The days of our years are threescore years and ten. Yet is life long enough for virtue and piety, and all too long for vice and blasphemy. The words may be rendered, *The days of our years! In them seventy years:* as much as to say, The days of our years? What about them? Are they worth mentioning? The account is utterly insignificant. Their full tale is but seventy. **And if by reason of strength they be fourscore years, yet is their strength labour and sorrow.** The unusual strength which overlaps the bound of threescore and ten only lands the aged man in a region where life is a weariness and a woe. What panting for breath! What toiling to move! What a failing of the senses! What a crushing sense of weakness! The evil days are come and the years wherein a man cries, *I have no pleasure in them.* The grasshopper has become a burden and desire faileth. Such is old age.

Yet mellowed by hallowed experience, and solaced by immortal hopes, the latter days of aged Christians are not so much to be pitied as envied. The sun is setting and the heat of the day is over, but sweet is the calm and the cool of eventide. The fair day melts away, not into a dark and dreary night, but into a glorious, unclouded, eternal day. The mortal fades to make room for the immortal. The old man falls asleep to wake up in the region of perennial youth. **For it is soon cut off, and we fly away.** The chain is snapped and the eagle mounts to its native air above the clouds. The words are more nearly rendered, *He drives us fast and we fly away.* Let the Lord's winds drive fast, if he so ordains. They waft us the more swiftly to himself, and to our own dear country.

So teach us to number our days, that we apply our hearts unto wisdom. *Psalm 90:12.*

So teach us to number our days. Instruct us to set store by time, mourning for that time past wherein we have wrought the will of the flesh, using diligently the time present, which is the accepted hour and the day of salvation, and reckoning the time which lieth in the future to be too uncertain to allow us safely to delay any gracious work or prayer. Numeration is a child's exercise in arithmetic. But in order to **number** their days aright the best of men need the Lord's teaching. We are more anxious to count the stars than our days, and yet the latter is by far more practical.

That we may apply our hearts unto wisdom. Men are led by reflections upon the brevity of time to give their earnest attention to eternal things. They become humble as they look into the grave which is so soon to be their bed. Their passions cool in the presence of mortality, and they yield themselves up to the dictates of unerring **wisdom.** But this is only the case when the Lord himself is the teacher. He alone can teach to real and lasting profit. Thus Moses prayed that the dispensations of justice might be sanctified in mercy. *The law is our schoolmaster to bring us to Christ,* when the Lord himself speaks by the law. It is most meet that the heart, which will so soon cease to beat, should while it moves be regulated by wisdom's hand. A short life should be wisely spent. We have not enough time at our disposal to justify us in misspending a single quarter of an hour. Neither are we sure of enough of life to justify us in procrastinating for a moment. If we were wise in heart we should see this. But mere head wisdom will not guide us aright.

O satisfy us early with thy mercy; that we may rejoice and be glad all our days. *Psalm 90:14.*

O satisfy us early with thy mercy. Since they must die, and die soon, the Psalmist pleads for speedy **mercy** upon himself and his brethren. Good men know how to turn the darkest trials into arguments at the throne of grace. He who has but the heart to pray need never be without pleas in prayer. The only satisfying food for the

Lord's people is the favour of God. This Moses earnestly seeks for. As the manna fell in the morning he beseeches the Lord to send at once his satisfying favour, that all through the little day of life he might be filled therewith. Are we so soon to die? Then, Lord, do not starve us while we live. **Satisfy us** at once, we pray thee. Our day is short and the night hastens on. O give us in the early morning of our days to be satisfied with thy favour, that all through our little day we may be happy.

That we may rejoice and be glad all our days. Being filled with divine love, their brief life on earth would become a joyful festival, and would continue so as long as it lasted. When the Lord refreshes us with his presence, our joy is such that no man can take it from us. Apprehensions of speedy death are not able to distress those who enjoy the present favour of God. Though they know that the night cometh, they see nothing to fear in it. They continue to live while they live, triumphing in the present favour of God and leaving the future in his loving hands. Since the whole generation which came out of Egypt had been doomed to die in the wilderness, they would naturally feel despondent, and therefore their great leader seeks for them that blessing which, beyond all others, consoles the heart, namely, the presence and favour of the Lord.

Make us glad according to the days wherein thou hast afflicted us, and the years wherein we have seen evil. *Psalm 90:15.*

None can gladden the heart as thou canst, O Lord. Therefore as thou hast made us sad, be pleased to make us glad. Fill the other scale. Proportion thy dispensations. Give us the lamb, since thou has sent us the bitter herbs. Make our days as long as our nights. The prayer is original, childlike, and full of meaning. It is moreover based upon a great principle in providential goodness, by which the Lord puts the good over against the evil in due measure. Great trial enables us to bear great joy, and may be regarded as the herald of extraordinary grace.

God's dealings are according to scale. Small lives are small throughout, and great histories are great both in sorrow and happiness. Where there are high hills, there are also deep valleys. As God provides the sea for leviathan, so does he find a pool for the minnow. In the sea all things are in fit proportion for the mighty monster, while in the little brook all things befit the tiny fish. If we have fierce afflictions, we may look for overflowing delights. Our faith may boldly ask for them. God is great in justice when he chastens. He will not be little in mercy when he blesses. He will be great all through. Let us appeal to him with unstaggering faith.

Let the beauty of the Lord our God be upon us: and establish
thou the work of our hands upon us; yea, the work of our hands
establish thou it. *Psalm 90:17*.

Let the beauty of the Lord our God be upon us. Even upon us who
must not see thy glory in the land of Canaan. It shall suffice us if in our
characters the holiness of God is reflected, and if over all our camp the
lovely excellences of our God shall cast a sacred beauty. Sanctification
should be the daily object of our petitions. And establish thou the
work of our hands upon us; yea, the work of our hands establish
thou it. Let what we do be done in truth, and last when we are in the
grave. May the work of the present generation minister permanently
to the building up of the nation. Good men are anxious not to work in
vain. They know that without the Lord they can do nothing. Therefore
they cry to him for help in the work, for acceptance of their efforts, and
for the establishment of their designs.

The church as a whole earnestly desires that the hand of the Lord
may so work with the hand of his people, that a substantial, yea, an
eternal edifice to the praise and glory of God may be the result. We
come and go. But the Lord's work abides. We are content to die, so
long as Jesus lives and his kingdom grows. Since the Lord abides for
ever the same, we trust our work in his hands, and feel that since it is
far more his work than ours he will secure its immortality. When we
have withered like grass, our holy service, like gold, silver, and precious
stones, will survive the fire.

PSALM 91

He that dwelleth in the secret place of the most High shall abide
under the shadow of the Almighty. *Psalm 91:1*.

He that dwelleth in the secret place of the most High. Every child
of God looks towards the inner sanctuary and the mercy-seat, yet all
do not *dwell* in the most holy place. They run to it at times, and enjoy
occasional approaches, but they do not habitually reside in the mysterious presence. Outer-court worshippers little know what belongs
to the inner sanctuary, or surely they would press on until the place
of nearness and divine familiarity became theirs. Those who are the
Lord's constant guests shall find that he will never suffer any to be
injured within his gates. He has eaten the covenant salt with them, and
is pledged for their protection.

Shall abide under the shadow of the Almighty. The Omnipotent
Lord will shield all those who dwell with him. They shall remain under
his care as guests under the protection of their host. In the most holy

place the wings of the cherubim were the most conspicuous objects, and they probably suggested to the Psalmist the expression here employed. Those who commune with God are safe with him, for the outstretched wings of his power and love cover them from all harm. This protection is constant—they **abide** under it, and it is all-sufficient, for it is the shadow of **the Almighty**, whose omnipotence will surely screen them from all attack. No shelter can be imagined at all comparable to the protection of Jehovah's own **shadow**. The Almighty himself is where his shadow is. Hence those who dwell in his secret place are shielded by himself. What a shade in the day of noxious heat! What a refuge in the hour of deadly storm! Communion with God is safety. The more closely we cling to our Almighty Father the more confident may we be.

I will say of the Lord, He is my refuge and my fortress: my God; in him I will trust. *Psalm 91:2.*

I will say of the Lord, He is my refuge and my fortress. It is but poor comfort to say 'the Lord is *a* refuge'. But to say **he is *my* refuge** is the essence of consolation. Those who believe should also speak— **I will say.** Such bold avowals honour God and lead others to seek the same confidence. Men are apt enough to proclaim their doubts, and even to boast of them. Hence it becomes the duty of all true believers to speak out and testify with calm courage to their own well-grounded reliance upon their God. Let others say what they will, be it ours to say of the Lord, *He is our refuge.* But what we say we must prove by our actions. We must fly to the Lord for shelter, and not to an arm of flesh. Let us, when we are secure in the Lord, rejoice that our position is unassailable, for he is our **fortress** as well as our refuge. Foes in flesh, and foes in ghostly guise are alike baulked of their prey when the Lord of Hosts stands between us and their fury, and all other evil forces are turned aside. Walls cannot keep out the pestilence, but the Lord can.

As if it were not enough to call the Lord his refuge and fortress, he adds, **My God! in him will I trust.** Now he can say no more. **My God** means all, and more than all, that heart can conceive by way of security. He who dwells in an impregnable fortress, naturally trusts in it. Shall not he who dwells in God feel himself well at ease, and repose his soul in safety? O that we more fully carried out the Psalmist's resolve! To trust in man is natural to fallen nature. To trust in God should be as natural to regenerated nature. Pray for grace to say, **In** *him* **will I trust.**

Because thou hast made the Lord, which is my refuge, even the most High, thy habitation; there shall no evil befall thee, neither shall any plague come nigh thy dwelling. *Psalm 91:9–10.*

In the year 1854, when I had been in London scarcely twelve months, the neighbourhood in which I laboured was visited by Asiatic cholera. My congregation suffered from its inroads. Family after family summoned me to the bedside of the smitten. Almost every day I was called to visit the grave. I gave myself up with youthful ardour to the visitation of the sick, and was sent for from all corners of the district by persons of all ranks and religions. I became weary in body and sick at heart. My friends seemed falling one by one, and I felt or fancied that I was sickening like those around me. A little more work and weeping would have laid me low among the rest. I felt that my burden was heavier than I could bear. I was ready to sink under it.

As God would have it, I was returning mournfully from a funeral, when my curiosity led me to read a paper which was wafered up in a shoemaker's window in the Dover Road. It did not look like a trade announcement. Nor was it. It bore in a good bold handwriting these words: **Because thou hast made the Lord, which is my refuge, even the most High, thy habitation; there shall no evil befall thee, neither shall any plague come nigh thy dwelling.** The effect upon my heart was immediate. Faith appropriated the passage as her own. I felt secure, refreshed, girt with immortality. I went on with my visitation of the dying in a calm and peaceful spirit. I felt no fear of evil. I suffered no harm. The providence which moved the tradesman to place those verses in his window I gratefully acknowledge, and in the remembrance of its marvellous power I adore the Lord my God.

He shall give his angels charge over thee, to keep thee in all thy ways. *Psalm 91:11.*

He shall give his angels charge over thee. Not one guardian angel, as some fondly dream, but all the angels are here alluded to. They are the bodyguard of the princes of the blood imperial of heaven. They have received commission from their Lord and ours to watch carefully over all the interests of the faithful. When men have a charge they become doubly careful, and therefore the angels are represented as bidden by God himself to see to it that the elect are secured. It is down in the marching orders of the hosts of heaven that they take special note of the people who dwell in God. It is not to be wondered at that the servants are bidden to be careful of the comfort of their Master's guests. We may be quite sure that when they are specially charged by the Lord himself, they will carefully discharge the duty imposed upon them.

To keep thee in all thy ways. To be a bodyguard, a garrison to the body, soul, and spirit of the saint. The limit of this protection **in all thy ways** is yet no limit to the heart which is right with God. It is not the way of the believer to go out of his way. He keeps in the way. Then the angels keep him. The protection here promised is exceeding broad as to place. It refers to *all* our ways. What do we wish for more? How angels thus keep us we cannot tell. Whether they repel demons, counteract spiritual plots, or even ward off the subtler physical forces of disease, we do not know. Perhaps we shall one day stand amazed at the multiplied services which the unseen bands have rendered to us.

Because he hath set his love upon me, therefore will I deliver him: I will set him on high, because he hath known my name. *Psalm 91:14.*

Here we have the Lord himself speaking of his own chosen one. **Because he hath set his love upon me, therefore will I deliver him.** Not because he deserves to be thus kept, but because with all his imperfections he does love his God. Therefore not the angels of God only, but the God of angels himself will come to his rescue in all perilous times, and will effectually deliver him. When the heart is enamoured of the Lord, all taken up with him, and intensely attached to him, the Lord will recognise the sacred flame, and preserve the man who bears it in his bosom. It is love—love set upon God, which is the distinguishing mark of those whom the Lord secures from ill.

I will set him on high, because he hath known my name. The man has known the attributes of God so as to trust in him, and then by experience has arrived at a yet deeper knowledge. This shall be regarded by the Lord as a pledge of his grace. He will set the owner of it above danger or fear, where he shall dwell in peace and joy. None abide in intimate fellowship with God unless they possess a warm affection towards God, and an intelligent trust in him. These gifts of grace are precious in Jehovah's eyes. Wherever he sees them he smiles upon them. How elevated is the standing which the Lord gives to the believer! We ought to covet it right earnestly. If *we climb* on high, it may be dangerous. But if *God sets us* there it is glorious.

He shall call upon me, and I will answer him: I will be with him in trouble; I will deliver him, and honour him. With long life will I satisfy him, and show him my salvation. *Psalm 91:15–16.*

He shall call upon me, and I will answer him. He will have need to pray. He will be led to pray aright. The answer shall surely come.

Saints are first called *of* God, and then they call *upon* God. Such calls as theirs always obtain answers. Not without prayer will the blessing come to the most favoured. But by means of prayer they shall receive all good things. **I will be with him in trouble,** or I *am* **with him in trouble.** Heirs of heaven are conscious of a special divine presence in times of severe trial. God is always near in sympathy and in power to help his tried ones. **I will deliver him, and honour him.** The man honours God, and God honours him. Believers are not delivered or preserved in a way which lowers them, and makes them feel themselves degraded. Far from it. The Lord's salvation bestows honour upon those it delivers. God first gives us conquering grace, and then rewards us for it.

With long life will I satisfy him. The man described in this Psalm fills out the measure of his days. Whether he dies young or old he is quite satisfied with life, and is content to leave it. He shall rise from life's banquet as a man who has had enough, and would not have more even if he could. **And show him my salvation.** The full sight of divine grace shall be his closing vision. Not with destruction before him black as night, but with **salvation** bright as noonday smiling upon him he shall enter into his rest.

PSALM 92

It is a good thing to give thanks unto the Lord, and to sing praises unto thy name, O most High. *Psalm 92:1.*

It is a good thing to give thanks unto the Lord, or *Jehovah*. It is good ethically, for it is the Lord's right. It is good emotionally, for it is pleasant to the heart. It is good practically, for it leads others to render the same homage. When duty and pleasure combine, who will be backward? **To give thanks** to God is but a small return for the great benefits wherewith he daily loadeth us. Yet as he by his Spirit calls it **a good thing,** we must not despise it, or neglect it. We thank men when they oblige us. How much more ought we to bless the Lord when he benefits us! Devout praise is always good. It is never out of season, never superfluous. But it is especially suitable to the Sabbath. A Sabbath without thanksgiving is a Sabbath profaned.

And to sing praises unto thy name, O most High. It is good to give thanks in the form of vocal song. Nature itself teaches us thus to express our gratitude to God. Do not the birds sing, and the brooks warble as they flow? To give his gratitude a tongue is wise in man. Silent worship is sweet, but vocal worship is sweeter. To deny the tongue the privilege of uttering the praises of God involves an unnatural strain upon the most commendable promptings of our

175

renewed manhood. Our personal experience has confirmed us in the belief that it is good to sing unto the Lord. We have often felt like Luther when he said, *Come, let us sing a Psalm, and drive away the devil.*

To show forth thy lovingkindness in the morning, and thy faithfulness every night. *Psalm 92:2.*

To show forth thy lovingkindness in the morning. The day should begin with praise. No hour is too early for holy song. **Lovingkindness** is a most appropriate theme for those dewy hours when morn is sowing all the earth with orient pearl. Eagerly and promptly should we magnify the Lord. We leave unpleasant tasks as long as we can, but our hearts are so engrossed with the adoration of God that we would rise betimes to attend to it. There is a peculiar freshness and charm about early morning praises. The day is loveliest when it first opens its eyelids. God himself seems then to make distribution of the day's manna, which tastes most sweetly if gathered ere the sun is hot. It seems most meet that if our hearts and harps have been silent through the shades of night, we should be eager again to take our place among the chosen choir who ceaselessly hymn the Eternal One.

And thy faithfulness every night. No hour is too late for praise. The end of the day must not be the end of gratitude. When nature seems in silent contemplation to adore its Maker, it ill becomes the children of God to refrain their thanksgiving. Evening is the time for retrospect. Memory is busy with the experience of the day. Hence the appropriate theme for song is the divine **faithfulness,** of which another day has furnished fresh evidences. **Every night,** clouded or clear, moonlit or dark, calm or tempestuous, is alike suitable for a song upon the faithfulness of God. Shame on us that we are so backward in magnifying the Lord, who in the daytime scatters bounteous love, and in the night season walks his rounds of watching care.

O Lord, how great are thy works! and thy thoughts are very deep. *Psalm 92:5.*

O Lord, how great are thy works! The Psalmist is lost in wonder. He utters an exclamation of amazement. How vast! How stupendous are the doings of Jehovah! Great for number, extent, and glory and design are all the creations of the Infinite One. **And thy thoughts are very deep.** The Lord's plans are as marvellous as his acts. His designs are as profound as his doings are vast. Creation is immeasurable, and the wisdom displayed in it unsearchable.

Some men think, but cannot work. Others are mere drudges working without thought. In the Eternal the conception and the execution go together. Providence is inexhaustible, and the divine decrees which originate it are inscrutable. Redemption is grand beyond conception, and the thoughts of love which planned it are infinite. Man is superficial; God is inscrutable. Man is shallow; God is deep. Dive as we may, we shall never fathom the mysterious plan, or exhaust the boundless wisdom of the all-comprehending mind of the Lord. We stand by the fathomless sea of divine wisdom, and exclaim with holy awe, *Oh, the depth!*

Mine eye also shall see my desire on my enemies, and mine ears shall hear my desire of the wicked that rise up against me. *Psalm 92:11.*

Mine eye also shall see my desire on mine enemies. The words **my desire,** inserted by the translators, had far better have been left out. He does not say what he should see concerning his enemies. He leaves that blank, and we have no right to fill in the vacant space with words which look vindictive. He would see that which would be for God's glory, and that which would be eminently right and just.

   And mine ears shall hear my desire of the wicked that rise up against me. Here again the words **my desire** are not inspired, and are a needless and perhaps a false interpolation. The good man is quite silent as to what he expected to hear. He knew that what he should hear would vindicate his faith in his God. He was content to leave his cruel foes in God's hands, without an expression concerning his own desire one way or the other. It is always best to leave Scripture as we find it. The broken sense of inspiration is better let alone than pieced out with additions of a translator's own invention. It is like repairing pure gold with tinsel, or a mosaic of gems with painted wood. The holy Psalmist had seen the beginning of the ungodly, and expected to see their end. He felt sure that God would right all wrongs, and clear his Providence from the charge of favouring the unjust. This confidence he here expresses, and sits down contentedly to wait the issues of the future.

The righteous shall flourish like the palm tree: he shall grow like a cedar in Lebanon. *Psalm 92:12.*

The song contrasts the condition of the righteous with that of the graceless. The wicked *spring as the grass* (verse 7), but **The righteous shall flourish like the palm tree,** whose growth may not be so rapid, but whose endurance for centuries is in fine contrast with the transitory verdure of the meadow. When we see a noble palm standing erect, sending all its strength upward in one bold column, and growing amid the dearth and drought of the desert, we have a fine picture of the godly man, who in his uprightness aims alone at the glory of God; and, independent of outward circumstances, is made by divine grace to live and thrive where all things else perish. The text tells us not only what **the righteous** is, but what he shall be. Come what may, the good man **shall flourish,** and flourish after the noblest manner.

He shall grow like a cedar in Lebanon. This is another noble and long-lived tree. *As the days of a tree are the days of my people*, saith the Lord. On the summit of the mountain, unsheltered from the blast, the cedar waves its mighty branches in perpetual verdure. So the truly godly man under all adversities retains the joy of his soul, and continues to make progress in the divine life. Grass, which makes hay for oxen, is a good enough emblem of the unregenerate. But cedars, which build the temple of the Lord, are none too excellent to set forth the heirs of heaven.

They shall still bring forth fruit in old age; they shall be fat and flourishing. *Psalm 92:14.*

They shall still bring forth fruit in old age. Nature decays, but grace thrives. **Fruit,** as far as nature is concerned, belongs to days of vigour. But in the garden of grace, when plants are weak in themselves, they become strong in the Lord, and abound in fruit acceptable to God. Aged believers possess a ripe experience. By their mellow tempers and sweet testimonies they feed many. Even if bedridden, they bear the fruit of patience. If poor and obscure, their lowly and contented spirit becomes the admiration of those who know how to appreciate modest worth. Grace does not leave the saint when the keepers of the house do tremble. The promise is still sure, though the eyes can no longer read it. The bread of heaven is fed upon when the grinders fail. The voice of the Spirit in the soul is still melodious when the daughters of music are brought low. Blessed be the Lord for this! Because even to hoar hairs he is the *I am*, who made his people, he therefore bears and carries them.

They shall be fat and flourishing. They do not drag out a wretched, starveling existence, but are like trees full of sap, which bear luxuriant foliage. God does not pinch his poor servants, and diminish their consolations when their infirmities grow upon them. Rather does he see to it that they shall renew their strength, for their mouths shall be satisfied with his own good things. Such an one as Paul the aged would not ask our pity, but invite our sympathetic gratitude. However feeble his outward man may be, his inner man is so renewed day by day that we may well envy his perennial peace.

The Lord reigneth, he is clothed with majesty; the Lord is clothed with strength, wherewith he hath girded himself. *Psalm 93: 1.*

The Lord reigneth, or *Jehovah reigns.* Whatever opposition may arise, his throne is unmoved. He has reigned, does reign, and will reign for ever and ever. Whatever turmoil and rebellion there may be beneath the clouds, the eternal King sits above all in supreme serenity. What can give greater joy to a loyal subject than a sight of the king in his beauty? Let us repeat the proclamation, **the Lord reigneth,** whispering it in the ears of the desponding, and publishing it in the face of the foe. **He is clothed with majesty.** Not with emblems of majesty, but with majesty itself. His is not the semblance but the reality of sovereignty. In nature, providence, and salvation the Lord is infinite in majesty.

The Lord is clothed with strength. His garments of glory are not his only array. He wears **strength** also as his girdle. He is always strong. But sometimes he displays his power in a special manner, and may therefore be said to be **clothed** with it. **Wherewith he hath girded himself.** As men gird up their loins for running or working, so the Lord appears in the eyes of his people to be preparing for action, girt with his omnipotence. Strength always dwells in the Lord Jehovah. But he hides his power full often, until, in answer to his children's cries, he puts on strength, assumes the throne, and defends his own.' It should be a constant theme for prayer, that in our day the reign of the Lord may be conspicuous, and his power displayed in his church and on her behalf. *Thy kingdom come* should be our daily prayer. That the Lord Jesus does actually reign should be our daily praise.

The floods have lifted up, O Lord, the floods have lifted up their voice; the floods lift up their waves. The Lord on high is mightier than the noise of many waters, yea, than the mighty waves of the sea. *Psalm 93: 3-4.*

The floods have lifted up, O Lord. Men have raged like angry waves of the sea, but vain has been their tumult. Observe that the Psalmist turns to the Lord when he sees the billows foam, and hears the breakers roar. He does not waste his breath by talking to the waves, or to violent men. Like Hezekiah he spreads the blasphemies of the wicked before the Lord. **The floods have lifted up their voice; the floods lift up their waves.** These repetitions are needed for the sake both of the poetry and the music. But they also suggest the frequency and the violence of wicked assaults upon the government of God, and the repeated defeats which they sustain. Sometimes men are furious in words—**they lift up their voice.** At other times they rise to acts of violence—**they lift up their waves.** But the Lord has control over them in either case. The ungodly are all foam and fury, noise and bluster, during their little hour. Then the tide turns or the storm is hushed, and we hear no more of them, while the kingdom of the Eternal abides in the grandeur of its power.

The Lord on high is mightier than the noise of many waters. The utmost of their power is to him but a sound and he can readily master it. Therefore he calls it a **noise** by way of contempt. **Yea, than the mighty waves of the sea.** When the storm raises Atlantic billows, and drives them on with terrific force, the Lord is still able to restrain them. So also when impious men are haughty and full of rage, the Lord is able to subdue them and over-rule their malice. Kings or mobs, emperors or savages, all are in the Lord's hands, and he can forbid their touching a hair of the heads of his saints.

Thy testimonies are very sure: holiness becometh thine house, O Lord, for ever. *Psalm 93: 5.*

Thy testimonies are very sure. As in providence the throne of God is fixed beyond all risk, so in revelation his truth is beyond all question. Other teachings are uncertain, but the revelations of heaven are infallible. As the rocks remain unmoved amid the tumult of the sea, so does divine truth resist all the currents of man's opinion and the storms of human controversy. They are not only *sure*, but **very sure.** Glory be to God, we have not been deluded by a cunningly-devised fable. Our faith is grounded upon the eternal truth of the Most High.

Holiness becometh thine house, O Lord, for ever. Truth changes not in its doctrines, which are very sure, nor **holiness** in its precepts, which are incorruptible. The teaching and the character of God are both unaltered. God has not admitted evil to dwell with him. He will not tolerate it in his house, He is eternally its enemy, and is for ever the sworn friend of holiness. The church must remain unchanged, and for ever be holiness unto the Lord. Yea, her King will preserve her undefiled by the intruder's foot. Sacred unto the Lord is the church of Jesus Christ, and so shall she be kept evermore. *Jehovah reigns* is the first word and the main doctrine of the Psalm, and **holiness** is the final result. A due esteem for the great King will lead us to adopt a behaviour becoming his royal presence. Divine sovereignty both confirms the promises as sure testimonies, and enforces the precepts as seemly and becoming in the presence of so great a Lord.

Lord, how long shall the wicked, how long shall the wicked triumph? How long shall they utter and speak hard things? and all the workers of iniquity boast themselves? *Psalm 94:3-4.*

Lord, how long shall the wicked, how long shall the wicked triumph? Shall wrong for ever rule? Are slavery, robbery, tyranny, never to cease? Since there is certainly a just God in heaven, armed with almighty power, surely there must be sooner or later an end to the ascendancy of evil. Innocence must one day find a defender. This **how long?** of the text is the bitter plaint of all the righteous in all ages. It expresses wonder caused by that great enigma of providence, the existence and predominance of evil. In due time God will publish his reply. But the full end is not yet.

How long shall they utter and speak hard things? The ungodly are not content with deeds of injustice. They add hard speeches, threatening, and insulting over the saints. Words often wound more than swords. They are as hard to the heart as stones to the flesh. These are poured forth by the ungodly in redundance, for such is the force of the word translated **utter.** They use them so commonly that they become their common speech (they **utter and speak** them). Will this always be endured? **And all the workers of iniquity boast themselves?** They even soliloquise and talk to themselves, and of themselves, in arrogance of spirit. It is the nature of workers of iniquity to **boast,** just as it is a characteristic of good men to be humble. Long, very long, have they had the platform to themselves, and loud, very loud, have been their blasphemies of God, and their railings at his saints. Will not the day soon come when the threatened heritage of shame and everlasting contempt shall be meted out to them?

They say, The Lord shall not see, neither shall the God of Jacob regard it. *Psalm 94:7.*

They say, the Lord shall not see. This was the reason of men's arrogance, and the climax of their wickedness. They were blindly wicked because they dreamed of a blind God. When men believe that the eyes of God are dim, there is no reason to wonder that they give full licence to their brutal passions. The persons mentioned above not only cherished an infidel unbelief, but dared to avow it, uttering the monstrous doctrine that God is too far away to take notice of the actions of men.

Neither shall the God of Jacob regard it. Abominable blasphemy and transparent falsehood! If God has actually become his people's God, and proved his care for them by a thousand acts of grace, how dare the ungodly assert that he will not notice the wrongs done to them? There is no limit to the proud man's profanity, reason itself cannot restrain him. He has broken through the bounds of common sense. Jacob's God heard him at the brook Jabbok. Jacob's God led him and kept him all his life long, and said concerning him and his family, *Touch not mine anointed, and do my prophets no harm.* Yet these brutish ones profess to believe that he neither sees nor regards the injuries wrought upon the elect people! Surely in such unbelievers is fulfilled the saying of the wise, that those whom the Lord means to destroy he leaves to the madness of their corrupt hearts.

The Lord knoweth the thoughts of man, that they are vanity. *Psalm 94:11.*

Whether men admit or deny that God knows, one thing is here declared, namely, that **The Lord knoweth the thoughts of man, that they are vanity.** Not their words alone are heard, and their works seen, but he reads the secret motions of their minds. Men themselves are not hard to be discerned of him. Before his glance they themselves are but vanity. It is in the Lord's esteem no great matter that he **knoweth the thoughts** of such transparent pieces of vanity as mankind are. He sums them up in a moment as poor vain things. This is the sense of the original. But that given in the authorised version is also true—**the thoughts,** the best part, the most spiritual portion of man's nature, even these **are vanity** itself, and nothing better.

Poor man! And yet such a creature as this boasts, plays at monarch, tyrannises over his fellow worms, and defies his God! Madness is mingled with human vanity, like smoke with the fog, to make it fouler but not more substantial than it would have been alone. How foolish are those who think that God does not know their actions, when the truth is that their vain thoughts are all perceived by him! How absurd to make nothing of God when in fact we ourselves are as nothing in his sight!

Blessed is the man whom thou chastenest, O Lord, and teachest him out of thy law. *Psalm 94:12.*

Blessed is the man whom thou chastenest, O Lord. The Psalmist's mind is growing quiet. He no longer complains to God or argues with men, but tunes his harp to softer melodies, for his faith perceives that with the most afflicted believer all is well. Though he may not feel blessed while smarting under the rod of chastisement, yet **blessed** he is. He is precious in God's sight, or the Lord would not take the trouble to correct him, and right happy will the results of his correction be. The Psalmist calls the chastened one a **man** in the best sense, using the Hebrew word which implies strength. He is a man, indeed, who is under the teaching and training of the Lord.

And teachest him out of thy law. The book and the rod, the law and the chastening, go together, and are made doubly useful by being found in connection. Affliction without the word is a furnace for the metal, but there is no flux to aid the purifying. The word of God supplies that need, and makes the fiery trial effectual. After all, the blessing of God belongs far rather to those who suffer under the divine hand than to those who make others suffer. Better far to lie and cry out as a **man** under the hand of our heavenly Father, than to roar and rave as a brute, and to bring down upon one's self a death blow from the destroyer of evil. The afflicted believer is under tuition. He is in training for something higher and better. All that he meets with is working out his highest good. Therefore is he a blessed man, however much his outward circumstances may argue the reverse.

When I said, My foot slippeth; thy mercy, O Lord, held me up. *Psalm 94:18.*

When I said, My foot slippeth—is slipping even now. I perceived my danger, and cried out in horror, and then, at the very moment of my extremity, came the needed help: **thy mercy, O Lord, held me up.** Often enough is this the case. We feel our weakness, and see our danger, and in fear and trembling we cry out. At such times nothing can help us but **mercy.** We can make no appeal to any fancied merit, for we feel that it is our inbred sin which makes our feet so ready to fail us. Our joy is that mercy endureth for ever, and is always at hand to pluck us out of the danger, and hold us up, where else we should fall to our destruction.

Ten thousand times has this verse been true in relation to some of us, and especially to the writer of this comment. The danger was imminent. It was upon us. We were going. The peril was apparent. We saw it, and were aghast at the sight. Our own heart was failing, and we concluded that it was all over with us. But then came the almighty interposition. We did not fall. We were held up by an unseen hand. The devices of the enemy were frustrated, and we sang for joy. O faithful Keeper of our souls, be thou extolled for ever and ever! We will bless the Lord at all times, his praise shall continually be in our mouths.

PSALM 95

O come, let us sing unto the Lord: let us make a joyful noise to the rock of our salvation. *Psalm 95:1.*

O come, let us sing unto the Lord. Other nations sing unto their gods. Let us sing unto Jehovah. We love him, we admire him, we reverence him. Let us express our feelings with the choicest sounds, using our noblest faculty for its noblest end. It is well thus to urge others to magnify the Lord. But we must be careful to set a worthy example ourselves, so that we may be able not only to cry **Come,** but also to add **let us sing,** because we are singing ourselves. It is to be feared that very much even of religious singing is not unto the Lord, but unto the ear of the congregation. Above all things we must in our service of song take care that all we offer is with the heart's sincerest and most fervent intent directed **unto the Lord** himself.

Let us make a joyful noise to the rock of our salvation. With holy enthusiasm let us sing, making a sound which shall indicate our earnestness. With abounding joy let us lift up our voices, actuated by that happy and peaceful spirit which trustful love is sure to foster. As the children of Israel sang for joy when the smitten rock poured forth its cooling streams, so let us make a joyful noise **to the rock of our salvation.** The author of this song had in his mind's eye the rock, the tabernacle, the Red Sea, and the mountains of Sinai, and he alludes to them all in this first part of his hymn. God is our abiding, immutable, and mighty rock. In him we find deliverance and safety. Therefore it becomes us to praise him with heart and with voice from day to day. Especially should we delight to do this when we assemble as his people for public worship.

Let us come before his presence with thanksgiving, and make a joyful noise unto him with psalms. *Psalm 95:2.*

Let us come before his presence with thanksgiving. Here is probably a reference to the peculiar **presence** of God in the Holy of Holies above the mercy-seat, and also to the glory which shone forth out of the cloud which rested above the tabernacle. We may make bold to come before the immediate presence of the Lord—for the voice of the Holy Ghost in this Psalm invites us. When we do draw near to him we should remember his great goodness to us and cheerfully confess it. Our worship should have reference to the past as well as to the future. If we do not bless the Lord for what we have already received, how can we reasonably look for more? We are permitted to bring our petitions, and therefore we are in honour bound to bring our thanksgivings.

And make a joyful noise unto him with psalms. We should shout as exultingly as those do who triumph in war, and as solemnly as those whose utterance is a Psalm. It is not always easy to unite enthusiasm with reverence, and it is a frequent fault to destroy one of these qualities while straining after the other. The perfection of singing is that which unites joy with gravity, exultation with humility, fervency with sobriety. One can imagine David in earnest tones persuading his people to go up with him to the worship of Jehovah with sound of harp and hymn, and holy delight. The gladsomeness of his exhortation is noteworthy: the noise is to be **joyful.** This quality he insists upon twice. It is to be feared that this is too much overlooked in ordinary services. People are so impressed with the idea that they ought to be serious that they put on the aspect of misery. They quite forget that joy is as much a characteristic of true worship as solemnity itself.

In his hand are the deep places of the earth: the strength of the hills is his also. *Psalm 95:4.*

In his hand are the deep places of the earth. He is the God of the valleys and the hills, the caverns, and the peaks. Far down where miners sink their shafts, deeper yet where lie the secret oceans by which springs are fed, and deepest of all in the unknown abyss where rage and flame the huge central fires of earth, there Jehovah's power is felt, and all things are under the dominion of his hand. As princes hold the mimic globe in their hands, so does the Lord in every deed hold the earth. When Israel drank of the crystal fount which welled up from the great deep, below the smitten rock, the people knew that in the Lord's hands were **the deep places of the earth.**

The strength of the hills is his also. When Sinai was altogether on a smoke the tribes learned that Jehovah was God of the hills as well as of the valleys. Everywhere and at all times is this true. The Lord rules upon the high places of the earth in lonely majesty. The vast foundations, the gigantic spurs, the incalculable masses, the untrodden heights of the mountains are all the Lord's. These are his fastnesses and treasure-houses, where he stores the tempest and the rain; whence also he pours the ice-torrents and looses the avalanches. The granite peaks are his, and his the precipices and the beetling crags. **Strength** is the main thought which strikes the mind when gazing on those vast ramparts of cliff which front the raging sea, or peer into the azure sky, piercing the clouds. But it is to the devout mind the strength of God. Hints of Omnipotence are given by those stern rocks which brave the fury of the elements, and like walls of brass defy the assaults of nature in her wildest rage.

Today if ye will hear his voice, harden not your heart, as in the provocation, and as in the day of temptation in the wilderness. *Psalm 95:7–8.*

Today if ye will hear his voice. Dreadful **if.** Many would not hear. They put off the claims of love, and provoked their God. **Today,** in the hour of grace, in the day of mercy, we are tried as to whether we have an ear for the voice of our Creator. Nothing is said of tomorrow. *He limiteth a certain day,* he presses for immediate attention, for our own sakes he asks instantaneous obedience. Shall we yield it? The Holy Ghost saith **Today.** Will we grieve him by delay? **Harden not your heart.** If ye will hear, learn to fear also. The sea and the land obey him. Do not prove more obstinate than they! We cannot soften our hearts, but we can **harden** them, and the consequences will be fatal. Today is too good a day to be profaned by the hardening of our hearts against our own mercies. While mercy reigns let not obduracy rebel.

As in the provocation, and as in the day of temptation in the wilderness (or, *like Meribah, like the day of Massah in the wilderness*). Be not wilfully, wantonly, repeatedly, obstinately rebellious. Let the example of that unhappy generation serve as a beacon to you. Do not repeat the offences which have already more than enough provoked the Lord. God remembers men's sins, and the more memorably so when they are committed by a favoured people, against frequent warnings, in defiance of terrible judgments, and in the midst of superlative mercies. Such sins write their record in marble. Reader, this verse is for you, for you even if you can say, *He is our God, and we are the people of his pasture.* Do not seek to turn aside the edge of the warning. Thou hast good need of it. Give good heed to it.

PSALM 96

O sing unto the Lord a new song: sing unto the Lord, all the earth. *Psalm 96:1.*

O sing unto the Lord a new song. New joys are filling the hearts of men, for the glad tidings of blessing to all people are proclaimed. Therefore let them sing **a new song.** Angels inaugurated the new dispensation with new songs. Shall not we take up the strain? Men are made new creatures, and their song is new also. The foolish ditty and the cruel war-song are alike forgotten. The song is holy, heavenly, pure, and pleasant. The Psalmist speaks as if he would lead the strain and be the chief musician, and cries with all his heart, *O sing unto Jehovah a new song.*

Sing unto the Lord, all the earth. National jealousies are dead. A Jew invites the Gentiles to adore, and joins with them, so that all the earth may lift up one common Psalm as with one heart and voice unto Jehovah, who hath visited it with his salvation. No corner of the world is to be discordant, no race of heathen to be dumb. **All the earth** Jehovah made, and all the earth must sing to him. As the sun shines on all lands, so are all lands to delight in the light of the Sun of Righteousness. The multitudinous languages of the sons of Adam, who were scattered at Babel, will blend in the same song when the people are gathered at Zion. Nor men alone, but the earth itself is to praise its Maker. Made subject to vanity for a while by a sad necessity, the creation itself also is to be delivered from the bondage of corruption, and brought into the glorious liberty of the children of God, so that sea and forest, field and flood, are to be joyful before the Lord. Is this a dream? Then let us dream again. Blessed are the eyes which shall see the kingdom, and the ears which shall hear its songs. Hasten thine advent, good Lord!

O worship the Lord in the beauty of holiness: fear before him, all the earth. *Psalm 96:9.*

O worship the Lord in the beauty of holiness. This is the only **beauty** which he cares for in our public services, and it is one for which no other can compensate. Beauty of architecture and apparel he does not regard. Moral and spiritual beauty is that in which his soul delighteth. Worship must not be rendered to God in a slovenly, sinful, superficial manner. We must be reverent, sincere, earnest, and pure in heart both in our prayers and praises. Purity is the white linen of the Lord's choristers. Righteousness is the comely garment of his priests. **Holiness** is the royal apparel of his servitors.

Fear before him, all the earth. *Tremble* is the word in the original, and it expresses the profoundest awe, just as the word **worship** does, which would be more accurately translated by *bow down.* Even the bodily frame would be moved to trembling and prostration if men were thoroughly conscious of the power and glory of Jehovah. Men of the world ridiculed the Quakers for trembling when under the power of the Holy Spirit. Had they been able to discern the majesty of the

Eternal they would have quaked also. There is a sacred trembling which is quite consistent with joy. The heart may even quiver with an awful excess of delight. The sight of the King in his beauty caused no alarm to John in Patmos, and yet it made him fall at his feet as dead. Oh, to behold him and worship him with prostrate awe and sacred fear!

PSALM 97

Clouds and darkness are round about him: righteousness and judgment are the habitation of his throne. *Psalm 97:2.*

Clouds and darkness are round about him. So the Lord revealed himself at Sinai. So must he ever surround his essential Deity when he shows himself to the sons of men, or his excessive glory would destroy them. There must be a veiling of his infinite splendour if anything is to be seen by finite beings. It is often thus with the Lord in providence. When working out designs of unmingled love, he conceals the purpose of his grace that it may be the more clearly discovered at the end. *It is the glory of God to conceal a thing.* Wisdom veils her face and adores the mercy which conceals the divine purpose. Folly rushes in and perishes, first blinded, and by-and-by consumed by the blaze of glory.
Righteousness and judgment are the habitation of his throne. There he abides. He never departs from strict justice and right. **His throne** is fixed upon the rock of eternal holiness. **Righteousness** is his immutable attribute, and **judgment** marks his every act. What though we cannot see or understand what he doeth, yet we are sure that he will do no wrong to us or any of his creatures. Is not this enough to make us rejoice in him and adore him? Divine sovereignty is never tyrannical. Jehovah is an autocrat, but not a despot. Absolute power is safe in the hands of him who cannot err, or act unrighteously. When the roll of the decrees, and the books of the divine providence shall be opened, no eye shall there discern one word that should be blotted out, one syllable of error, one line of injustice, one letter of unholiness. Of none but the Lord of all can this be said.

Rejoice in the Lord, ye righteous; and give thanks at the remembrance of his holiness. *Psalm 97:12.*

Rejoice in the Lord, ye righteous. The Psalmist had earlier bidden the earth rejoice. Here he turns to the excellent of the earth and bids them lead the song. If all others fail to praise the Lord, the godly must not. To them God is peculiarly revealed. By them he should be specially

adored. **And give thanks at the remembrance of his holiness—**
which is the harmony of all his attributes, the superlative wholeness of
his character. This is a terror to the wicked, and a cause of thankfulness
to the gracious. To remember that Jehovah is holy is becoming in
those who dwell in his courts. To **give thanks** in consequence of that
remembrance is the sure index of their fitness to abide in his presence.

In reference to the triumphs of the gospel, this text teaches us to
rejoice greatly in its purifying effect. It is the death of sin and the life
of virtue. An unholy gospel is no gospel. The **holiness** of the religion
of Jesus is its glory. It is that which makes it glad tidings, since while
man is left in his sins no bliss can be his portion. Salvation from sin is
the priceless gift of our thrice holy God. Therefore let us magnify him
for ever and ever. He will fill the world with holiness, and so with
happiness. Therefore let us glory in his holy name, world without end.
Amen.

PSALM 98

**O sing unto the Lord a new song; for he hath done marvellous
things: his right hand, and his holy arm, hath gotten him the
victory.** *Psalm 98:1.*

**O sing unto the Lord a new song; for he hath done marvellous
things.** Jesus, our King, has lived a marvellous life, died a marvellous
death, risen by a marvellous resurrection, and ascended marvellously
into heaven. By his divine power he has sent forth the Holy Spirit
doing marvels, and by that sacred energy his disciples have also wrought
marvellous things and astonished all the earth. For all this he deserves
the highest praise. His acts have proved his Deity. Jesus is Jehovah,
and therefore we sing unto him as the Lord.

His right hand, and his holy arm, hath gotten him the victory.
Not by the aid of others, but by his own unweaponed hand his marvellous conquests have been achieved. Sin, death, and hell all fell
beneath his solitary prowess. The victories of Jesus among men are all
the more wonderful because they are accomplished by means to all
appearance most inadequate. They are due not to physical but to moral
power—the energy of goodness, justice, truth. In a word, to the power
of his *holy* arm. His holy influence has been the sole cause of success.
Jesus never stoops to use policy, or brute force. His unsullied perfections secure to him a real and lasting victory over all the powers of
evil. That victory will be gained as dexterously and easily as when a
warrior strikes his adversary with **his right hand** and stretches him
prone upon the earth. The salvation which Jesus has accomplished is

wrought out with wonderful wisdom. Hence it is ascribed to **his right hand**. It meets the requirements of justice. Hence we read of **his holy arm**. It is his own unaided work. Hence all the glory is ascribed to him. It is **marvellous** beyond degree. Hence it deserves a **new song**.

Make a joyful noise unto the Lord, all the earth: make a loud noise, and rejoice, and sing praise. *Psalm 98:4.*

Make a joyful noise unto the Lord, all the earth. Every tongue must applaud, and that with the vigour which joy of heart alone can arouse to action. As men shout when they welcome a king, so must we. Loud hosannas, full of happiness, must be lifted up. If ever men shout for joy, it should be when the Lord comes among them in the proclamation of his gospel reign. John Wesley said to his people, *Sing lustily, and with a good courage. Beware of singing as if you were half dead or half asleep. Lift up your voice with strength. Be no more afraid of your voice now, nor more ashamed of its being heard, than when you sung the songs of Satan.*

Make a loud noise, and rejoice, and sing praise; or *Burst forth, and sing, and play.* Let every form of exultation be used, every kind of music pressed into the service, till the accumulated praise causes the skies to echo the joyful tumult. There is no fear of our being too hearty in magnifying the God of our salvation. Only we must take care that the song comes from the heart. Otherwise the music is nothing but a noise in his ears, whether it be caused by human throats, or organ pipes, or far-resounding trumpets. **Loud** let our hearts ring out the honours of our conquering Saviour. With all our might let us extol the Lord who has vanquished all our enemies, and led our captivity captive. He will do this best who is most in love with Jesus.

PSALM 99

Let them praise thy great and terrible name; for it is holy. *Psalm 99:3.*

Let them praise thy great and terrible name. Let all the dwellers in Zion and all the nations upon the earth praise the Lord, or *acknowledge thankfully* the goodness of his divine nature, albeit that there is so much in it which must inspire their awe. Under the most terrible aspect the Lord is still to be praised. Many profess to admire the milder beams of the sun of righteousness, but burn with rebellion against its more flaming radiance. It ought not to be so. We are bound to praise a terrible God and worship him who casts the wicked down to hell.

Did not Israel praise him *who overthrew Pharaoh and his hosts in the Red Sea, for his mercy endureth for ever*? The terrible Avenger is to be praised, as well as the loving Redeemer. Against this the sympathy of man's evil heart with sin rebels. It cries out for an effeminate God in whom pity has strangled justice. The well-instructed servants of Jehovah praise him in all the aspects of his character, whether terrible or tender. Grace streaming from the mercy-seat can alone work in us this admirable frame of mind. **For it is holy.** or *He is holy*. In him is no flaw or fault, excess or deficiency, error or iniquity. He is wholly excellent, and is therefore called **holy**. In his words, thoughts, acts, and revelations as well as in himself, he is perfection itself. O come let us worship and bow down before him.

Moses and Aaron among his priests, and Samuel among them that call upon his name; they called upon the Lord, and he answered them. *Psalm 99:6.*

Moses and Aaron among his priests, and Samuel among them that call upon his name. Though not ordained to the typical priest-hood, Moses was a true priest, even as Melchizedek had been before him. God has ever had a priesthood beside and above that of the law. The three holy men here mentioned all stood in his courts, and saw his holiness, each one after his own order. Moses saw the Lord in flaming fire revealing his perfect law. Aaron full often watched the sacred fire devour the sin-offering. Samuel witnessed the judgment of the Lord on Eli's house, because of the error of his way. These each one stood in the gap when the wrath of God broke forth, because his holiness had been insulted. Acting as intercessors, they screened the nation from the great and terrible God, who otherwise would in a dreadful manner have executed judgment in Jacob.

Let these men, or such as these, lead us in our worship. Let us approach the Lord at the mercy-seat as they did, for he is as accessible to us as to them. They made it their life's business to call upon him in prayer, and by so doing brought down innumerable blessings upon themselves and others. Does not the Lord call us also to come up into the mount with Moses, and to enter the most holy place with Aaron? Do we not hear him call us by our name as he did Samuel? And do we not answer, *Speak, Lord, for thy servant heareth*? **They called upon the Lord, and he answered them.** Not in vain were their prayers. But being a holy God he was true to his promises, and hearkened to them from off the mercy-seat. Here is reason for praise. Answers to the petitions of some are proofs of God's readiness to hear others.

Know ye that the Lord he is God: it is he that hath made us, and not we ourselves; we are his people, and the sheep of his pasture. *Psalm 100:3.*

Know that the Lord he is God. Our worship must be intelligent. We ought to **know** whom we worship and why. To prove our knowledge by obedience, trust, submission, zeal, and love is an attainment which only grace can bestow. Only those who practically recognise his Godhead are at all likely to offer acceptable praise. **It is he that hath made us, and not we ourselves.** Shall not the creature reverence its Maker? Some men live as if they made themselves. They call themselves self-made men—and they adore their supposed creators. But Christians recognise the origin of their being and their well-being, and take no honour to themselves either for being, or for being what they are. Neither in our first or second creation dare we put so much as a finger upon the glory, for it is the sole right and property of the Almighty. To disclaim honour for ourselves is as necessary a part of true reverence as to ascribe glory to the Lord.

We are his people, and the sheep of his pasture. It is our honour to have been chosen from all the world to be **his people,** and our privilege to be therefore guided by his wisdom, tended by his care, and and fed by his bounty. **Sheep** gather around their shepherd and look up to him. In the same manner let us gather around the great Shepherd of mankind. The avowal of our relation to God is in itself praise. When we recount his goodness, we are rendering to him the best adoration. Our songs require none of the inventions of fictions. The bare facts are enough. The simple narration of the mercies of the Lord is more astonishing than the productions of imagination. That we are **the sheep of his pasture** is a plain truth, and at the same time the very essence of poetry.

The Lord is good; his mercy is everlasting; and his truth endureth to all generations. *Psalm 100:5.*

The Lord is good. This sums up his character and contains a mass of reasons for praise. He is good, gracious, kind, bountiful, loving. Yea, God is love. He who does not praise the good is not good himself. The kind of praise inculcated in the Psalm, viz., that of joy and gladness, is most fitly urged upon us by an argument from the goodness of God. **His mercy is everlasting.** God is not mere justice, stern and cold. He has bowels of compassion, and wills not the sinner's death. Towards his own people **mercy** is still more conspicuously displayed. It has been theirs from all eternity, and shall be theirs world without end. **Everlasting** mercy is a glorious theme for sacred song.

And his truth endureth to all generations. No fickle being is he, promising and forgetting. He has entered into covenant with his people, and he will never revoke it, nor alter the thing that has gone out of his lips. As our fathers found him faithful, so will our sons, and their seed for ever. A changeable God would be a terror to the righteous. They would have no sure anchorage. Amid a changing world they would be driven to and fro in perpetual fear of shipwreck. Our heart leaps for joy as we bow before One who has never broken his word or changed his purpose. Resting on his sure word, we feel that joy which is here commanded. In the strength of it we come into his presence even now, and speak good of his name.

PSALM 101

I will sing of mercy and judgment: unto thee, O Lord, will I sing.
Psalm 101:1.

I will sing of mercy and judgment. The Psalmist would extol both the love and the severity, the sweets and the bitters, which the Lord had mingled in his experience. He would admire the justice and the goodness of the Lord. Such a song would fitly lead up to godly resolutions as to his own conduct, for that which we admire in our superiors we naturally endeavour to imitate. Mercy and judgment would temper the administration of David, because he had adoringly perceived them in the dispensations of his God. Everything in God's dealings with us may fittingly become the theme of song. We have not viewed it aright until we feel we can sing about it. We ought as much to bless the Lord for the **judgment** with which he chastens our sin, as for the **mercy** with which he forgives it. There is as much love in the blows of his hand as in the kisses of his mouth.

Upon a retrospect of their lives instructed saints scarcely know which to be most grateful for—the comforts which have cheered them, or the afflictions which have purged them. **Unto thee, O Lord, will I sing.** Jehovah shall have all our praise. The secondary agents of either the mercy or the judgment must hold a very subordinate place in our memory, and the Lord alone must be hymned by our hearts. Our soul's sole worship must be the lauding of the Lord. The Psalmist resolves that, come what may, he will sing, and sing to the Lord too, whatever others may do.

I will behave myself wisely in a perfect way. O when wilt thou come unto me ? I will walk within my house with a perfect heart. *Psalm 101:2.*

I will behave myself wisely in a perfect way. To be holy is to be wise. **A perfect way** is a wise way. David's resolve was excellent. But his practice did not fully tally with it. Alas! he was not always wise or perfect, but it was well that it was in his heart. He who does not even resolve to do well is likely to do very ill. Householders, employers, and especially ministers, should pray for both wisdom and holiness. They will need them both. **O when wilt thou come unto me ?**—an ejaculation, but not an interruption. He feels the need not merely of divine help, but also of the divine presence, that so he may be instructed, and sanctified, and made fit for the discharge of his high vocation. If God be with us, we shall neither err in judgment nor transgress in character. His presence brings us both wisdom and holiness. Away from God we are away from safety. Good men are so sensible of infirmity that they cry for help from God, so full of prayer that they cry at all seasons, so intense in their desires that they cry with sighs and groanings which cannot be uttered, saying, **O when wilt thou come unto me ?**

I will walk within my house with a perfect heart. Piety must begin at home. Our first duties are those within our own abode. We must have **a perfect heart** at home, or we cannot keep a perfect way abroad. Notice that these words are a part of a song. There is no music like the harmony of a gracious life, no Psalm so sweet as the daily practice of holiness. Reader, how fares it with your family? Do you sing in the choir and sin in the chamber? Are you a saint abroad and a devil at home? For shame! What we are at home, that we are indeed.

PSALM 102

Hide not thy face from me in the day when I am in trouble; incline thine ear unto me: in the day when I call answer me speedily. *Psalm 102:2.*

Hide not thy face from me in the day when I am in trouble. Do not seem as if thou didst not see me, or wouldst not own me. Smile now at any rate. Reserve thy frowns for other times when I can bear them better, if, indeed, I can ever bear them. But now in my distress, favour me with looks of compassion. **Incline thine ear unto me.** Bow thy greatness to my weakness. If because of sin thy face is turned away, at least let me have a side view of thee: lend me thine ear if I may not see thine eye. Turn thyself to me again if my sin has turned thee away. Give to thine ear an inclination to my prayers.

In the day when I call answer me speedily. Because the case is urgent, and my soul little able to wait. We may ask to have answers to prayer as soon as possible. But we may not complain of the Lord if he should think it more wise to delay. We have permission to request and to use importunity, but no right to dictate or to be petulant. If it be important that the deliverance should arrive at once, we are quite right in making an early time a point of our entreaty. God is as willing to grant us a favour now as tomorrow, and he is not slack concerning his promise. It is a proverb concerning favours from human hands that *he gives twice who gives quickly*, because a gift is enhanced in value by arriving in a time of urgent necessity. We may be sure that our heavenly Patron will grant us the best gifts in the best manner, granting us grace to help in time of need. When answers come upon the heels of our prayers, they are all the more striking, more consoling, and more encouraging.

I am like a pelican of the wilderness: I am like an owl of the desert. I watch, and am as a sparrow alone upon the house top. *Psalm 102:6–7.*

I am like a pelican of the wilderness, a mournful and even hideous object, the very image of desolation. **I am like an owl of the desert,** moping among ruins, hooting discordantly. The Psalmist likens himself to two birds which were commonly used as emblems of gloom and wretchedness. On other occasions he had been like the *eagle*. But the griefs of his people had pulled him down. Should not we also lament when the ways of Zion mourn and her strength languishes? Were there more of this holy sorrow we should soon see the Lord returning to build up his church. It is ill for men to be playing the peacock with wordly pride, when the ills of the times should make them mournful.

   I watch, and am as a sparrow alone upon the house top. The Psalmist compared himself to a bird—a bird when it has lost its mate or its young, or is for some other reason made to mope alone in a solitary place. The **sparrow** is happy in company. If it were alone, the sole one of its species in the neighbourhood, there can be little doubt that it would become very miserable, and sit and pine away. He who has felt himself to be so weak and inconsiderable as to have no more power over his times than a sparrow over a city, has also, when bowed down with despondency concerning the evils of the age, sat himself down in utter wretchedness to lament the ills which he could not heal. Christians of an earnest, watchful kind often find themselves among those who have no sympathy with them. Even in the church they look in vain for kindred spirits. Then do they persevere in their prayers and labours, but feel themselves to be as lonely as the poor bird which looks from the ridge of the roof, and meets with no friendly greeting from any of its kind.

This shall be written for the generation to come: and the people which shall be created shall praise the Lord. *Psalm 102:18.*

This shall be written for the generation to come. A note shall be made of it, for there will be destitute ones in future generations. It will make glad their eyes to read the story of the Lord's mercy to the needy in former times. Registers of divine kindness ought to be made and preserved. We write down in history the calamities of nations—wars, famines, pestilences, and earthquakes. How much rather then should we set up memorials of the Lord's lovingkindnesses! Those who have in their own souls endured spiritual destitution, and have been delivered out of it, cannot forget it. They are bound to tell others of it.

And the people which shall be created shall praise the Lord. Revivals of religion not only cause great joy to those who are immediately concerned in them. They give encouragement and delight to the people of God long after, and are indeed perpetual incentives to adoration throughout the church of God. This verse teaches us that we ought to have an eye to posterity. Especially should we endeavour to perpetuate the memory of God's love to his church and to his poor people, so that young people as they grow up may know that the Lord God of their fathers is good and full of compassion. Sad as the Psalmist was when he wrote, he was not so absorbed in his own sorrow, or so distracted by the national calamity, as to forget the claims of coming generations. This, indeed, is a clear proof that he was not without hope for his people. He who is making arrangements for the good of a future generation has not yet despaired of his nation. The praise of God should be the great object of all that we do. To secure him a revenue of glory both from the present and the future is the noblest aim of intelligent beings.

Thou art the same, and thy years shall have no end. *Psalm 102:27.*

Thou art the same, or, *Thou art he.* As a man remains the same when he has changed his clothing, so is the Lord evermore the unchanging One, though his works in creation may be changed, and the operations of his providence may vary. When heaven and earth shall flee away from the dread presence of the great Judge, he will be unaltered by the terrible confusion, and the world in conflagration will effect no change in him. Even so, the Psalmist remembered that when Israel was vanquished, her capital destroyed, and her temple levelled with the ground, her God remained the same self-existent, all-sufficient being, and would restore his people. So he will restore the heavens and the earth, bestowing at the same time a new glory never known before. The doctrine of the immutability of God should be more considered than it is. The neglect of it tinges the theology of many religious teachers, and makes them utter many things of which they would have seen the absurdity long ago if they had remembered the divine declaration, *I am God, I change not, therefore ye sons of Jacob are not consumed.*

And thy years shall have no end. God lives on, no decay can happen to him, or destruction overtake him. What a joy is this! We may lose our dearest earthly friends, but not our heavenly Friend. Men's days are often suddenly cut short, and at the longest they are but few. But the years of the right hand of the Most High cannot be counted, for they have neither first nor last, beginning nor end. O my soul, rejoice thou in the Lord always, since he is always the same.

PSALM 103

Bless the Lord, O my soul: and all that is within me, bless his holy name. *Psalm 103:1.*

Bless the Lord, O my soul. Soul music is the very soul of music. Jehovah is worthy to be praised by us in that highest style of adoration which is intended by the term **bless**—All thy works praise thee, O God, but thy saints shall bless thee. Our very life and essential self should be engrossed with this delightful service, and each one of us should arouse his own heart to the engagement. Let others forbear if they can: **Bless the Lord, O** *my* **soul.** Let others murmur, but do thou *bless.* Let others bless themselves and their idols, but do thou bless *the Lord.* Let others use only their tongues, but as for me I will cry, **Bless the Lord, O my** *soul.*

And all that is within me, bless his holy name. Many are our faculties, emotions, and capacities. But God has given them all to us, and they ought all to join in chorus to his praise. Half-hearted, ill-conceived, unintelligent praises are not such as we should render to our loving Lord. If the law of justice demanded all our heart and soul and mind for the Creator, much more may the law of gratitude put in a comprehensive claim for the homage of our whole being to the God of grace. It is instructive to note how the Psalmist dwells upon the *holy* name of God, as if his holiness were dearest to him. Or, perhaps, because the holiness or wholeness of God was to his mind the grandest

197

motive for rendering to him the homage of his nature in its wholeness. Babes may praise the divine goodness, but fathers in grace magnify his holiness. By *the name* we understand the revealed character of God, and assuredly those songs which are suggested, not by our fallible reasoning and imperfect observation, but by unerring inspiration, should more than any others arouse all our consecrated powers.

Who satisfieth thy mouth with good things; so that thy youth is renewed like the eagle's. *Psalm 103:5.*

Who satisfieth thy mouth with good things, or rather *filling with good thy soul.* No man is ever filled to satisfaction but a believer, and only God himself can satisfy even him. Many a worldling is satiated, but not one is satisfied. God satisfies the very soul of man, his noblest part, his ornament and glory; and of consequence he satisfies his mouth, however hungry and craving it might otherwise be. Our good Lord bestows really **good things,** not vain toys and idle pleasures. And these he is always giving, so that from moment to moment he is *satisfying* our soul with good. Shall we not be still praising him? If we never cease to bless him till he ceases to bless us, our employment will be eternal.

So that thy youth is renewed like the eagle's. Renewal of strength, amounting to a grant of a new lease of life, was granted to the Psalmist. He was so restored to his former self that he grew young again, and looked as vigorous as an eagle, whose eye can gaze upon the sun, and whose wing can mount above the storm. Our version refers to the annual moulting of the eagle, after which it looks fresh and young. But the original does not appear to allude to any such fact of natural history, but simply to describe the diseased one as so healed and strengthened, that he became as full of energy as the bird which is strongest of the feathered race, most fearless, most majestic, and most soaring. He who sat moping with the owl in the previous Psalm, here flies on high with the eagle. The Lord works marvellous changes in us, and we learn by such experiences to bless his holy name. To grow from a sparrow to an eagle, and leave the wilderness of the pelican to mount among the stars, is enough to make any man cry, *Bless the Lord, O my soul.*

He will not always chide: neither will he keep his anger for ever. *Psalm 103:9.*

He will not always chide. He will sometimes, for he cannot endure that his people should harbour sin in their hearts. But not for ever will he chasten them. As soon as they turn to him and forsake their evil ways he will end the quarrel. He might find constant cause for striving with us, for we have always something in us which is contrary to his holy mind. But he refrains himself lest our spirits should fail before him. It will be profitable for any one of us who may be at this time out of conscious fellowship with the Lord to enquire at his hands the reason for his anger, saying, *Show me wherefore thou contendest with me?* For he is easily entreated of, and soon ceaseth from his wrath. When his children turn from their sins he soon turns from his chidings.

Neither will he keep his anger for ever. He bears no grudges. The Lord would not have his people harbour resentments, and in his own course of action he sets them a grand example. When the Lord has chastened his child he has done with his anger. He is not punishing as a judge, else might his wrath burn on. But he is acting as a father, and, therefore, after a few blows he ends the matter, and presses his beloved one to his bosom as if nothing had happened. Or if the offence lies too deep in the offender's nature to be thus overcome, he continues to correct, but he never ceases to love, and he does not suffer his anger with his people to pass into the next world, but receives his erring child into his glory.

As the heaven is high above the earth, so great is his mercy toward them that fear him. *Psalm 103:11.*

Boundless in extent towards his chosen is the mercy of the Lord. It is no more to be measured than the height of heaven or the heaven of heavens. *Like the height of the heaven* is the original language, which implies other points of comparison besides extent, and suggests sublimity, grandeur, and glory. As the lofty heavens canopy the earth, water it with dews and rains, enlighten it with sun, moon, and stars, and look down upon it with unceasing watchfulness, even so the Lord's mercy from above covers all his chosen, enriches them, embraces them, and stands for ever as their dwelling-place. Who can reach the first of the fixed stars, and who can measure the utmost bounds of the starry universe? Yet **so great is his mercy!** Oh, that great little word *so*!

All this mercy is for **them that fear him.** There must be a humble, hearty reverence of his authority, or we cannot taste of his grace. Godly fear is one of the first products of the divine life in us. It is the beginning of wisdom, yet it fully ensures to its possessor all the benefits of divine mercy. Many a true child of God is full of filial fear, and yet at the same time stands trembling as to his acceptance with God. This trembling is groundless. But it is infinitely to be preferred to that base-born presumption which incites men to boast of their adoption and consequent security, when all the while they are in the gall of bitterness.

Those who are presuming upon the infinite extent of divine mercy should here be led to consider that although it is wide as the horizon and high as the stars, yet it is only meant for them that fear the Lord.

PSALM 104

O Lord my God, thou art very great; thou art clothed with honour and majesty. *Psalm 104:1.*

O Lord my God, thou art very great. This ascription has in it a remarkable blending of the boldness of faith, and the awe of holy fear. The Psalmist calls the infinite Jehovah **my God,** and at the same time, prostrate in amazement at the divine greatness, he cries out in utter astonishment, **Thou art very great.** God was great on Sinai, yet the opening words of his law were, *I am the Lord thy God.* His greatness is no reason why faith should not put in her claim, and call him all her own. Observe that the wonder expressed does not refer to the creation and its greatness, but to Jehovah himself. It is not *the universe* is very great but *Thou* **art very great.** Many stay at the creature, and so become idolatrous in spirit. To pass onward to the Creator himself is true wisdom.

Thou art clothed with honour and majesty. Garments both conceal and reveal a man; and so does the creation of God. The Lord is seen in his works as worthy of **honour** for his skill, his goodness, and his power, and as claiming **majesty,** for he has fashioned all things in sovereignty, doing as he wills, and asking no man's permit. He must be blind indeed who does not see that nature is the work of a king. These are broad lines of inscrutable mystery, which make creation's picture a problem never to be solved, except by admitting that he who drew it giveth no account of his matters, but ruleth all things according to the good pleasure of his will. His **majesty** is, however, always so displayed as to reflect **honour** upon his whole character. He does as he wills, but he wills only that which is thrice holy, like himself. The very robes of the unseen Spirit teach us this, and it is ours to recognise it with humble adoration.

He sendeth the springs into the valleys, which run among the hills. They give drink to every beast of the field: the wild asses quench their thirst. *Psalm 104:10-11.*

He sendeth the springs into the valleys, which run among the hills. This is a beautiful part of the Lord's arrangement of the subject waters. They find vents through which they leap into liberty where their presence will be beneficial in the highest degree. When the waters are confined in the abyss, *the Lord* sets their bound. When they sport at liberty, *he* sends them forth.

They give drink to every beast of the field. Who else would water them if the Lord did not? They are *his* cattle, and therefore he leads them forth to watering. Not one of them is forgotten of him. **The wild asses quench their thirst.** The good Lord gives them enough and to spare. They know their Master's crib. Though bit or bridle of man they will not brook, and man denounces them as unteachable, they learn of the Lord, and know better far than man where flows the cooling crystal of which they must drink or die. They are only asses, and wild, yet our heavenly Father careth for them. Will he not also care for us? We see here, also, that nothing is made in vain. Though no human lip is moistened by the brooklet in the lone valley, yet are there other creatures which need refreshment, and these slake their thirst at the stream. Is this nothing? Must everything exist for man, or else be wasted? What but our pride and selfishness could have suggested such a notion? It is not true that flowers which blush unseen by human eye are wasting their sweetness. The bee finds them out, and other winged wanderers live on their luscious juices. Man is but one creature of the many whom the heavenly Father feedeth and watereth.

The young lions roar after their prey, and seek their meat from God. *Psalm 104:21.*

This is the poetic interpretation of a roar. To whom do **the young lions roar**? Certainly not *to* **their prey,** for the terrible sound tends to alarm their victims, and drive them away. They after their own fashion express their desire for food, and the expression of desire is a kind of prayer. Out of this fact comes the devout thought of the wild beast's appealing to its Maker for food. But neither with lions nor men will the seeking of prayer suffice, there must be practical seeking too, and the lions are well aware of it. What they have in their own language asked for they go forth to **seek.** In this they are far wiser than many men who offer formal prayers not half so earnest as those of the young lions, and then neglect the means in the use of which the object of their petitions might be gained. The lions roar and seek. Too many are liars before God, and roar but never seek.

How comforting is the thought that the Spirit translates the voice of a lion, and finds it to be a seeking of meat from God! May we not hope that our poor broken cries and groans, which in our sorrow we have called *the voice of our roaring* (Ps. 22:1), will be understood by him, and interpreted in our favour. Evidently he considers the meaning rather than the music of the utterance, and puts the best construction upon it.

O Lord, how manifold are thy works! in wisdom hast thou made them all: the earth is full of thy riches. *Psalm 104:24.*

O Lord, how manifold are thy works! Works in the heavens above and in the earth beneath, and in the waters under the earth, works which abide the ages, works which come to perfection and do not outlive a day, works within works, and works within these—who can number one of a thousand? God is the great worker, and ordainer of variety. It is ours to study his works, for they are great, and sought out of all them that have pleasure therein. The kingdom of grace contains as manifold and as great works as that of nature, but the chosen of the Lord alone discern them. **In wisdom hast thou made them all,** or *wrought* **them all.** They are all his works, wrought by his own power, and they all display his wisdom. It was wise to make them—none could be spared. Every link is essential to the chain of nature—wild beasts as much as men, poisons as truly as odoriferous herbs. As a whole, the *all* of creation is a wise achievement, and however it may be chequered with mysteries, and clouded with terrors, it all works together for good, and as one complete harmonious piece of workmanship it answers the great Worker's end.

The earth is full of thy riches. It is not a poor-house, but a palace. In the bowels of **the earth** are hidden mines of wealth, and on her surface are teeming harvests of plenty. All these riches are the Lord's. We ought to call them not *the wealth of nations,* but **thy riches,** O Lord! Not in one clime alone are these riches of God to be found, but in all lands. Even the Arctic ocean has its precious things which men endure much hardness to win, and the burning sun of the equator ripens a produce which flavours the food of all mankind. If his house below is so full of riches, what must his house above be?

PSALM 105

Sing unto him, sing psalms unto him: talk ye of all his wondrous works. *Psalm 105:2.*

Sing unto him. Bring your best thoughts and express them in the best language to the sweetest sounds. Take care that your singing is **unto him,** and not merely for the sake of the music or to delight the ears of others. Singing is so delightful an exercise that it is a pity so much of it should be wasted upon trifles. O ye who can emulate the nightingale, and almost rival the angels, we do most earnestly pray that your hearts may be renewed that so your floods of melody may be poured out at your Maker's and Redeemer's feet.

Talk ye of all his wondrous works. Men love to speak of marvels. Surely the believer in the living God has before him the most amazing series of wonders ever heard of or imagined. His themes are inexhaustible and they are such as should hold men spellbound. You all know something by experience of the marvellous lovingkindness of the Lord—**talk** *ye*. In this way, by all dwelling on this blessed subject, *all* his wondrous works will be published. One cannot do it, nor ten thousand times ten thousand. But if all speak to the Lord's honour, they will at least come nearer to accomplishing the deed. We ought to have a wide range when conversing upon the Lord's doings, and should not shut our eyes to any part of them. **Talk ye of all his wondrous works** in creation and in grace, in judgment and in mercy, in providential interpositions and in spiritual comfortings. Leave out none, or it will be to your damage. Obedience to this verse will give every sanctified tongue some work to do. The trained musicians can *sing*, and the commoner voices can *talk*. In both ways the Lord will receive a measure of the thanks due to him, and his deeds will be made known among the people.

Unto thee will I give the land of Canaan, the lot of your inheritance: when they were but a few men in number; yea, very few, and strangers in it. *Psalm 105:11-12.*

Unto thee will I give the land of Canaan, the lot of your inheritance. This repetition of the great covenant promise is recorded in Gen. 35:9-12 in connection with the change of Jacob's name, and very soon after that slaughter of the Shechemites, which had put the patriarch into such great alarm and caused him to use language almost identical with that of the next verse. **When they were but a few men in number; yea, very few, and strangers in it.** Thus the fears of the man of God declared themselves, and they were reasonable, if we look only at the circumstances in which he was placed. But they are soon seen to be groundless, when we remember that the covenant promise, which guaranteed the possession of the land, necessarily implied the preservation of the race to whom the promise was made. We often fear where no fear is.

The blessings promised to the seed of Abraham were not dependent upon the number of his descendants, or their position in this world. The covenant was made with one man, and consequently the number could never be less. That one man was not the owner of a foot of soil in all the land, save only a cave in which to bury his dead. Therefore his seed could not have less inheritance than he. The smallness of a church, and the poverty of its members, are no barriers to the divine blessing, if it be sought earnestly by pleading the promise. Were not the apostles few, and the disciples feeble, when the good work began?

Until the time that his word came: the word of the Lord tried him. *Psalm 105:19.*

Until the time that his word came. God has his times, and his children must wait till his **until** is fulfilled. Joseph was tried as in a furnace, until the Lord's assaying work was fully accomplished. The word of the chief butler was nothing, he had to wait until God's word came, and meanwhile **the word of the Lord tried him.** He believed the promise. But his faith was sorely exercised. A delayed blessing tests men, and proves their metal, whether their faith is of that precious kind which can endure the fire. Of many a choice promise we may say with Daniel *the thing was true, but the time appointed was long.* If the vision tarry it is good to wait for it with patience.

There is a *trying* word and a *delivering* word, and we must bear the one till the other comes to us. How meekly Joseph endured his afflictions, and with what fortitude he looked forward to the clearing of his slandered character we may readily imagine. It will be better still if under similar trials we are able to imitate him, and come forth from the furnace as thoroughly purified as he was, and as well prepared to bear the yet harder ordeal of honour and power.

He brought them forth also with silver and gold: and there was not one feeble person among their tribes. *Psalm 105:37.*

He brought them forth also with silver and gold. This they asked of the Egyptians, perhaps even demanded, and well they might, for they had been robbed and spoiled for many a day, and it was not meet that they should go forth empty-handed. Glad were the Egyptians to hand over their jewels to propitiate a people who had such a terrible friend above. They needed no undue pressure. They feared them too much to deny them their requests. The Israelites were compelled to leave their houses and lands behind them. It was but justice that they should be able to turn these into portable property.

And there was not one feeble person among their tribes—a great marvel indeed. The number of their army was very great and yet there was not one in hospital, not one carried in an ambulance, or limping in the rear. Poverty and oppression had not enfeebled them.

Jehovah Rophi had healed them. They carried none of the diseases of Egypt with them, and felt none of the exhaustion which sore bondage produces. When God calls his people to a long journey he fits them for it. In the pilgrimage of life our strength shall be equal to our day. See the contrast between Egypt and Israel—in Egypt one dead in every house, and among the Israelites not one so much as limping.

PSALM 106

Remember me, O Lord, with the favour that thou bearest unto thy people. O visit me with thy salvation. *Psalm 106:4.*

Remember me, O Lord, with the favour which thou bearest unto thy people. Insignificant as I am, do not forget me. Think of me with kindness, even as thou thinkest of thine own elect. I cannot ask more, nor would I seek less. Treat me as the least of thy saints are treated and I am content. We may be well content both to live as they live, and die as they die. This feeling would prevent our wishing to escape trial, persecution, and chastisement. These have fallen to the lot of saints, and why should we escape them? At the same time we pray to have their sweets as well as their bitters. If the Lord smiled upon their souls, we cannot rest unless he smile upon us also. We would dwell where they dwell, rejoice as they rejoice, sorrow as they sorrow, and in all things be for ever one with them in the favour of the Lord. The sentence before us is a sweet prayer, at once humble and aspiring, submissive and expansive. It might be used by a dying thief or a living apostle. Let us use it now.

O visit me with thy salvation. Bring it home to me. Come to my house and to my heart. Give me the **salvation** which thou hast prepared, and art alone able to bestow. There is no salvation apart from the Lord, and he must **visit** us with it or we shall never obtain it. We are too sick to visit our Great Physician, and therefore he visits us. Sometimes the second prayer of this verse seems to be too great for us. We feel that we are not worthy that the Lord should come under our roof. **Visit me, Lord!** Can it be? Dare I ask for it? And yet I must, for thou alone canst bring me salvation. Therefore, Lord, I entreat thee to come unto me, and abide with me for ever.

Our fathers understood not thy wonders in Egypt; they remembered not the multitude of thy mercies; but provoked him at the sea, even at the Red sea. *Psalm 106:7.*

Our fathers understood not thy wonders in Egypt. The Israelites saw the miraculous plagues and ignorantly wondered at them. Their design of love, their deep moral and spiritual lessons, and their revelation of the divine power and justice they were unable to perceive. A long sojourn among idolaters had blunted the perceptions of the chosen family, and cruel slavery had ground them down into mental sluggishness. Alas, how many of God's wonders are not understood, or misunderstood by us still. A want of understanding is no excuse for sin, but is itself one count in the indictment against Israel.

They remembered not the multitude of thy mercies. The sin of the understanding leads on to the sin of the memory. What is not understood will soon be forgotten. Men feel little interest in preserving husks. If they know nothing of the inner kernel, they will take no care of the shells. It was an aggravation of Israel's sin that when God's mercies were so numerous they yet were able to forget them all. Surely some out of such a multitude of benefits ought to have remained engraven upon their hearts. But if grace does not give us understanding, nature will soon cast out the memory of God's great goodness. **But provoked him at the sea, even at the Red Sea.** To fall out at starting was a bad sign. Those who did not begin well can hardly be expected to end well. Israel is not quite out of Egypt, and yet she begins to provoke the Lord by doubting his power to deliver, and questioning his faithfulness to his promise. The sea was only *called* Red, but their sins were scarlet in reality. It was known as the Sea of weeds. But far worse weeds grew in their hearts.

PSALM 107

Then they cried unto the Lord in their trouble, and he delivered them out of their distresses. *Psalm 107:6.*

Then they cried unto the Lord in their trouble. Not till they were in extremities did they pray. But the mercy is that they prayed **then,** and prayed in the right manner, with a *cry,* and to the right person, even *to the Lord.* Nothing else remained for them to do. They could not help themselves, or find help in others, and therefore they cried to God. Supplications which are forced out of us by stern necessity are none the less acceptable with God. But, indeed, they have all the more prevalence, since they are evidently sincere, and make a powerful appeal to the divine pity. Some men will never pray till they are half-starved, and for their best interests it is far better for them to be empty and faint than to be full and stout-hearted. If hunger brings us to our knees, it is more useful to us than feasting. If thirst drives us to the fountain, it is better than the deepest draughts of worldly joy. If fainting leads to crying, it is better than the strength of the mighty.

And he delivered them out of their distresses. Deliverance follows prayer most surely. The cry must have been very feeble. They were faint, and their faith was as weak as their cry. But yet they were heard, and heard at once. A little delay would have been their death. But there was none, for the Lord was ready to save them. The Lord delights to come in when no none else can be of the slightest avail. The case was hopeless till Jehovah interposed, and then all was changed immediately. The people were shut up, straitened, and almost pressed to death. But enlargement came to them at once when they began to remember their God, and look to him in prayer.

They that go down to the sea in ships, that do business in great waters; these see the works of the Lord, and his wonders in the deep. *Psalm 107:23–24.*

They that go down to the sea in ships. Navigation was so little practised among the Israelites that the occupation was looked upon as one of singular daring and peril. He who had sailed to Ophir or to Tarshish and had returned alive was looked upon as a man of renown, an ancient mariner to be listened to with reverent attention. Voyages were looked on as descending to an abyss, *going down* **to the sea in ships,** whereas now our bolder and more accustomed sailors talk of the *high seas*. **That do business in great waters.** If they had not had business to do, they would never have ventured on the ocean, for we never read in the Scriptures of any man taking his pleasure on the sea.

These see the works of the Lord. Instead of the ocean proving to be a watery wilderness, it is full of God's creatures, and if we were to attempt to escape from his presence by flying to the uttermost parts of it, we should only rush into Jehovah's arms, and find ourselves in the very centre of his workshop. **And his wonders in the deep.** The ocean contains many of the more striking of God's creatures, and it is the scene of many of the more tremendous of the physical phenomena by which the power and majesty of the Lord are revealed among men. All believers have not the same deep experience. But for wise ends, that they may do business for him, the Lord sends some of his saints to the sea of soul-trouble. There they see, as others do not, the wonders of divine grace. Sailing over the deeps of inward depravity, the waste waters of poverty, the billows of persecution, and the rough waves of temptation, they need God above all others, and they find him.

He maketh the storm a calm, so that the waves thereof are still. Then are they glad because they be quiet; so he bringeth them unto their desired haven. *Psalm 107:29–30.*

He maketh the storm a calm. He reveals his power in the sudden and marvellous transformations which occur at his bidding. He commanded **the storm** and now he ordains **a calm.** God is in all natural phenomena, and we do well to recognise his working. **So that the waves thereof are still.** They bow in silence at his feet. Where huge billows leaped aloft, there is scarce a ripple to be seen. When God makes peace it is peace indeed, the peace of God which passeth all understanding. He can in an instant change the condition of a man's mind, so that it shall seem an absolute miracle to him that he has passed so suddenly from hurricane to calm. O that the Lord would thus work in the reader, should his heart be stormbeaten with outward troubles or inward fears. Lord, say the word and peace will come at once.

Then are they glad because they be quiet. No one can appreciate this verse unless he has been in a storm at sea. No music can be sweeter than the rattling of the chain as the shipmen let down the anchor. No place seems more desirable than the little cove, or the wide bay, in which the ship rests in peace. **So he bringeth them unto their desired haven.** By storms and by favourable breezes, through tempest and fair weather, the great Pilot and Ruler of the sea brings mariners to port, and his people to heaven. We should long ago have been wrecked if it had not been for his preserving hand. Our only hope of outliving the storms of the future is based upon his wisdom, faithfulness, and power. Our heavenly haven shall ring with shouts of grateful joy when once we reach its blessed shore.

PSALM 108

O God, my heart is fixed; I will sing and give praise, even with my glory. *Psalm 108:1.*

O God, my heart is fixed. Though I have many wars to disturb me, and many cares to toss me to and fro, yet I am settled in one mind and cannot be driven from it. My heart has taken hold and abides in one resolve. Thy grace has overcome the fickleness of nature, and I am now in a resolute and determined frame of mind. **I will sing and give praise.** Both with voice and music will I extol thee—*I will sing and play,* as some read it. Even though I have to shout in the battle, I will also sing in my soul. If my fingers must needs be engaged with the bow, yet shall they also touch the ten-stringed instrument and show forth thy praise. **Even with my glory**—with my intellect, my tongue, my poetic faculty, my musical skill, or whatever else causes me to be renowned, and confers honour upon me. It is **my glory** to be able to speak and not to be a dumb animal. Therefore my voice shall show forth thy praise. It is my glory to know God and not to be a heathen. Therefore my instructed intellect shall adore thee. It is my glory to be a saint and no more a rebel. Therefore the grace I have received shall bless thee. It is my glory to be immortal and not a mere brute which perisheth. Therefore my inmost life shall celebrate thy majesty. When he says **I will,** he supposes that there might be some temptation to refrain. But this he puts on one side, and with fixed heart prepares himself for the joyful engagement. He who sings with a fixed heart is likely to sing on, and all the while to sing well.

Through God we shall do valiantly: for he it is that shall tread down our enemies. *Psalm 108:13.*

God's help shall inspire us to help ourselves. Faith is neither a coward nor a sluggard. She knows that God is with her, and therefore she does valiantly. She knows that he will tread down her enemies, and therefore she arises to tread them down in his name. Where praise and prayer have preceded the battle, we may expect to see heroic deeds and decisive victories. **Through God** is our secret support. From that source we draw all our courage, wisdom, and strength. **We shall do valiantly.** This is the public outflow from that secret source. Our inward and spiritual faith proves itself by outward and valorous deeds.

He shall tread down our enemies. They shall fall before him, and as they lie prostrate he shall march over them, and all the hosts of his people with him. This is a prophecy. It was fulfilled to David. But it remains true to the Son of David and to all who are on his side. The church shall yet arouse herself to praise her God with all her heart, and then with songs and hosannas she will advance to the great battle. Her foes shall be overthrown and utterly crushed by the power of her God, and the Lord's glory shall be above all the earth. Send it in our time, we beseech thee, O Lord!

PSALM 109

Hold not thy peace, O God of my praise. For the mouth of the wicked and the mouth of the deceitful are opened against me: they have spoken against me with a lying tongue. *Psalm 109:1–2.*

Hold not thy peace. Mine enemies speak. Be thou pleased to speak too. Break thy solemn silence, and silence those who slander me. It is the cry of a man whose confidence in God is deep, and whose communion with him is very close and bold. Note that he asks the Lord only to speak. A word from God is all a believer needs. **O God of my praise.** If we take care of God's honour he will take care of ours. If we live to God's praise, he will in the long run give us praise among men.

For the mouth of the wicked and the mouth of the deceitful are opened against me. Wicked men must needs say wicked things, and these we have reason to dread. But in addition they utter false and deceitful things, and these are worst of all. The misery caused to a good man by slanderous reports no heart can imagine but that which is wounded by them. In all Satan's armoury there are no worse weapons than deceitful tongues. To have a reputation, over which we have watched with daily care, suddenly bespattered with the foulest aspersions, is painful beyond description. But when wicked and deceitful men get their mouths fully opened we can hardly expect to escape any more than others. **They have spoken against me with a lying tongue.** Lying tongues cannot lie still. Here is reason enough for prayer. The heart sinks when assailed with slander. We know not what may be said next, what friend may be alienated, what evil may be threatened, or what misery may be caused to us and others. What ill can be worse than to be assailed with slander?

But do thou for me, O God the Lord, for thy name's sake: because thy mercy is good, deliver thou me. *Psalm 109:21.*

But do thou for me, O God the Lord, for thy name's sake. How eagerly he turns from his enemies to his God! He sets the great **Thou** in opposition to all his adversaries, and you see at once that his heart is at rest. The words are very indistinct, and though our version may not precisely translate them, yet it in a remarkable manner hits upon the sense and upon the obscurity which hang over it. **Do thou for me—** what shall he do? Why, do whatever he thinks fit. He leaves himself in the Lord's hands, dictating nothing, but quite content so long as his God will but undertake for him. His plea is not his own merit, but **thy name.** The saints have always felt this to be their most mighty plea. God himself has performed his grandest deeds of grace for the honour of his name, and his people know that this is the most potent argument with him. What the Lord himself has guarded with sacred jealousy we should reverence with our whole hearts and rely upon without distrust.

Because thy mercy is good, deliver thou me. Not because I am good, but because thy mercy is good. See how the saints fetch their pleadings in prayer from the Lord himself. God's **mercy** is the star to which the Lord's people turn their eye when they are tossed with tempest and not comforted, for the peculiar bounty and goodness of that mercy have a charm for weary hearts. When *man* has no mercy, we shall still find it in *God*. When man would devour we may look to God to deliver. His name and his mercy are two firm grounds for hope, and happy are those who know how to rest upon them.

Thy people shall be willing in the day of thy power, in the beauties of holiness from the womb of the morning: thou hast the dew of thy youth. *Psalm 110:3.*

Let but the gospel be preached with divine unction, and the chosen of the Lord respond to it like troops in the day of the mustering of armies. They come arrayed by grace in shining uniforms of holiness. For number, freshness, beauty, and purity, they are as the dewdrops which come mysteriously from the morning's womb. Some refer this passage to the resurrection. But even if it be so, the work of grace in regeneration is equally well described by it, for it is a spiritual resurrection. Even as the holy dead rise gladly into the lovely image of their Lord, so do quickened souls put on the glorious righteousness of Christ, and stand forth to behold their Lord and serve him. How truly beautiful is **holiness!** God himself admires it. How wonderful also is the eternal **youth** of the mystical body of Christ! As **the dew** is new every morning, so is there a constant succession of converts to give to the church perpetual juvenility. Her young men have a dew from the Lord upon them, and arouse in her armies an undying enthusiasm for him whose *locks are bushy and black as a raven* with unfailing youth.

Since Jesus ever lives, so shall his church ever flourish. As his strength never faileth, so shall the vigour of his true people be renewed day by day. As he is a Priest-King, so are his people all priests and kings. **The beauties of holiness** are their priestly dress, their garments for glory and for beauty. The realisation of this **day of power** during the time of the Lord's tarrying is that which we should constantly pray for. We may legitimately expect it since he ever sits in the seat of honour and power, and puts forth his strength, according to his own word, *My Father worketh hitherto, and I work.*

The Lord hath sworn, and will not repent. Thou art a priest for ever after the order of Melchizedek. *Psalm 110:4.*

The declaration runs in the present tense as being the only time with the Lord, and comprehending all other times. **Thou art,** i.e., thou wast and art, and art to come, in all ages a priestly King. **The order of Melchizedek's** priesthood was the most ancient and primitive, and at the same time the most honourable. There has never arisen another like to him since his days, for whenever the kings of Judah attempted to seize the sacerdotal office they were driven back to their confusion. God would have no king-priest save his son. Melchizedek's office was exceptional.

The Lord hath sworn. It must be a solemn and a sure matter which leads the Eternal to swear. With him an oath fixes and settles the decree for ever. As if to make assurance a thousand times sure, it is added, **and will not repent.** Jesus is sworn in to be the priest of his people. His commission is sealed by the unchanging oath of the immutable Jehovah. If his priesthood could be revoked, and his authority removed, it would be the end of all hope and life for the people whom he loves. But this sure rock is the basis of our security—the oath of God establishes our glorious Lord both in his priesthood and in his throne. Our Lord Jesus, like Melchizedek, stands forth before us a priest of divine ordaining, not made a priest by fleshy birth, as the sons of Aaron. He mentions neither father, mother, nor descent, as his right to the sacred office. He stands upon his personal merits, by himself alone. The King-priest has been here and left his blessing upon the believing seed. Now he sits in glory in his complete character, atoning for us by the merit of his blood, and exercising all power on our behalf.

PSALM III

The works of the Lord are great, sought out of all them that have pleasure therein. *Psalm III:2.*

The works of the Lord are great. In design, in size, in number, in excellence, all the works of the Lord are great. Even the little things of God are great. **Sought out of all them that have pleasure therein.** Those who love their Maker delight in his handiworks. They perceive that there is more in them than appears upon the surface. They bend their minds to study and understand them. God's works are worthy of our researches. They yield us instruction and pleasure wonderfully blended, and they grow upon, appearing to be far greater, after investigation than before. Men's works are noble from a distance. God's works are great when **sought out.** Delitzsch reads the passage, *Worthy of being sought after in all their purposes,* and this also is a grand truth. The end and design which God hath in all that he makes or does is equally admirable with the work itself.

The hidden wisdom of God is the most marvellous part of his works. Hence those who do not look below the surface miss the best part of what he would teach us. Because the works are great they cannot be seen all at once, but must be looked into with care. This seeking out is of essential service to us by educating our faculties, and strengthening our spiritual eye gradually to bear the light of the divine glory. It is well for us that all things cannot be seen at a glance, for the search into their mysteries is as useful to us as the knowledge which we thereby attain. The history of the Lord's dealings with his people is especially a fit subject for the meditation of reverent minds who find therein a sweet solace, and a never failing source of delight.

The fear of the Lord is the beginning of wisdom: a good understanding have all they that do his commandments: his praise endureth for ever. *Psalm III:10.*

The fear of the Lord is the beginning of wisdom. It is its first principle, but it is also its head and chief attainment. The word **beginning** in Scripture sometimes means the chief; and true religion is at once the first element of **wisdom,** and its chief fruit. To know God so as to walk aright before him is the greatest of all the applied sciences. Holy reverence of God leads us to praise him, and this is the point which the psalm drives at, for it is a wise act on the part of a creature towards his Creator. **A good understanding have all they that do his commandments.** Practical godliness is the test of wisdom. Men may know and be very orthodox. They may talk and be very eloquent. They may speculate and be very profound. But the best proof of their intelligence must be found in their actually doing the will of the Lord. The former part of the Psalm taught us the doctrine of God's nature and character, by describing his works. The second part supplies the practical lesson by drawing the inference that to worship and obey him is the dictate of true wisdom. We joyfully own that it is so.

His praise endureth for ever. The praises of God will never cease, because his works will always excite adoration, and it will always be the wisdom of men to extol their glorious Lord. Some regard this sentence as referring to those who fear the Lord: *their praise shall endure for ever.* Indeed, it is true that those who lead obedient lives shall obtain honour of the Lord, and commendations which will abide for ever. A word of approbation from the mouth of God will be a mede of honour which will outshine all the decorations which kings and emperors can bestow.

Wealth and riches shall be in his house: and his righteousness endureth for ever. *Psalm 112:3.*

Wealth and riches shall be in his house. Understood literally this is rather a promise of the old covenant than of the new, for many of the best of the people of God are very poor. Yet it has been found true that uprightness is the road to success, and, all other things being equal, the honest man is the rising man. Many are kept poor through knavery and profligacy. But godliness hath the promise of the life that now is. If we understand the passage spiritually, it is abundantly true. What **wealth** can equal that of the love of God? What **riches** can rival a contented heart? It matters nothing that the roof is thatched, and the floor is of cold stone. The heart which is cheered with the favour of heaven is *rich to all the intents of bliss.*

And his righteousness endureth for ever. Often when gold comes in the gospel goes out. But it is not so with the blessed man. Prosperity does not destroy the holiness of his life, or the humility of his heart. His character stands the test of examination, overcomes the temptations of wealth, survives the assaults of slander, outlives the afflictions of time, and endures the trial of the last great day. The **righteousness** of a true saint endureth for ever, because it springs from the same root as the righteousness of God, and is, indeed, the reflection of it. So long as the Lord abideth righteous he will maintain by his grace the righteousness of his people. They shall hold on their way, and wax stronger and stronger. There is also another righteousness which belongs to the Lord's chosen, which is sure to endure for ever, namely, the imputed righteousness of the Lord Jesus, which is called *everlasting righteousness,* belonging as it does to the Son of God himself, who is *the Lord our righteousness.*

Unto the upright there ariseth light in the darkness. *Psalm 112:4.*

The upright man does not lean to injustice in order to ease himself, but like a pillar stands erect. He shall be found so standing when the ungodly, who are as a bowing wall and a tottering fence, shall lie in ruins. He will have his days of darkness. He may be sick and sorry, poor and pining, as well as others. His former riches may take to themselves wings and fly away, while even his righteousness may be cruelly suspected. Thus the clouds may lower around him. But his gloom shall not last for ever. The Lord will bring him light in due season. As surely as a good man's sun goes down it shall rise again.

If the darkness be caused by depression of spirit, the Holy Ghost will comfort him. If by pecuniary loss or personal bereavement, the presence of Christ shall be his solace. If by the cruelty and malignity of men, the sympathy of his Lord shall be his support. It is as ordinary for the righteous to be comforted as for the day to dawn. Wait for the **light** and it will surely come. For even if our heavenly Father should in our last hours put us to bed in the dark, we shall find it morning when we awake.

PSALM 113

Blessed be the name of the Lord from this time forth and for evermore. *Psalm 113:2.*

Blessed be the name of the Lord. While praising him aloud, the people were also to *bless* him in the silence of their hearts, wishing glory to his name, success to his cause, and triumph to his truth. By mentioning **the name,** the Psalmist would teach us to bless each of the attributes of the Most High, which are as it were the letters of his name; not quarrelling with his justice or his severity, nor servilely dreading his power, but accepting him as we find him revealed in the inspired word and by his acts, and loving him and praising him as such. Every time we think of the God of Scripture we should bless him, and his august name should never be pronounced without joyful reverence. **From this time forth.** If we have never praised him before, let us begin now. As the Passover stood at the beginning of the year it was well to commence the new year with blessing him who wrought deliverance for his people. Every solemn feast had its own happy associations, and might be regarded as a fresh starting-place for adoration. Are there not reasons why the reader should make the present day the opening of a year of praise? When the Lord says, *From this time will I bless you,* we ought to reply, **Blessed be the name of the Lord from this time forth.**

And for evermore: eternally. The Psalmist could not have intended that the divine praise should cease at a future date however remote. **For evermore** in reference to the praise of God must signify endless duration. Can our hearts ever cease to praise the name of the Lord? Can we imagine a period in which the praises of Israel shall no more surround the throne of the Divine Majesty? Impossible. For ever, and more than for ever, if more can be, let him be magnified.

He maketh the barren woman to keep house, and to be a joyful mother of children. *Psalm 113:9.*

The strong desire of the easterns to have children caused the birth of offspring to be hailed as the choicest of favours. Barrenness was regarded as a curse. The glorious Lord displays his condescending grace in regarding those who are despised on account of their barrenness, whether it be of body or of soul. Sarah, Rachel, the wife of Manoah, Hannah, Elizabeth, and others were all instances of the miraculous power of God in literally fulfilling the statement of the Psalmist. Women were not supposed to have a **house** till they had children. But in certain cases, where childless women pined in secret, the Lord visited them in mercy, and made them not only to have a house, but to **keep** it. The Gentile church is a spiritual example upon a large scale of the gift of fruitfulness after long years of hopeless barrenness. The Jewish church in the latter days will be another amazing display of the same quickening power. Long forsaken for her spiritual adultery, Israel shall be forgiven, and restored, and joyously shall she keep that house which now is left unto her desolate.

Nor is this all. Each believer in the Lord Jesus must at times have mourned his lamentable barrenness. He has appeared to be a dry tree yielding no fruit to the Lord. Yet when visited by the Holy Ghost, he has found himself suddenly to be like Aaron's rod, which budded, and blossomed, and brought forth almonds. Our graces have been multiplied, as if many children had come to us at a single birth. Then have we marvelled greatly at the Lord. Like Mary, we have lifted up our Magnificat, and like Hannah, we have said *There is none holy as the Lord; for there is none beside thee: neither is there any rock like our God.*

PSALM 114

Tremble, thou earth, at the presence of the Lord, at the presence of the God of Jacob; which turned the rock into a standing water, the flint into a fountain of waters. *Psalm 114:7–8.*

Tremble, thou earth, at the presence of the Lord, at the presence of the God of Jacob. Or *from before the Lord, the Adonai, the Master and King.* Very fitly does the Psalm call upon all nature again to feel a holy awe because its Ruler is still in its midst. Let the believer feel that God is near, and he will serve the Lord with fear and rejoice with trembling. Awe is not cast out by faith, but the rather it becomes deeper and more profound. The Lord is most reverenced where he is most loved.

Which turned the rock into a standing water, causing a mere or lake to stand at its foot, making the wilderness a pool. So abundant was the supply of water from the rock that it remained like water in a reservoir. The flint into a fountain of waters, which flowed freely in streams, following the tribes in their devious marches. Behold what God can do! It seemed impossible that the flinty rock should become a fountain. But he speaks, and it is done. Not only do mountains move, but rocks yield rivers when the God of Israel wills that it should be so. O magnify the Lord with me, and let us exalt his name together, for he it is and he alone who doeth such wonders as these. He supplies our temporal needs from sources of the most unlikely kind, and never suffers the stream of his liberality to fail. As for our spiritual necessities they are all met by the water and the blood which gushed of old from the riven rock, Christ Jesus. Therefore let us extol the Lord our God.

PSALM 115

Not unto us, O Lord, not unto us, but unto thy name give glory, for thy mercy, and for thy truth's sake. *Psalm 115:1.*

Not unto us, O Lord, not unto us, but unto thy name give glory. The people undoubtedly wished for relief from the contemptuous insults of idolaters. But their main desire was that Jehovah himself should no longer be the object of heathen insults. The saddest part of all their trouble was that their God was no longer feared and dreaded by their adversaries. When Israel marched into Canaan, a terror was upon all the people round about, because of Jehovah, the mighty God. But this dread the nations had shaken off since there had been of late no remarkable display of miraculous power. Therefore Israel cried unto her God that he would again make bare his arm. Because of their past unfaithfulness they hardly dared to appeal to the covenant, and to ask blessings for themselves. But they fell back upon the honour of the Lord their God—an old style of argument which their great lawgiver, Moses, had used with such effect. In such manner also let us pray when no other plea is available because of our sense of sin. The Lord is always jealous of his honour, and will work for his name's sake when no other motive will move him.

For thy mercy, and for thy truth's sake. These attributes seemed most in jeopardy. How could the heathen think Jehovah to be a merciful God if he gave his people over to the hands of their enemies? How could they believe him to be faithful and true if, after all his solemn covenant engagements, he utterly rejected his chosen nation? God is very jealous of the two glorious attributes of grace and truth, and the plea that these may not be dishonoured has great weight with him. We may not desire the triumph of our opinions, for our own sakes, or for the honour of a sect. But we may confidently pray for the triumph of truth, that God himself may be honoured.

The Lord hath been mindful of us: he will bless us; he will bless the house of Israel; he will bless the house of Aaron. *Psalm 115:12.*

The Lord hath been mindful of us, or *Jehovah hath remembered us.* His past mercies prove that we are on his heart, and though for the present he may afflict us, yet he does not forget us. We have not to put him in remembrance as though he found it hard to recollect his children, but he hath remembered us and therefore he will in future deal well with us. **He will bless us.** The word **us** is supplied by the translators, and is superfluous, the passage should run, **He will bless; he will bless the house of Israel; he will bless the house of Aaron.** The repetition of the word **bless** adds great effect to the passage. The Lord has many blessings, each one worthy to be remembered, he blesses and blesses and blesses again. Where he has once bestowed his favour he continues it; his blessing delights to visit the same house very often and to abide where it has once lodged.

Blessing does not impoverish the Lord. He has multiplied his mercies in the past, and he will pour them forth thick and threefold in the future. He will have a general blessing for all who fear him, a peculiar blessing for the whole house of Israel, and a double blessing for the sons of Aaron. It is his nature to bless. It is his prerogative to bless. It is his glory to bless. It is his delight to bless. He has promised to bless, and therefore be sure of this, that he will bless and bless and bless without ceasing.

PSALM 116

I love the Lord, because he hath heard my voice and my supplications. *Psalm 116:1.*

I love the Lord. A blessed declaration. Every believer ought to be able to declare without the slightest hesitation, **I love the Lord.** The sweetest of all graces and the surest of all evidences of salvation is love. It is great goodness on the part of God that he condescends to be loved by such poor creatures as we are. **Because he hath heard my voice and my supplications.** The Psalmist not only knows that he loves God, but he knows why he does so. When love can justify itself with a reason, it is deep, strong, and abiding. David's reason for his love was the love of God in hearing his prayers. The Psalmist had used his **voice** in prayer, and the habit of doing so is exceedingly helpful to devotion. If we can pray aloud without being overheard, it is well to do so.

Sometimes, however, when the Psalmist had lifted up his voice, his utterance had been so broken and painful that he scarcely dared to call it prayer. Words failed him. He could produce only a groaning sound. But the Lord heard his moaning voice. At other times his prayers were more regular and better formed. These he calls **supplications.** David had praised as best he could, and when one form of devotion failed him he tried another. He had gone to the Lord again and again, hence he uses the plural and says **my supplications.** But as often as he had gone, so often had he been welcome. Jehovah had **heard,** that is to say, accepted, and answered both his broken cries and his more composed and orderly supplications. Hence he loved God with all his heart. Answered prayers are silken bonds which bind our hearts to God. When a man's prayers are answered, love is the natural result.

Return unto thy rest, O my soul; for the Lord hath dealt bountifully with thee. *Psalm 116:7.*

Return unto thy rest, O my soul. He calls the **rest** still his own, and feels full liberty to **return** to it. The Psalmist had evidently been somewhat disturbed in mind. His troubles had ruffled his spirit. But now with a sense of answered prayer upon him he quiets his soul. He had rested before, for he knew the blessed repose of faith, and therefore he returns to the God who had been the refuge of his soul in former days. Whenever a child of God even for a moment loses his peace of mind, he should be concerned to find it again, not by seeking it in the world or in his own experience, but in **the Lord** alone. When the believer prays, and the Lord inclines his ear, the road to the old rest is before him. Let him not be slow to follow it.

For the Lord hath dealt bountifully with thee. Thou hast served a good God, and built upon a sure foundation. Go not about to find any other rest, but come back to him who in former days hath condescended to enrich thee by his love. What a text is this! and what an exposition of it is furnished by the biography of every believing man and woman! **The Lord hath dealt bountifully with** *us.* He hath given us his Son, and in him he hath given us all things. He hath sent us his Spirit, and by him he conveys to us all spiritual blessings. God dealeth with us like a God. He lays his fullness open to us, and of that fullness have we all received, and grace for grace. We have sat at no niggard's table. We have been clothed by no penurious hand. We have been equipped by no grudging provider. Let us come back to him who has treated us with such excellent kindness.

I said in my haste, All men are liars. *Psalm 116: 11.*

In a modified sense the expression **All men are liars** will bear justification, even though hastily uttered, for all men will prove to be liars if we unduly trust in them—some from want of truthfulness, and others from want of power. But from the expression **I said in my haste** it is clear that the Psalmist did not justify his own language, but considered it as the ebullition of a hasty temper. In the sense in which he spoke his language was unjustifiable. He had no right to distrust *all* men, for many of them are honest, truthful, and conscientious. There are faithful friends and loyal adherents yet alive. If sometimes they disappoint us, we ought not to call them liars for failing when the failure arises entirely from want of power, and not from lack of will. Under great affliction our temptation will be to form hasty judgments of our fellow-men. Knowing this to be the case we ought carefully to watch our spirit, and to keep the door of our lips.

The Psalmist had believed, and therefore he spoke. He had doubted, and therefore he spoke in haste. He believed, and therefore he rightly prayed to God. He disbelieved, and therefore he wrongfully accused mankind. Speaking is as ill in some cases as it is good in others. Speaking in haste is generally followed by bitter repentance. It is much better to be quiet when our spirit is disturbed and hasty, for it is so much easier to say than to unsay. We may repent of our words, but we cannot so recall them as to undo the mischief they have done. If even David had to eat his own words, when he spoke in a hurry, none of us can trust our tongue without a bridle.

Precious in the sight of the Lord is the death of his saints. *Psalm 116:15.*

Precious in the sight of the Lord is the death of his saints. Therefore he did not suffer the Psalmist to die, but delivered his soul from death. This seems to indicate that the song was meant to remind Jewish families of the mercies received by any one of the household, supposing him to have been sore sick and to have been restored to health, for the Lord values the lives of his saints, and often spares them where others perish. They shall not die prematurely. They shall be immortal till their work is done. When their time shall come to die, then their deaths shall be precious. The Lord watches over their dying beds, smooths their pillows, sustains their hearts, and receives their souls.

Those who are redeemed with precious blood are so dear to God that even their deaths are precious to him. The death-beds of saints are very precious to the church, she often learns much from them. They are very precious to all believers, who delight to treasure up the last words of the departed. But they are most of all precious to the Lord Jehovah himself, who views the triumphant deaths of his gracious ones with sacred delight. If we have walked before him in the land of the living, we need not fear to die before him when the hour of our departure is at hand.

O praise the Lord, all ye nations: praise him, all ye people. *Psalm 117:1.*

O praise the Lord, all ye nations. The nations could not be expected to join in the praise of Jehovah unless they were also to be partakers of the benefits which Israel enjoyed. Hence this Psalm was an intimation to Israel that the grace and mercy of their God were not to be confined to one nation. In happier days it would be extended to all the race of man, even as Moses had prophesied when he said, *Rejoice, O ye nations, his people* (Deut. 32:43), for so the Hebrew has it. The **nations** were to be his **people.** He would call them a people that were not a people, and her beloved that was not beloved. We know and believe that no one tribe of men shall be unrepresented in the universal song which shall ascend unto the Lord of all. Individuals have already been gathered out of every kindred and people and tongue by the preaching of the gospel. They have right heartily joined in magnifying the grace which sought them out, and brought them to know the Saviour. These are but the advance-guard of a number, which no man can number, who will come ere long to worship the all-glorious One.

Praise him, all ye people. Having done it once, do it again, and do it still more fervently, daily increasing in the reverence and zeal with which you extol the Most High. Not only **praise him** nationally by your rulers, but popularly in your crowds. The multitude of the common folk shall bless the Lord. Inasmuch as the matter is spoken of twice, its certainty is confirmed. The Gentiles must and shall extol Jehovah—all of them, without exception. Under the gospel dispensation we worship no new god. The God of Abraham is our God for ever and ever. The God of the whole earth shall he be called.

O give thanks unto the Lord; for he is good: because his mercy endureth for ever. *Psalm 118:1.*

O give thanks unto the Lord. It is always well to trace our mercies to him who bestows them. If we cannot give him anything else, let us at any rate give him our **thanks.** Have we been of a forgetful or murmuring spirit? Let us hear the lively language of the text, and allow it to speak to our hearts: *Give thanks unto the Lord.* **For he is good.** This is reason enough for giving him thanks. Goodness is his essence and nature, and therefore he is always to be praised whether we are receiving anything from him or not. Those who only praise God because he *does* them good should rise to a higher note and give thanks to him because he *is* good. His dispensations may vary, but his nature is always the same, and always good. It is not only that he was good, and will be good, but he *is* good, let his providence be what it may.

Because his mercy endureth for ever. Mercy is a great part of his goodness, and one which more concerns us than any other, for we are sinners and have need of his mercy. Angels may say that he is good, but they need not his mercy and cannot therefore take an equal delight in it. Inanimate creation declares that **he is good,** but it cannot feel **his mercy,** for it has never transgressed. But man, deeply guilty and graciously forgiven, beholds mercy as the very focus and centre of the goodness of the Lord. The endurance of the divine mercy is a special subject for song. Notwithstanding our sins, our trials, our fears, his mercy **endureth for ever.** The best of earthly joys pass away, and even the world itself grows old and hastens to decay. But there is no change in the mercy of God.

It is better to trust in the Lord than to put confidence in man.
Psalm 118:8.

It is better in all ways. First of all it is wiser. God is infinitely more able to help, and more likely to help, than man. Therefore prudence suggests that we put our confidence in him above all others. It is also morally better to do so, for it is the duty of the creature to trust in the Creator. God has a claim upon his creatures' faith. He deserves to be trusted. To place our reliance upon another rather than upon himself is a direct insult to his faithfulness. It is better in the sense of safer, since we can never be sure of our ground if we rely upon mortal man. But we are always secure in the hands of our God. It is better in its effect upon ourselves. To trust in man tends to make us mean, crouching, dependent. But confidence in God elevates, produces a sacred quiet of spirit, and sanctifies the soul.

It is, moreover, much better to trust in God, as far as the result is concerned. In many cases the human object of our trust fails from want of ability, from want of generosity, from want of affection, or from want of memory. But the Lord, so far from failing, does for us exceeding abundantly above all that we ask or even think. This verse is written out of the experience of many who have first of all found the broken reeds of the creature break under them, and have afterwards joyfully found the Lord to be a solid pillar sustaining all their weight.

The Lord is my strength and song, and is become my salvation. *Psalm 118:14.*

The Lord is my strength and song. My strength while I was in the conflict, **my song** now that it is ended. **My strength** against the strong, and **my song** over their defeat. He is far from boasting of his own valour. He ascribes his victory to its real source. He has no song concerning his own exploits. All his paeans are unto *Jehovah Victor,* the Lord whose right hand and holy arm had given him the victory. **And is become my salvation.** The poet warrior knew that he was saved, and he not only ascribed that salvation unto God, but he declared God himself to be his salvation. It is an all-comprehending expression, signifying that from beginning to end, in the whole and in the details of it, he owed his deliverance entirely to the Lord. Thus can all the Lord's redeemed say, *Salvation is of the Lord.*

We cannot endure any doctrine which puts the crown upon the wrong head and defrauds the glorious King of his revenue of praise. Jehovah has done it all. Yea, in Christ Jesus he *is* all, and therefore in our praises let him alone be extolled. It is a happy circumstance for us when we can praise God as alike our **strength, song,** and **salvation.** God sometimes gives a secret strength to his people, and yet they question their own salvation, and cannot, therefore, sing of it. Many are, no doubt, truly saved, but at times they have so little strength, that they are ready to faint, and therefore they cannot sing. When strength is imparted and salvation is realised then the song is clear and full.

I will praise thee: for thou hast heard me, and art become my salvation. *Psalm 118:21.*

I will praise thee, not *I will praise the Lord,* for now he vividly realises the divine presence, and addresses himself directly to Jehovah. How well it is in all our songs of praise to let the heart have direct and distinct communion with God himself! The Psalmist's song was personal praise too: *I will* **praise thee.** Resolute praise, for he firmly resolved to offer it; spontaneous praise, for he voluntarily and cheerfully rendered it; continuous praise, for he did not intend soon to have done with it. It was a life-long vow to which there would never come a close, **I will praise thee.**

For thou hast heard me, and art become my salvation. He praises God by mentioning his favours, weaving his song out of the divine goodness which he had experienced. In these words he gives the reason for his praise: his answered prayer, and the deliverance which he had received in consequence. How fondly he dwells upon the personal interposition of God! *Thou* hast heard me. How heartily he ascribes the whole of his victory over his enemies to God. Nay, he sees God himself to be the whole of it: *Thou* art become my salvation. It is well to go directly to God himself, and not to stay even in his mercy, or in the acts of his grace. Answered prayers bring God very near to us. Realised salvation enables us to realise the immediate presence of God. Considering the extreme distress through which the worshipper had passed, it is not at all wonderful that he should feel his heart full of gratitude at the great salvation which God had wrought for him, and should at his first entrance into the temple lift up his voice in thankful praise for personal favours so great, so needful, so perfect.

This is the day which the Lord hath made; we will rejoice and be glad in it. *Psalm 118:24.*

This is the day which the Lord hath made. A new era has commenced. The day of David's enthronement was the beginning of better times for Israel. In a far higher sense the day of our Lord's resurrection is a new day of God's own making, for it is the dawn of a blessed dispensation. No doubt the Israelitish nation celebrated the victory of its champion with a day of feasting, music and song. Surely it is but meet that we should reverently keep the feast of the triumph of the Son of David. We observe the Lord's day as henceforth our true Sabbath, a day made and ordained of God, for the perpetual remembrance of the achievements of our Redeemer.

We will rejoice and be glad in it. What else can we do? Having obtained so great a deliverance through our illustrious leader, and having seen the eternal mercy of God so brilliantly displayed, it would ill become us to mourn and murmur. Rather will we exhibit a double joy, rejoice in heart and be glad in face, rejoice in secret and be glad in public, for we have more than a double reason for being glad in the Lord. We ought to be specially joyous on the Sabbath. It is the queen of days, and its hours should be clad in royal apparel of delight. Entering into the midst of the church of God, and beholding the Lord Jesus as all in all in the assemblies of his people, we are bound to overflow with joy. Is it not written, *then were the disciples glad when they saw the Lord?* When the King makes the house of prayer to be a banqueting

224

house, and we have grace to enjoy fellowship with him, both in his sufferings and in his triumphs, we feel an intense delight, and we are glad to express it with the rest of his people.

Blessed are they that keep his testimonies. *Psalm 119:2.*

Blessedness is ascribed to those who treasure up the **testimonies** of the Lord: in which is implied that they search the Scriptures, that they come to an understanding of them, that they love them, and then that they continue in the practice of them. We must first *get* a thing before we can *keep* it. We cannot keep in the heart that which we have not heartily embraced by the affections. God's word is his witness or testimony to grand and important truths which concern himself and our relation to him. This we should desire to know. Knowing it, we should believe it. Believing it, we should love it. Loving it, we should hold it fast against all comers. There is a doctrinal keeping of the word when we are ready to die for its defence, and a practical keeping of it when we actually live under its power. Revealed truth is precious as diamonds, and should be kept or treasured up in the memory and in the heart as jewels in a casket. This however is not enough, for it is meant for practical use, and therefore it must be kept or followed, as men keep to a path, or to a line of business. If we keep God's testimonies, they will keep us. They will keep us right in opinion, comfortable in spirit, holy in conversation, and hopeful in expectation.

We are bound to keep with all care the word of God, because it is **his testimonies.** He gave them to us, but they are still his own. We shall have to give an account, for we are put in trust with the gospel, and woe to us if we be found unfaithful. We cannot fight a good fight, nor finish our course, unless we keep the faith. To this end the Lord must keep us. Only those who are kept by the power of God unto salvation will ever be able to keep his testimonies.

Wherewithal shall a young man cleanse his way? by taking heed thereto according to thy word. *Psalm 119:9.*

Wherewithal shall a young man cleanse his way? Among all the questions which a young man asks, and they are many, let this be the first and chief. This is a question suggested by common sense, and pressed home by daily occurrences. But it is not to be answered by unaided reason, nor, when answered, can the directions be carried out by unsupported human power. It is ours to ask the question. It is

God's to give the answer and enable us to carry it out. **By taking heed thereto according to thy word.** Young man, you must take heed to your daily life, as well as study your Bible, and you must study your Bible that you may take heed to your daily life. With the greatest care a man will go astray if his map misleads him. But with the most accurate map he will still lose his road if he does not take heed to it. The narrow way was never hit upon by chance, neither did any heedless man ever lead a holy life. We can sin without thought, we have only to neglect the great salvation and ruin our souls. But to obey the Lord and walk uprightly will need all our heart and soul and mind.

Yet the **word** is absolutely necessary. Otherwise care will darken into morbid anxiety, and conscientiousness may become superstition. It is not enough to desire to be right. Let each man, whether young or old, who desires to be holy have a holy watchfulness in his heart, and keep his Holy Bible before his open eye. There he will find every turn of the road marked down, every slough and miry place pointed out, with the way to go through unsoiled. There, too, he will find light for his darkness, comfort for his weariness, and company for his loneliness.

I will meditate in thy precepts, and have respect unto thy ways. *Psalm 119:15.*

I will meditate in thy precepts. He who has an inward delight in anything will not long withdraw his mind from it. As the miser often returns to look upon his treasure, so does the devout believer by frequent meditation turn over the priceless wealth which he has discovered in the book of the Lord. To some men meditation is a task. To the man of cleansed way it is a joy. He who has meditated will meditate. He who saith, *I have rejoiced*, is the same who adds, *I will meditate*. No spiritual exercise is more profitable to the soul than that of devout meditation. Why are many of us so exceeding slack in it? It is worthy of observation that the preceptory part of God's word was David's special subject of meditation. This was the more natural because the question was still upon his mind as to *how* a young man should cleanse his way. Practical godliness is vital godliness.

And have respect unto thy ways, that is to say, I will think much about them so as to know what thy ways are. I will think much of them so as to have thy ways in great reverence and high esteem. I will see what thy ways are towards me that I may be filled with reverence, gratitude, and love. I will observe what are those ways which thou hast prescribed for me, thy ways in which thou wouldest have me follow thee. These I would watch carefully that I may become obedient, and prove myself to be a true servant of such a Master.

My hands also will I lift up unto thy commandments, which I have loved; and I will meditate in thy statutes. *Psalm 119:48.*

My hands also will I lift up unto thy commandments. He will stretch out towards perfection as far as he can, hoping to reach it one day. When his hands hang down, he will cheer himself out of languor by the prospect of glorifying God by obedience. He will give solemn sign of his hearty assent and consent to all that his God commands. **Which I have loved.** Again he declares his love. A true heart loves to express itself. It is a kind of fire which must send forth its flames. It was natural that he should reach out towards a law which he delighted in, even as a child holds out his hands to receive a gift which it longs for. When such a lovely object as holiness is set before us, we are bound to rise towards it with our whole nature. Till that is fully accomplished we should at least lift up our hands in prayer towards it. Where holy hands and holy hearts go, the whole man will one day follow.

And I will meditate in thy statutes. He can never have enough of meditation upon the mind of God. Loving subjects wish to be familiar with their sovereign's statutes, for they are anxious that they may not offend through ignorance. Prayer with lifted hands, and meditation with upward-glancing eyes will in happy union work out the best inward results. The whole of this verse is in the future, and may be viewed not only as a determination of David's mind, but as a result which he knew would follow from the Lord's sending him his mercies and his salvation. When mercy comes down, our hands will be lifted up. When God in favour thinks upon us, we are sure to think of him. Happy is he who stands with hands uplifted both to receive the blessing and to obey the precept. He shall not wait upon the Lord in vain.

I thought on my ways, and turned my feet unto thy testimonies. *Psalm 119:59.*

While studying the word he was led to study his own life, and this caused a mighty revolution. He came to the word, and then he came to himself, and this made him arise and go to his father. Consideration is the commencement of conversion. First we *think*, and then we *turn*. When the mind repents of ill ways, the feet are soon led into good ways. But there will be no repenting until there is deep, earnest thought. Many men are averse to thought of any kind, and as to thought upon their ways, they cannot endure it, for their ways will not bear thinking of. David's ways had not been all that he could have wished them to be, and so his thoughts were sobered o'er with the pale cast of regret. But he did not end with idle lamentations. He set about a practical amendment. He turned and returned. He sought the testimonies of the Lord, and hastened to enjoy once more the conscious favour of his heavenly friend.

Action without thought is folly, and thought without action is sloth. To think carefully and then to act promptly is a happy combination. He had entreated for renewed fellowship. How he proved the genuineness of his desire by renewed obedience. If we are in the dark, and mourn an absent God, our wisest method will be not so much to think upon our sorrows as upon our ways. Though we cannot turn the course of providence, we can turn the way of our walking, and this will soon mend matters. If we can get our feet right as to holy walking, we shall soon get our hearts right as to happy living. God will turn to his saints when they turn to him. Yea, he has already favoured them with the light of his face when they begin to think and turn.

The law of thy mouth is better unto me than thousands of gold and silver. *Psalm 119:72.*

The law of thy mouth. A sweetly expressive name for the word of God. It comes from God's own *mouth* with freshness and power to our souls. Things written are as dried herbs. But speech has a liveliness and dew about it. We do well to look upon the word of the Lord as though it were newly spoken into our ear. In very truth it is not decayed by years, but is as forcible and sure as though newly uttered. Precepts are prized when it is seen that they come forth from the lips of our Father who is in heaven.

Is better unto me than thousands of gold and silver. If a poor man had said this, the world's witlings would have hinted that the grapes are sour. But this is the verdict of a man who owned his **thousands,** and could judge by actual experience of the value of money and the value of truth. He speaks of great riches. He heaps it up by thousands. He mentions the varieties of its forms, **gold and silver.** Then he sets the word of God before it all, as better *to him*, even if others did not think it better to them. Wealth is good in some respects, but obedience is better in all respects. It is well to keep the treasures of this life; but far more commendable to keep the law of the Lord. The law is better than gold and silver, for these may be stolen from us, but not the word. These take to themselves wings, but the word of God remains. These are useless in the hour of death, but then it is that the promise is most dear. It is a sure sign of a heart which has learned God's statutes when it prizes them above all earthly possessions. It is **an**

equally certain mark of grace when the precepts of Scripture are as precious as its promises.

O how I love thy law! it is my meditation all the day. *Psalm 119:97.*

O how love I thy law! It is a note of exclamation. He loves so much that he must express his love, and in making the attempt he perceives that it is inexpressible—and therefore cries, **O how I love!** We not only reverence but love the law. We obey it out of love, and even when it chides us for disobedience we love it none the less. The law is God's law, and therefore it is our love. We love it for its holiness, and pine to be holy. We love it for its wisdom, and study to be wise. We love it for its perfection, and long to be perfect. Those who know the power of the gospel perceive an infinite loveliness in the law as they see it fulfilled and embodied in Christ Jesus.

It is my meditation all the day. This was both the effect of his love and the cause of it. He meditated in God's word because he loved it, and then loved it the more because he meditated in it. He could not have enough of it, so ardently did he love it. **All the day** was not too long for his converse with it. His matin prayer, his noonday thought, his evensong were all out of Holy Writ. Yea, in his worldly business he still kept his mind saturated with the law of the Lord. It is said of some men that the more you know them the less you admire them. But the reverse is true of God's word. Familiarity with the word of God breeds affection, and affection seeks yet greater familiarity. When **thy law,** and **my meditation** are together all the day, the day grows holy, devout, and happy, and the heart lives with God. David turned away from all else. In the preceding verse he tells us that he had seen an end of all perfection; but he turned in unto the law and tarried there the whole day of his life on earth, growing henceforth wiser and holier.

Thy word is a lamp unto my feet, and a light unto my path. *Psalm 119:105.*

Thy word is a lamp unto my feet. We are walkers through the city of this world, and we are often called to go out into its darkness. Let us never venture there without the light-giving **word,** lest we slip with our feet. Each man should use the word of God personally, practically, and habitually, that he may see his way and see what lies in it. When darkness settles down upon all around me, the word of the Lord, like a flaming torch, reveals my way. Having no fixed lamps in eastern towns, in old time each passenger carried a lantern with him. This is a true picture of our path through this dark world. We should not know the way, or how to walk in it, if the Scripture did not reveal it. One of the most practical benefits of Holy Writ is guidance in the acts of daily life. It is not sent to astound us with its brilliance, but to guide us by its instruction. It is true the head needs illumination. But even more the feet need direction, else head and feet may both fall into a ditch. Happy is the man who personally appropriates God's word, and practically uses it as his comfort and counsellor, **a lamp** to his own feet.

And a light unto my path. It is a **lamp** by night, a **light** by day, and a delight at all times. David guided his own steps by it, and also saw the difficulties of his road by its beams. He who walks in darkness is sure, sooner or later, to stumble. He who walks by the light of day, or by the lamp of night, stumbleth not, but keeps his uprightness. Ignorance is painful upon practical subjects. It breeds indecision and suspense, and these are uncomfortable. The word of God, by imparting heavenly knowledge, leads to decision, and when that is followed by determined resolution, as in this case, it brings with it great restfulness of heart.

Thou art my hiding-place and my shield: I hope in thy word. *Psalm 119:114.*

Thou art my hiding-place and my shield. To his God he ran for shelter from vain thoughts. There he hid himself away from their tormenting intrusions, and in solemn silence of the soul he found God to be his **hiding-place.** When called into the world, if he could not be alone with God as his hiding-place, he could have the Lord with him as his **shield,** and by this means he could ward off the attacks of wicked suggestions. This is an experimental verse. It testifies to that which the writer knew of his own personal knowledge. He could not fight with his own thoughts, or escape from them, till he flew to his God. Then he found deliverance. Observe that he does not speak of God's *word* as being his double defence, but he ascribes that to God *himself.* When we are beset by very spiritual assaults, such as those which arise out of vain thoughts, we shall do well to fly distinctly to the person of our Lord, and to cast ourselves upon his real presence. Happy is he who can truly say to the triune God, **Thou art my hiding-place.** He has beheld God under that glorious covenant aspect which ensures to the beholder the surest consolation.

I hope in thy word. And well he might, since he had tried and proved it. He looked for protection from all danger, and preservation from all temptation to him who had hitherto been the tower of his defence on former occasions. It is easy to exercise *hope* where we have experienced *help.* Sometimes when gloomy thoughts afflict us, the only thing we can do is to hope. Happily, the word of God always sets before us objects of hope and reasons for hope, so that it becomes the very sphere and support of hope, and thus tiresome thoughts are overcome. Amid fret and worry a hope of heaven is an effectual quietus.

The entrance of thy words giveth light; it giveth understanding unto the simple. *Psalm 119:130.*

The entrance of thy words giveth light. No sooner do they gain admission into the soul than they enlighten it. What light may be expected from their prolonged indwelling! Their very entrance floods the mind with instruction, for they are so full, so clear. But, on the other hand, there must be such an **entrance,** or there will be no illumination. The mere *hearing* of the word with the external ear is of small value by itself. But when the words of God enter into the chambers of the heart, then light is scattered on all sides. The word finds no entrance into some minds because they are blocked up with self-conceit, or prejudice, or indifference. But where due attention is given, divine illumination must surely follow upon knowledge of the mind of God. Oh, that **thy words,** like the beams of the sun, may enter through the window of my understanding, and dispel the darkness of my mind!

It **giveth understanding unto the simple.** The sincere and candid are the true disciples of the word. To such it gives not only knowledge, but understanding. These simple-hearted ones are frequently despised, and their simplicity has another meaning infused into it, so as to be made the theme of ridicule. But what matters it? Those whom the world dubs as fools are among the truly wise if they are taught of God. What a divine power rests in the word of God, since it not only bestows light, but gives that very mental eye by which the light is received—**It giveth understanding.** Hence the value of the words of God to the simple, who cannot receive mysterious truth unless their minds are aided to see it and prepared to grasp it.

Consider mine affliction, and deliver me: for I do not forget thy law. *Psalm 119:153.*

Consider mine affliction, and deliver me. There is no impatience: he does not ask for hasty action, but for consideration. In effect he cries—'Look into my grief, and see whether I do not need to be delivered. From my sorrowful condition, judge as to the proper method and time for my rescue.' It should be the desire of every gracious man who is in adversity that the Lord should look upon his need, and relieve it in such a way as shall be most for the divine glory, and for his own benefit. The words **mine affliction** are picturesque. They seem to portion off a special spot of woe as the writer's own inheritance. He possesses it as no one else had ever done, and he begs the Lord to have that special spot under his eye—even as a husbandman looking over all his fields may yet take double care of a certain selected plot. His prayer is eminently practical, for he seeks to be delivered. That is, brought out of the trouble and preserved from sustaining any serious damage by it. For God to consider is to act in due season. Men **consider** and do nothing. But such is never the case with our God.

For I do not forget thy law. His affliction was not sufficient, with all its bitterness, to drive out of his mind the memory of God's law. Nor could it lead him to act contrary to the divine command. He forgot prosperity, but he did not forget obedience. This is a good plea when it can be honestly urged. If we are kept faithful to God's **law,** we may be sure that God will remain faithful to his promise. If we do not forget his *law,* the Lord will not forget *us.* He will not long leave that man in trouble whose only fear in trouble is lest he should leave the way of right.

Great peace have they which love thy law: and nothing shall offend them. *119:165.*

Great peace have they which love thy law. What a charming verse is this! It deals not with those who perfectly *keep* the **law,** for where should such men be found? but with those who *love* it, whose hearts and hands are made to square with its precepts and demands. These men are ever striving, with all their hearts, to walk in obedience to the law. Though they are often persecuted, they have peace, yea, *great* **peace.** They have learned the secret of the reconciling blood. They have felt the power of the comforting Spirit. They stand before the Father as men accepted. The Lord has given them to feel his peace, which passes all understanding. They have many troubles, and are likely to be persecuted by the proud. But their usual condition is that of deep calm—a peace too great for this little world to break.

And nothing shall offend them, or, *shall really injure them.* All things work together for good to them that love God, to them who are the called according to his purpose. It must needs be that offences come. But these lovers of the law are peacemakers, and so they neither give nor take offence. That peace which is founded upon conformity to God's will is a living and lasting one, worth writing of with enthusiasm, as the Psalmist here does.

Deliver my soul, O Lord, from lying lips, and from a deceitful tongue. *Psalm 120:2.*

Deliver my soul, O Lord, from lying lips. It will need divine power to save a man from these deadly instruments. Lips are soft. But when they are *lying* **lips** they suck away the life of character and are as murderous as razors. David says, **Deliver my soul:** the **soul,** the life of the man, is endangered by **lying lips.** Cobras are not more venomous, nor devils themselves more pitiless. Some seem to lie for lying's sake. It is their sport and spirit. Their lips deserve to be kissed with a hot iron. But it is not for the friends of Jesus to render to men according to their deserts. Oh for a dumb generation rather than a lying one! The faculty of speech becomes a curse when it is degraded into a mean weapon for smiting men behind their backs. We need to be delivered from slander by the Lord's restraint upon wicked tongues, or else to be delivered out of it by having our good name cleared from the liar's calumny.

And **from a deceitful tongue.** This is rather worse than downright falsehood. Better to meet wild beasts and serpents than deceivers. These are a kind of monster whose birth is from beneath, and whose end lies far below. Here is to the believer good cause for prayer. *Deliver us from evil* may be used with emphasis concerning this business. From gossips, talebearers, writers of anonymous letters, forgers of newspaper paragraphs, and all sorts of liemongers, good Lord deliver us!

He will not suffer thy foot to be moved: he that keepeth thee will not slumber. *Psalm 121:3.*

He will not suffer thy foot to be moved. Though the paths of life are dangerous and difficult, yet we shall stand fast, for Jehovah will not permit our feet to slide. If *he* will not suffer it, *we* shall not suffer it. If our **foot** will be thus kept, we may be sure that our head and heart will be preserved also. In the original the words express a wish or prayer: *May he not suffer thy foot to be moved.* Promised preservation should be the subject of perpetual prayer. And we may pray believingly, for those who have God for their keeper shall be safe from all perils of the way. Among the hills and ravines of Palestine the literal keeping of the feet is a great mercy. But in the slippery ways of a tried and afflicted life, the boon of upholding is of priceless value. A single false step might cause us a fall fraught with awful danger. To stand erect and pursue the even tenor of our way is a blessing which only God can give, which is worthy of the divine hand, and worthy also of perennial gratitude. Our feet shall move in progress. But they shall not **be moved** to their overthrow.

He that keepeth thee will not slumber, or *thy keeper shall not slumber.* We should not stand a moment if our keeper were to sleep. We need him by day and by night. Not a single step can be safely taken except under his guardian eye. This is a choice stanza in a pilgrim song. When dangers are awake around us we are safe, for our Preserver is awake also, and will not permit us to be taken unawares. No fatigue or exhaustion can cast our God into sleep. His watchful eyes are never closed.

The Lord shall preserve thy going out and thy coming in from this time forth, and even for evermore. *Psalm 121:8.*

When we go out in the morning to labour, and come home at eventide to rest, Jehovah shall keep us. When we go out in youth to begin life, and come in at the end to die, we shall experience the same keeping. Our exits and our entrances are under one protection. Three times in this Psalm have we the phrase, *Jehovah shall keep,* as if the sacred Trinity thus sealed the word to make it sure. Ought not all our fears to be slain by such a threefold flight of arrows? What anxiety can survive this triple promise? This keeping is eternal: continuing **from this time forth, and even for evermore.** The whole church is thus assured of everlasting security. The final perseverance of the saints is thus ensured. The glorious immortality of believers is guaranteed. Under the aegis of such a promise we may go on pilgrimage without trembling, and venture into battle without dread.

None is so safe as him whom God keeps. None is so much in danger as the self-secure. To goings out and comings in belong peculiar dangers, since every change of position turns a fresh quarter to the foe. It is for these weak points that an especial security is provided. Jehovah will keep the door when it opens and closes. This he will perseveringly continue to do, so long as there is left a single man that trusteth in him, as long as a danger survives, and, in fact, as long as time endures. Glory be unto the Keeper of Israel, who is endeared to us under that title, since our growing sense of weakness makes us feel more deeply than ever our need of being kept.

PSALM 122

I was glad when they said unto me, Let us go into the house of the Lord. *Psalm 122:1.*

Good children are pleased to go home, and glad to hear their brothers and sisters call them thither. David's heart was in the worship of God, and he was delighted when he found others inviting him to go where his desires had already gone. It helps the ardour of the most ardent to hear others inviting them to a holy duty. The word was not *go*, but **let us go**. Hence the ear of the Psalmist found a double joy in it. He was glad *for the sake of others*: glad that they wished to go themselves, glad that they had the courage and liberality to invite others. He knew that it would do them good. Nothing better can happen to men and their friends than to love the place where God's honour dwelleth.

David was glad *for his own sake*. He rejoiced that good people thought enough of him to extend their invitation to him. He was glad to go into the house of the Lord, glad to go in holy company, glad to find good men and women willing to have him in their society. He may have been sad before, but this happy suggestion cheered him up. Is it so with us? Are we glad when others invite us to public worship, or to church fellowship? Then we shall be glad when the spirits above shall call us to the house of the Lord not made with hands, eternal in the heavens. If we are glad to be called by others to our Father's house, how much more glad shall we be actually to go there. We love our Lord, and therefore we love his house.

Pray for the peace of Jerusalem: they shall prosper that love thee.
Psalm 122:6.

Pray for the peace of Jerusalem. Peace was her name (*Salem*). **Pray** that her condition may verify her title. Abode of Peace, peace be to thee. Here was a most sufficient reason for rejoicing at the thought of going up to the house of the Lord. That sacred shrine stood in the centre of an area of peace. Well might Israel pray that such peace should be continued. In a church peace is to be desired, expected, promoted, and enjoyed. If we may not say, *Peace at any price*, yet we may certainly cry, *Peace at the highest price*. Those who are daily fluttered by rude alarms are charmed to reach their nest in a holy fellowship, and abide in it. In a church one of the main ingredients of success is internal peace. Strife, suspicion, party-spirit, division—these are deadly things. Those who break the peace of the church deserve to suffer, and those who sustain it win a great blessing.

Peace in the church should be our daily prayer. In so praying we shall bring down peace upon ourselves, for the Psalmist goes on to say, **They shall prosper that love thee.** Whether the passage be regarded as a promise or as a prayer matters not, for prayer pleads the promise, and the promise is the ground of prayer. Prosperity of soul is already enjoyed by those who take a deep interest in the church and cause of God. They are men of peace, and find peace in their holy endeavours. God's people pray for them, and God himself delights in them. Prosperity of worldly condition often comes to the lovers of the church if they are able to bear it. No man shall ever be a permanent loser by the house of the Lord. In peace of heart alone, if in nothing else, we find recompense enough for all that we can do in promoting the interests of Zion.

PSALM 123

Behold, as the eyes of servants look unto the hand of their masters, and as the eyes of a maiden unto the hand of her mistress; so our eyes wait upon the Lord our God, until that he have mercy upon us. *Psalm 123:2.*

Behold, as the eyes of servants (or *slaves*) **look unto the hand of their masters.** Orientals speak less than we do, and prefer to direct their slaves by movements of their hands. Creation, providence, grace: these are all motions of Jehovah's hand, and from each of them a portion of our duty is to be learned. Therefore should we carefully study them, to discover the divine will.

So our eyes wait upon the Lord our God. Believers desire to be attentive to each and all of the directions of the Lord. Even those which concern apparently little things are not little to us, for we know that even for idle words we shall be called to account, and we are anxious to give in that account with joy, and not with grief. True saints, like obedient servants, look to the Lord their God *reverentially*: they have a holy awe and inward fear of the great and glorious One. They watch *obediently*, doing his commandments, guided by his eye. Their constant gaze is fixed *attentively* on all that comes from the Most High. They give earnest heed, and fear lest they should let anything slip through inadvertence or drowsiness. They look *continuously*, for there never is a time when they are off duty. At all times they delight to serve in all things. Upon the Lord they fix their eyes *expectantly*, looking for supply, succour, and safety from his hands, waiting that he may have mercy upon them. To him they look *singly*. They have no other confidence. They learn to look *submissively*, waiting patiently for the Lord, seeking both in activity and suffering to glorify his name.

PSALM 124

Our soul is escaped as a bird out of the snare of the fowlers: the snare is broken, and we are escaped. *Psalm 124:7.*

Our soul is escaped as a bird out of the snare of the fowlers.
Fowlers have many methods of taking small birds, and Satan has many
methods of entrapping souls. Some are decoyed by evil companions,
others are enticed by the love of dainties. Hunger drives many into the
trap, and fright impels numbers to fly into the net. Fowlers know their
birds, and how to take them. But the birds see not the snare so as to
avoid it, and they cannot break it so as to escape from it. Happy is the
bird that hath a deliverer strong, and mighty, and ready in the moment
of peril. Happier still is the soul over which the Lord watches day and
night to pluck its feet out of the net. What joy there is in this song,
Our soul is escaped! How the emancipated one sings and soars, and
soars and sings again. Blessed be God many of us can make joyous
music with these notes, **Our soul is escaped!** Escaped from our
natural slavery; escaped from the guilt, the degradation, the habit, the
dominion of sin; escaped from the vain deceits and fascinations of
Satan; escaped from all that can destroy. We do indeed experience
delight. What a wonder of grace it is! The Lord has heard the prayer
which he taught us to pray, and he hath delivered us from evil.

The snare is broken, and we are escaped. The song is worth
repeating. We see not the mercy while we are in the snare. The gratitude comes when we perceive what we have escaped from, and by
what hand we have been set free. Then our Lord has a song from our
mouths and hearts as we make heaven and earth ring with the notes,
the snare is broken, and we are escaped.

Our help is in the name of the Lord, who made heaven and earth.
Psalm 124: 8.

Our help, our hope for the future, our ground of confidence in all trials
present and to come. **Is in the name of the Lord.** Jehovah's revealed
character is our foundation of confidence, his person is our sure
fountain of strength. **Who made heaven and earth.** Our Creator is
our preserver. He is immensely great in his creating work. He has not
fashioned a few little things alone, but all heaven and the whole round
earth are the works of his hands. When we worship the Creator let us
increase our trust in our Comforter. Did he create all that we see, and
can he not preserve us from evils which we cannot see? Blessed be his
name, he that has fashioned us will watch over us. Yea, he has done so,
and rendered us help in the moment of jeopardy.

He is our help and our shield, even he alone. He will to the end
break every snare. He **made heaven** for us, and he will keep us for
heaven. He made the **earth,** and he will succour us upon it until the
hour cometh for our departure. Every work of his hand preaches to us

the duty and the delight of reposing upon him only. All nature cries, *Trust ye in the Lord for ever, for in the Lord Jehovah there is everlasting strength.* Wherefore comfort one another with these words.

As the mountains are round about Jerusalem, so the Lord is round about his people from henceforth even for ever. *Psalm 125:2.*

The hill of Zion is the type of the believer's constancy, and the surrounding **mountains** are made emblems of the all-surrounding presence of the Lord. The mountains around the holy city, though they do not make a circular wall, are, nevertheless, set like sentinels to guard her gates. God doth not enclose his people within ramparts and bulwarks, making their city to be a prison. Yet he so orders the arrangements of his providence that his saints are as safe as if they dwelt behind the strongest fortifications. What a double security the first two verses of this Psalm set before us! First, we are established, and then entrenched: settled, and then sentinelled: made like a mount, and then protected as if by mountains. This is no matter of poetry. It is so in fact.

And it is no matter of temporary privilege, but it shall be so for ever. Date when we please **from henceforth,** Jehovah encircles his people. Look on us as far as we please, the protection extends **even for ever.** Note, it is not said that Jehovah's power or wisdom defends believers, but he himself is **round about** them. They have his personality for their protection, his Godhead for their guard. The Lord's **people** are those who trust him, for the line of faith is the line of grace. They must abide where God has placed them, and God must for ever protect them from all evil. It would be difficult to imagine greater safety than is here set forth.

When the Lord turned again the captivity of Zion, we were like them that dream. *Psalm 126:1.*

So sudden and so overwhelming was their joy that they felt like men out of themselves, ecstatic, or in a trance. **The captivity** had been great, and great was the deliverance; for the great God himself had wrought it. It was not the freedom of an individual which the Lord in mercy had wrought, but of all **Zion,** of the whole nation. How often it has been true to ourselves! Let us look to the prison-houses from which we have been set free. At our first conversion what a turning again of captivity we experienced! Since then, from multiplied troubles, from depression of spirit, from miserable backsliding, from grievous doubt, we have been emancipated, and we are not able to describe the bliss which followed each emancipation.

This verse will have a higher fulfilment in the day of the final overthrow of the powers of darkness when the Lord shall come forth for the salvation and glorification of his redeemed. Then, in a fuller sense than even at Pentecost, our old men shall see visions, and our young men shall dream dreams. Yea, all things shall be so wonderful, so far beyond all expectation, that those who behold them shall ask themselves whether it be not all a **dream**. We shall again and again find ourselves amazed at the wonderful goodness of the Lord. Let our hearts gratefully remember the former lovingkindnesses of the Lord. We were sadly low, sorely distressed, and completely past hope. But when Jehovah appeared, he did not merely lift us out of despondency. He raised us into wondering happiness. The Lord who alone turns our captivity, does nothing by halves. Those whom he saves from hell he brings to heaven. He turns exile into ecstasy, and banishment into bliss.

They that sow in tears shall reap in joy. *Psalm 126:5.*

Present distress must not be viewed as if it would last for ever. It is not the end, by any means, but only a means to the end. *Sorrow* is our sowing, *rejoicing* shall be our reaping. If there were no sowing in tears, there would be no reaping in joy. If we were never captives, we could never lead our captivity captive. Our mouth had never been filled with holy laughter, if it had not been first filled with the bitterness of grief. We must **sow**. We may have to sow in the wet weather of sorrow. But we shall **reap,** and reap in the bright summer season of **joy.** Let us keep to the work of this present sowing time, and find strength in the promise which is here so positively given us. Here is one of the Lord's shalls and wills. It is freely given both to workers, waiters, and weepers, and they may rest assured that it will not fail: *in due season they shall reap.*

It is not every sowing which is thus insured against all danger, and guaranteed a harvest. But the promise specially belongs to sowing **in tears.** When a man's heart is so stirred that he weeps over the sins of others, he is elect to usefulness. Winners of souls are first weepers for souls. As there is no birth without travail, so is there no spiritual harvest without painful tillage. When our own hearts are broken with grief at man's transgression we shall break other men's hearts. Tears of earnestness beget tears of repentance: *deep calleth unto deep.*

It is in vain for you to rise up early, to sit up late, to eat the bread of sorrows: for so he giveth his beloved sleep. *Psalm 127:2.*

It is vain for you to rise up early, to sit up late, to eat the bread of sorrows. Because the Lord is mainly to be rested in, all carking care is mere vanity and vexation of spirit. We are bound to be diligent, for this the Lord blesses. We ought not to be anxious, for that dishonours the Lord, and can never secure his favour. Some deny themselves needful rest. Nor is their sleeplessness the only index of their daily fret. They stint themselves in their meals, for they fear that daily bread will fail them. Not thus, not thus, would the Lord have his children live. Let them take a fair measure of rest and a due portion of food, for it is for their health. Faith brings calm with it, and banishes the disturbers who both by day and by night murder peace.

So he giveth his beloved sleep. Through faith the Lord makes his chosen ones to rest in him in happy freedom from care. The text may mean that God gives blessings to his beloved in sleep, even as he gave Solomon the desire of his heart while he slept. The meaning is much the same. Those whom the Lord loves are delivered from the fret and fume of life, and take a sweet repose upon the bosom of their Lord. He rests them; blesses them while resting; blesses them more in resting than others in their moiling and toiling. God is sure to give the best thing to his beloved, and we here see that he gives them **sleep** —that is, a laying aside of care, a forgetfulness of need, a quiet leaving of matters with God. This kind of sleep is better than riches and honour.

Thou shalt eat the labour of thine hands. *Psalm 128:2.*

This is the portion of God's saints: to work, and to find a reward in so doing. God is the God of labourers. We are not to leave our worldly callings because the Lord has called us by grace. We are not promised a blessing upon romantic idleness or unreasonable dreaming, but upon hard work and honest industry. Though we are in God's hands, we are to be supported by our own hands. He will give us daily bread, but it must be made our own by labour. All kinds of labour are here included. If one toils by the sweat of his brow, and another does so by the sweat of his brain, there is no difference in the blessing; save that it is generally more healthy to work with the body than with the mind only. Without

God it would be vain to labour. But when we are labourers together with God a promise is set before us. The promise is that labour shall be fruitful, and that he who performs it shall himself enjoy the recompense of it.

It is a grievous ill for a man to slave his life away and receive no fair remuneration for his toil. *The labourer is worthy of his hire.* Under the Theocracy the chosen people could see this promise literally fulfilled. But when evil rulers oppressed them, their earnings were withheld by churls, and their harvests were snatched away from them by marauders. Had they walked in the fear of the Lord they would never have known such great evils. Some men never enjoy their labour, for they give themselves no time for rest. Eagerness to get takes from them the ability to enjoy. Surely, if it is worth while to labour, it is worth while to eat of that labour.

PSALM 129

Many a time have they afflicted me from my youth: yet they have not prevailed against me. *Psalm 129:2.*

Many a time have they afflicted me from my youth. When in Canaan, at the first, the chosen household was often severely tried. In Egypt it was heavily oppressed; in the wilderness it was fiercely assailed; and in the promised land it was often surrounded by deadly enemies. It was something for the afflicted nation, that it survived to *say* **Many a time have they afflicted me.** The affliction began early— **from my youth;** and it continued late. The earliest years of Israel and of the church of God were spent in trial. Babes in grace are cradled in opposition. No sooner is the man-child born than the dragon is after it. It is, however, *good for a man that he bear the yoke in his youth.* He shall see it to be so when in after days he tells the tale.

Yet they have not prevailed against me. We seem to hear the beat of timbrels and the clash of cymbals here. The foe is derided. His malice has failed. That **yet** breaks in like the blast of trumpets, or the roll of kettledrums. *Cast down, but not destroyed,* is the shout of a victor. Israel has wrestled, and has overcome in the struggle. Who wonders? If Israel overcame the angel of the covenant, what man or devil shall vanquish him? The fight was oft renewed and long protracted. The champion severely felt the conflict, and was at times fearful of the issue. But at length he takes breath, and cries, **Yet they have not prevailed against me.** Many a time, yes, *many a time,* the enemy has had his opportunity and his vantage. But not so much as once has he gained the victory.

Out of the depths have I cried unto thee, O Lord. *Psalm 130:1.*

This is the Psalmist's statement and plea. He had never ceased to pray even when brought into the lowest state. **The depths** usually silence all they engulf. But they could not close the mouth of this servant of the Lord. Beneath the floods prayer lived and struggled. Yea, above the roar of the billows rose the cry of faith. It little matters where we are, if we can pray. But prayer is never more real and acceptable than when it rises out of the worst places. Depths of earnestness are stirred by depths of tribulation. The more distressed we are, the more excellent is the faith which trusts bravely in the Lord, and therefore appeals to him, and to him alone.

Good men may be in the depths of temporal and spiritual trouble. But good men in such cases look only to their God, and they stir themselves up to be more instant and earnest in prayer than at other times. The depth of their distress moves the depths of their being. From the bottom of their hearts an exceeding great and bitter cry rises unto the one living and true God. David had often been in the deep, and as often had he pleaded with Jehovah, his God, in whose hand are all deep places. He prayed, and remembered that he had prayed, and pleaded that he had prayed, hoping ere long to receive an answer. It would be dreadful to look back on trouble and feel forced to own that we did not cry unto the Lord in it. But it is most comforting to know that whatever we did not do, or could not do, yet we did pray, even in our worst times. He that prays in the depth will not sink out of his depth. He that cries out of the depths shall soon sing in the heights.

My soul waiteth for the Lord more than they that watch for the morning: I say, more than they that watch for the morning. *Psalm 130:6.*

My soul waiteth for the Lord more than they that watch for the morning. Men who guard a city, and women who wait by the sick, long for daylight. Worshippers tarrying for the morning sacrifice, the kindling of the incense and the lighting of the lamps, mingle fervent prayers with their holy vigils, and pine for the hour when the lamb shall smoke upon the altar. David, however, waited more than these, waited longer, waited more longingly, waited more expectantly. He was not afraid of the great *Adonai* before whom none can stand in their own righteousness, for he had put on the righteousness of faith, and therefore longed for gracious audience with the Holy One. God was no more dreaded by him than light is dreaded by those engaged in a lawful calling. He pined and yearned after his God.

I say, more than they that watch for the morning. The figure was not strong enough, though one can hardly think of anything more vigorous. He felt that his own eagerness was unique and unrivalled. Oh to be thus hungry and thirsty after God! Our version spoils the abruptness of the language. The original runs *My soul for the Lord more than those watching for the morning—watching for the morning.* This is a fine poetical repeat. We long for the favour of the Lord more than weary sentinels long for the morning light which will release them from their tedious watch. Indeed this is true. He that has once rejoiced in communion with God is sore tried by the hidings of his face, and grows faint with strong desire for the Lord's appearing.

PSALM 131

Let Israel hope in the Lord from henceforth and for ever. *Psalm 131:3.*

Let Israel hope in the Lord from henceforth and for ever. See how lovingly a man who is weaned from self thinks of others! David thinks of his people, and loses himself in his care for Israel. How he prizes the grace of **hope!** He has given up the things which are seen, and therefore he values the treasures which are not seen except by the eyes of hope. There is room for the largest hope when self is gone, ground for eternal hope when transient things no longer hold the mastery of our spirits. This verse is the lesson of experience. A man of God, who had been taught to renounce the world and live upon the Lord alone, here exhorts all his friends and companions to do the same. He found it a blessed thing to live by hope, and therefore he would have all his kinsmen do the same.

Let all the nation hope. Let all their hope be in Jehovah. Let them at once begin hoping **from henceforth,** and let them continue hoping **for ever.** Weaning takes the child out of a temporary condition into a state in which he will continue for the rest of his life. To rise above the world is to enter upon a heavenly existence which can never end. When we cease to hanker for the world we begin hoping in the Lord. O Lord, as a parent weans a child, so do thou wean me, and then shall I fix all my hope on thee alone.

PSALM 132

Lord, remember David, and all his afflictions. *Psalm 132:1.*

Lord, remember David, and all his afflictions. With David the covenant was made, and therefore his name is pleaded on behalf of his descendants, and the people who would be blessed by his dynasty. Jehovah, who changes not, will never forget one of his servants, or fail to keep his covenant. Yet for this thing he is to be entreated. That which we are assured the Lord will do must, nevertheless, be made a matter of prayer. The plea is urged with God that he would bless the family of David for the sake of their progenitor. How much stronger is our master-argument in prayer that God would deal well with us for Jesus' sake! David had no personal merit. The plea is based upon the covenant graciously made with him. But Jesus has deserts which are his own, and of boundless merit—these we may urge without hesitation. **Lord, remember** *Jesus,* **and all his afflictions.**

The **afflictions** of David here meant were those which came upon him as a godly man in his endeavours to maintain the worship of Jehovah. Since he zealously delighted in the worship of Jehovah, his God, he was despised and ridiculed by those who could not understand his enthusiasm. God will never forget what his people suffer for his sake. No doubt innumerable blessings descend upon families and nations through the godly lives and patient sufferings of the saints. We cannot be saved by the merits of others. But beyond all question we are benefited by their virtues. *God is not unrighteous to forget your work and labour of love, which ye have showed towards his name.*

Let thy priests be clothed with righteousness; and let thy saints shout for joy. *Psalm 132:9.*

Let thy priests be clothed with righteousness. No garment is so resplendent as that of a holy character. In this glorious robe our great High-priest is evermore arrayed. He would have all his people adorned in the same manner. Then only are **priests** fit to appear before the Lord, and to minister for the profit of the people, when their lives are dignified with goodness. They must ever remember that they are God's priests, and should therefore wear the livery of their Lord, which is holiness. They are not only to have **righteousness,** but to **be clothed** with it, so that upon every part of them righteousness shall be conspicuous. Whoever looks upon God's servants should see holiness, if they see nothing else. Now, this righteousness of the ministers of the temple is prayed for in connection with the presence of the Lord. This instructs us that holiness is only to be found among those who commune with God, and only comes to them through his visitation of their spirits. God will dwell among a holy people. On the other hand, where God is the people become holy.

And let thy saints shout for joy. Holiness and happiness go together. Where the one is found, the other ought never to be far away. Holy persons have a right to great and demonstrative joy. They may shout because of it. The sentence, while it may read as a permit, is also a precept: **saints** are commanded to rejoice in the Lord. Happy religion which makes it a duty to be glad! Where righteousness is the clothing, joy may well be the occupation.

I will abundantly bless her provision: I will satisfy her poor with bread. *Psalm 132:15.*

I will abundantly bless her provision. It must be so. How can we be without a blessing when the Lord is among us? We live upon his word. We are clothed by his charity. We are armed by his power. All sorts of **provision** are in him. How can they be otherwise than blessed? The provision the Lord will **abundantly bless.** Then it will be abundant and blessed. Daily provision, royal provision, satisfying provision, overflowingly joyful provision the church shall receive. The divine benediction shall cause us to receive it with faith, to feed upon it by experience, to grow upon it by sanctification, to be strengthened by it to labour, cheered by it to patience, and built up by it to perfection.

I will satisfy her poor with bread. The citizens of Zion are **poor** in themselves, poor in spirit, and often poor in pocket. But their hearts and souls shall dwell in such abundance that they shall neither need more nor desire more. They are to be satisfied with what the Lord himself calls **bread.** The bread of earth is the bread that perisheth. But the bread of God endureth to life eternal. In the church where God rests, his people shall not starve. The Lord would never rest if they did. He did not take rest for six days till he had prepared the world for the first man to live in. He would not stay his hand till all things were ready. Therefore, we may be sure if the Lord rests it is because *it is finished*, and the Lord hath prepared of his goodness for the poor. Where God finds his desire his people shall find theirs. If he is satisfied, they shall be.

PSALM 133

Behold, how good and how pleasant it is for brethren to dwell together in unity! *Psalm 133:1.*

Behold. It is a wonder seldom seen, therefore behold it! It may be seen, for it is the characteristic of real saints—therefore fail not to inspect it! God looks on with approval, therefore consider it with attention. **How good and how pleasant it is for brethren to dwell together in unity!** For a thing to be **good** is good. But for it also to be **pleasant** is better. All men love pleasant things, and yet it frequently happens that the pleasure is evil. But here the condition is as good as it is pleasant, as pleasant as it is good, for the same **how** is set before each qualifying word.

For **brethren** according to the flesh **to dwell together** is not always wise. Experience teaches that they are better a little apart, and it is shameful for them to dwell together in disunion. They had much better part in peace like Abraham and Lot, than dwell together in envy like Joseph's brothers. When brethren can and do dwell together **in unity**, then is their communion worthy to be gazed upon and sung of in holy psalmody. Such sights ought often to be seen among those who are near of kin, for they are brethren, and therefore should be united in heart and aim. They dwell together, and it is for their mutual comfort that there should be no strife. Yet how many families are rent by fierce feuds, and exhibit a spectacle which is neither good nor pleasant! As to brethren in spirit, they ought to dwell together in church fellowship, and in that fellowship one essential matter is unity. We can dispense with uniformity if we possess unity. Oneness of life, truth, and way; oneness in Christ Jesus; oneness of object and spirit—these we must have, or our assemblies will be synagogues of contention rather than churches of Christ.

PSALM 134

Behold, bless ye the Lord, all ye servants of the Lord, which by night stand in the house of the Lord. *Psalm 134:1.*

Behold. By this call the pilgrims bespeak the attention of the nightwatch. Let them look around them upon the holy place, and everywhere **behold** reasons for sacred praise. Let them look above them at night and magnify him that made heaven and earth, and lighted the one with stars and the other with his love. Let them see to it that their hallelujahs never come to an end. **Bless ye the Lord.** Be not content with praise, such as all his works render to him. But, as his saints, see that ye bless him. He blesses you. *Therefore*, be zealous to bless him. Oh to abound in blessing! May *blessed* and *blessing* be the two words which describe our lives. We will bless Jehovah, from whom all blessings flow.

All ye servants of the Lord. Servants should speak well of their masters. To be a servant in his temple, a domestic in his house, is a delight and a glory. If those who are ever with the Lord, and dwell in

246

his own temple, do not bless the Lord, who will? **Which by night stand in the house of the Lord.** To the silence and solemnity of night there was added the awful glory of the place where Jehovah had ordained that his worship should be celebrated. Blessed were the priests and Levites who were ordained to a service so sublime.

PSALM 135

Praise him, O ye servants of the Lord. Ye that stand in the house of the Lord, in the courts of the house of our God. *Psalm 135:1–2.*

Praise him, O ye servants of the Lord. If others are silent, you must not be. You know what a blessed Master he is, therefore speak well of him. Those who shun his service are sure to neglect his praise. But as grace has made you his own personal **servants,** let your hearts make you his court-musicians. We do not **praise** enough. We cannot praise too much. **Ye that stand in the house of the Lord, in the courts of the house of our God.** You are highly favoured. You are nearest to the Father of the heavenly family, privileged to find your home in his house. Therefore you must, beyond all others, abound in thanksgiving.

Should not ministers be celebrated for celebrating the praises of Jehovah? Should not church-officers and church-members excel all others in the excellent duty of adoration? Should not all of every degree who wait even in his outer courts unite in his worship? Ought not the least and feeblest of his people to proclaim his praises, in company with those who live nearest to him? Is it not a proper thing to remind them of their obligations? Is not the Psalmist wise when he does so in this case and in many others? Those who can call Jehovah **our God** are highly blessed, and therefore should abound in the work of blessing him. Perhaps this is the sweetest word in these two verses. *This God is our God for ever and ever.* **Our God** signifies possession, communion in possession, assurance of possession, delight in possession. Oh the unutterable joy of calling God our own!

PSALM 136

O give thanks unto the Lord; for he is good: for his mercy endureth for ever. *Psalm 136:1.*

O give thanks unto the Lord. Thanks are the least that we can offer, and these we ought freely to give. The inspired writer calls us to praise Jehovah for all his goodness to us, and all the greatness of his power in

247

blessing his chosen. We thank our parents. Let us praise our heavenly Father. We are grateful to our benefactors. Let us give thanks unto the Giver of all good. **For he is good.** Essentially he is goodness itself. Practically all that he does is good. Relatively he is good to his creatures. Let us thank him that we have seen, proved, and tasted that he is good. He is good beyond all others. Indeed, he alone is good in the highest sense. He is the source of good, the good of all good, the sustainer of good, the perfecter of good, and the rewarder of good. For this he deserves the constant gratitude of his people.

For his mercy endureth for ever. This is repeated in every verse of this Psalm, but not once too often. It is the sweetest stanza that a man can sing. What joy that there is **mercy,** mercy with Jehovah, enduring mercy, mercy that **endureth for ever.** We are ever needing it, trying it, praying for it, receiving it. Therefore let us for ever sing of it.

PSALM 137

If I do not remember thee, let my tongue cleave to the roof of my mouth; if I prefer not Jerusalem above my chief joy. *Psalm 137:6.*

If I do not remember thee, let my tongue cleave to the roof of my mouth. Thus the singers imprecate eternal silence upon their mouths if they forget Jerusalem to gratify Babylon. The players on instruments and the sweet songsters are of one mind. The enemies of the Lord will get no mirthful tune or song from them.

If I prefer not Jerusalem above my chief joy. The sacred city must ever be first in their thoughts, the queen of their souls. They had sooner be dumb than dishonour her sacred hymns, and give occasion to the oppressor to ridicule her worship. If such is the attachment of a banished Jew to his native land, how much more should we love the church of God of which we are children and citizens. How jealous should we be of her honour, how zealous for her prosperity. Never let us find jests in the words of Scripture, or make amusement out of holy things, lest we be guilty of forgetting the Lord and his cause. It is to be feared that many tongues have lost all power to charm the congregations of the saints because they have forgotten the gospel, and God has forgotten *them*.

PSALM 138

In the day when I cried thou answeredst me, and strengthenedst me with strength in my soul. *Psalm 138:3.*

In the day when I cried thou answeredst me. No proof is so convincing as that of experience. No man doubts the power of prayer after he has received an answer of peace to his supplication. It is the distinguishing mark of the true and living God that he hears the pleadings of his people, and answers them. Jehovah's memorial is— *the God that heareth prayer.* There was some special day in which David cried more vehemently than usual. He was weak, wounded, worried, and his heart was wearied. Then like a child he **cried**—cried unto his Father. It was a bitter, earnest, eager prayer, as natural and as plaintive as the cry of a babe. The Lord answered it. Our heavenly Father is able to interpret tears, and cries, and he replies to their inner sense in such a way as fully meets the case. The answer came **in the same day** as the cry ascended. So speedily does prayer rise to heaven. So quickly does mercy return to earth.

And strengthenedst me with strength in my soul. This was a true answer to his prayer. If the burden was not removed, yet strength was given wherewith to bear it. This is an equally effective method of help. It may not be best for us that the trial should come to an end. It may be far more to our advantage that by its pressure we should learn patience. By his word and Spirit the Lord can make the trembler brave, the sick whole, the weary bright. This soul-might will continue. The man having been strengthened for one emergency remains vigorous for life, and is prepared for all future labours and sufferings; unless, indeed, he throw away his force by unbelief, or pride, or some other sin. When God strengthens, none can weaken.

The Lord will perfect that which concerneth me: thy mercy, O Lord, endureth for ever: forsake not the works of thine own hands. *Psalm 138: 8.*

The Lord will perfect that which concerneth me. All my interests are safe in Jehovah's hands. God is concerned in all that concerns his servants. He will see to it that none of their precious things shall fail of completion. Their life, their strength, their hopes, their graces, their pilgrimage, shall each and all be perfected. **Thy mercy, O Lord, endureth for ever.** The first clause of the verse is the assurance of faith, and this second one reaches to the full assurance of understanding. God's work in us will abide unto perfection because God's mercy towards us thus abideth.

Forsake not the works of thine own hands. Our confidence does not cause us to live without prayer, but encourages us to pray all the more. Since we have it written upon our hearts that God will perfect his work in us, and we see it also written in Scripture that his mercy

249

changeth not, we with holy earnestness entreat that we may not be forsaken. If there be anything good in us, it is the work of God's own hands. Will he leave it? Why has he wrought so much in us if he means to give us up? It will be a sheer waste of effort. He who has gone so far will surely persevere with us to the end. Our hope for the final perseverance of the believer lies in the final perseverance of the believer's God. If the Lord begins to build, and does not finish, it will not be to his honour. He will have a desire to the work of his hands, for he knows what it has cost him already, and he will not throw away a vessel upon which he has expended so much of labour and skill.

PSALM 139

Thou knowest my downsitting and mine uprising, thou understandest my thought afar off. *Psalm 139:2.*

Thou knowest my downsitting and mine uprising. *Me* **thou knowest,** and all that comes of me. I am observed when I quietly sit down, and marked when I resolutely rise up. My most common and casual acts, my most needful and necessary movements, are noted by thee, and thou knowest the inward thoughts which regulate them. Whether I sink in lowly self-renunciation, or ascend in pride, thou seest the motions of my mind, as well as those of my body. This is a fact to be remembered every moment. Sitting down to consider, or rising up to act, we are still seen, known, and read by Jehovah our Lord.

Thou understandest my thought afar off. Before it is my own it is foreknown and comprehended by thee. Though **my thought** be invisible to the sight, though as yet I be not myself cognisant of the shape it is assuming, yet thou hast it under thy consideration. Thou perceivest its nature, its source, its drift, its result. Never dost thou misjudge or wrongly interpret me. My inmost thought is perfectly understood by thine impartial mind. Though thou shouldst give but a glance at my heart, and see me as one sees a passing meteor moving afar, yet thou wouldst by that glimpse sum up all the meanings of my soul, so transparent is everything to thy piercing glance.

Yea, the darkness hideth not from thee; but the night shineth as the day: the darkness and the light are both alike to thee. *Psalm 139:12.*

Yea, of a surety, beyond all denial. **The darkness hideth not from thee.** It veils nothing. It is not the medium of concealment in any degree whatever. It hides from men, but not from God. **But the night shineth as the day.** It is but another form of day. It shines, revealing all. It **shineth as the day,** quite as clearly and distinctly manifesting all that is done. **The darkness and the light are both alike to thee.** This sentence seems to sum up all that went before, and most emphatically puts the negative upon the faintest idea of hiding under the cover of night. Men cling to this notion, because it is easier and less expensive to hide under darkness than to journey to remote places. Therefore the foolish thought is here beaten to pieces by statements which in their varied forms effectually batter it.

Yet the ungodly are still duped by their grovelling notions of God, and enquire, *How doth God know?* They must fancy that he is as limited in his powers of observation as they are. Yet if they would but consider for a moment, they would conclude that he who could not see in the dark could not be God, and he who is not present everywhere could not be the Almighty Creator. Assuredly God is in all places, at all times, and nothing can by any possibility be kept away from his all-observing, all-comprehending mind. The Great Spirit comprehends within himself all time and space, and yet he is infinitely greater than these, or aught else that he has made.

Search me, O God, and know my heart; try me, and know my thoughts. *Psalm 139:23.*

Search me, O God, and know my heart. David is no accomplice with traitors. He has disowned them in set form, and now he appeals to God that he does not harbour a trace of fellowship with them. He will have God himself **search** him, and search him thoroughly, till every point of his being is known, and read, and understood. He is sure that even by such an investigation there will be found in him no complicity with wicked men. He challenges the fullest investigation, the innermost search. He had need be a true man who can put himself deliberately into such a crucible. Yet we may each one desire such searching. It would be a terrible calamity to us for sin to remain in our hearts unknown and undiscovered.

Try me, and know my thoughts. Exercise any and every test upon me. By fire and by water let me be examined. Read not alone the desires of my heart, but the fugitive **thoughts** of my head. Know with all-penetrating knowledge all that is or has been in the chambers of my mind. What a mercy that there is one being who can know us to perfection! He is intimately at home with us. He is graciously inclined towards us, and is willing to bend his omniscience to serve the end of our sanctification. Let us pray as David did, and let us be as honest as he. We cannot hide our sin. Salvation lies the other way, in a plain discovery of evil, and an effectual severance from it.

Keep me, O Lord, from the hands of the wicked; preserve me from the violent man; who have purposed to overthrow my goings. *Psalm 140:4.*

Keep me, O Lord, from the hands of the wicked. To fall into their hands would be a calamity indeed. David in his most pitiable plight chose to fall into the hand of a chastising God rather than to be left in the power of men. No creature among the wild beasts of the wood is so terrible an enemy to man as man himself when guided by evil, and impelled by violence. The Lord by providence and grace can keep us out of the power of the wicked. He alone can do this, for neither our own watchfulness nor the faithfulness of friends can secure us against the serpentine assaults of the foe. We have need to be preserved from the smooth as well as the rough hands of the ungodly. Their flatteries may harm us as much as their calumnies. The hands of their example may pollute us, and so do us more harm than the hands of their oppression. Jehovah must be our keeper, or evil hands will do what evil hearts have imagined and evil lips have threatened.

Preserve me from the violent man. His intense passion makes him terribly dangerous. He will strike anyhow, use any weapon, smite from any quarter. He is so furious that he is reckless of his own life, if he may accomplish his detestable design. Lord, preserve us by thine omnipotence when men attack us with their violence. **Who have purposed to overthrow my goings.** This is a forcible argument to use in prayer with God. He is the patron of holiness, and when the pure lives of his people are in danger of overthrow, he may be expected to interpose. Never let the pious forget to pray, for this is a weapon against which the most determined enemy cannot stand.

O God the Lord, the strength of my salvation, thou hast covered my head in the day of battle. *Psalm 140:7.*

When he looked back upon past dangers and deliverances, the good man felt that he should have perished had not the Lord held a shield over his head. **In the day** *of the clash of arms*, or *of putting on of armour* (as some read it), the glorious Lord had been his constant protector. Goliath had his armour-bearer, and so had Saul, and these each one guarded his master. Yet the giant and the king both perished, while

David, without armour or shield, slew the giant and baffled the tyrant. The shield of the Eternal is better protection than a helmet of brass. When arrows fly thick and the battleaxe crashes right and left, there is no covering for the head like the power of the Almighty.

See how the child of providence glorifies his Preserver! He calls him not only his **salvation,** but **the strength** of it, by whose unrivalled force he had been enabled to outlive the cunning and cruelty of his adversaries. He had obtained a deliverance in which the strength of the Omnipotent was clearly to be seen. This is a grand utterance of praise, a gracious ground of comfort, a prevalent argument in prayer. He that has covered our head aforetime will not now desert us. Wherefore let us fight a good fight, and fear no deadly wound. The Lord God is our shield, and our exceeding great reward.

Surely the righteous shall give thanks unto thy name: the upright shall dwell in thy presence. *Psalm 140:13.*

Surely the righteous shall give thanks unto thy name. As surely as God will slay the wicked he will save the oppressed, and fill their hearts and mouths with praises. Whoever else may be silent, the righteous will give thanks. Whatever they may suffer, the matter will end in their living through the trial, and magnifying the Lord for his delivering grace. On earth ere long, and in heaven for ever, the pure heart shall sing unto the Lord. How loud and sweet will be the songs of the redeemed in the millennial age, when the meek shall inherit the earth, and delight themselves in the abundance of peace!

The upright shall dwell in thy presence. Thus shall they give thanks in the truest and fullest manner. This abiding before the Lord shall render to him songs without words, and therefore all the more spiritual and true. Their living and walking with their God shall be their practical form of gratitude. Sitting down in holy peace, like children at their father's table, their joyful looks and language shall speak their high esteem and fervent love to him who has become their dwelling-place.

PSALM 141

Let my prayer be set forth before thee as incense; and the lifting up of my hands as the evening sacrifice. *Psalm 141:2.*

Let my prayer be set forth before thee as incense. As incense is carefully prepared, kindled with holy fire, and devoutly presented unto God, so let **my prayer** be. We are not to look upon prayer as easy work requiring no thought. It needs to be **set forth.** What is more, it must be set forth **before** *the Lord,* by a sense of his presence and a holy reverence for his name. Neither may we regard all supplication as certain of divine acceptance. It needs to be set forth before the Lord **as incense,** concerning the offering of which there were rules to be observed, otherwise it would be rejected of God.

And the lifting up of my hands as the evening sacrifice. Whatever form his prayer might take his one desire was that it might be accepted of God. Prayer is sometimes presented without words by the very motions of our bodies. Bended knees and lifted hands are the tokens of earnest, expectant prayer. Certainly work, or **the lifting up of** the **hands** in labour, is prayer if it be done in dependence upon God and for his glory. There is a hand-prayer as well as a heart-prayer. Our desire is that this may be sweet unto the Lord as the **sacrifice** of eventide. Holy hope, the lifting up of hands that hang down, is also a kind of worship. May it ever be acceptable with God. The Psalmist makes a bold request. He would have his humble cries and prayers to be as much regarded of the Lord as the appointed morning and evening sacrifices of the holy place. Yet the prayer is by no means too bold. The spiritual is in the Lord's esteem higher than the ceremonial. The calves of the lips are a truer sacrifice than the calves of the stall.

Set a watch, O Lord, before my mouth; keep the door of my lips. *Psalm 141:3.*

Set a watch, O Lord, before my mouth. That **mouth** had been used in prayer. It would be a pity it should ever be defiled with untruth, or pride, or wrath. Yet so it will become unless carefully watched, for these intruders are ever lurking about the door. David feels that with all his own watchfulness he may be surprised into sin, and so he begs the Lord himself to keep him. When Jehovah sets the watch the city is well guarded. When the Lord becomes the guard of our mouth the whole man is well garrisoned.

Keep the door of my lips. God has made our lips **the door** of the mouth. But we cannot keep that door of ourselves. Therefore do we entreat the Lord to take the rule of it. O that the Lord would both open and shut our lips! We can do neither the one nor the other aright if left to ourselves. In times of persecution by ungodly men we are peculiarly liable to speak hastily, or evasively, and therefore we should be specially anxious to be preserved in that direction from every form of sin. How condescending is the Lord! We are ennobled by being door-keepers for him, and yet he deigns to be a door-keeper for us.

Mine eyes are unto thee, O God the Lord: in thee is my trust; leave not my soul destitute. *Psalm 141:8.*

Mine eyes are unto thee, O God the Lord. He looked upward and kept his eyes fixed there. He regarded duty more than circumstances. He considered the promise rather than the external providence. He expected from **God** rather than from men. He did not shut his eyes in indifference or despair. Neither did he turn them to the creature in vain confidence. But he gave his eyes to his God, and saw nothing to fear. Jehovah his Lord is also his hope. Thomas called Jesus Lord and God, and David here speaks of his God and Lord. Saints delight to dwell upon the divine names when they are adoring or appealing.

In thee is my trust. Not alone in thine attributes or in thy promises, but in thyself. Others might confide where they chose, but David kept to his God. In him he trusted always, only, confidently, and unreservedly. **Leave not my soul destitute,** as it would be if the Lord did not remember and fulfil his promise. To be **destitute** in circumstances is bad. But to be destitute in **soul** is far worse. To be left of friends is a calamity. But to be left of God would be destruction. Destitute of God is destitution with a vengeance. The comfort is that God hath said, *I will never leave thee nor forsake thee.*

PSALM 142

I cried unto the Lord with my voice; with my voice unto the Lord did I make my supplication. *Psalm 142:1.*

I cried unto the Lord with my voice. It was a cry of such anguish that he remembers it long after, and makes a record of it. In the loneliness of the cave he could use his voice as much as he pleased. Therefore he made its gloomy vaults echo with his appeals to heaven. **With my voice unto the Lord did I make my supplication.** He dwells upon the fact that he spoke aloud in prayer. It was evidently well impressed upon his memory. Hence he doubles the word and says, **with my voice . . . with my voice.** It is well when our supplications are such that we find pleasure in looking back upon them. He that is cheered by the memory of his prayers will pray again.

See how the good man's appeal was to Jehovah only. He did not go round about to men, but he ran straight forward to Jehovah, his God. What true wisdom is here! Consider how the Psalmist's prayer grew into shape as he proceeded with it. He first poured out his natural longings. **I cried.** Then he gathered up all his wits and arranged his thoughts: **I made supplication.** True prayers may differ in their

diction, but not in their direction. An impromptu cry and a precon-
ceived supplication must alike ascend towards the one prayer-hearing
God. He will accept each of them with equal readiness. The intense
personality of the prayer is noteworthy. No doubt the Psalmist was
glad of the prayers of others, but he was not content to be silent himself.
See how everything is in the first person—*I cried with my voice; with
my voice did I make my supplication.* It is good to pray in the plural
—*Our Father.* But in times of trouble we shall feel forced to change our
note into *Let this cup pass from* me.

**I poured out my complaint before him; I showed before him my
trouble.** *Psalm 142:2.*

I poured out my complaint before him. He must pour out the
wormwood and the gall. He could not keep it in. But he took care
where he outpoured his complaint, lest he should do mischief, or receive
an ill return. If he poured it out before man, he might only receive
contempt from the proud, hard-heartedness from the careless, or
pretended sympathy from the false. Therefore he resolved upon an
outpouring before God alone, since *he* would pity and relieve. We may
complain *to* God, but not *of* God. When we complain, it should not be
before men, but before God alone.

    I showed before him my trouble. He exhibited his griefs to one
who could assuage them. He did not fall into the mistaken plan of so
many who publish their sorrows to those who cannot help them.
David first pours out his complaint, letting it flow forth in a natural,
spontaneous manner, and then afterwards he makes a more elaborate
show of his affliction. Praying men pray better as they proceed. Note
that we do not show our trouble before the Lord that *he* may see *it*, but
that *we* may see *him*. It is for *our* relief, and not for his information that
we make plain statements concerning our woes. It does us much good
to set out our sorrow in order. Much of it vanishes in the process, like
a ghost which will not abide the light of day. The rest loses much of its
terror, because the veil of mystery is removed by a clear and deliberate
stating of the trying facts. Pour out your thoughts and you will see
what they are. Show your trouble and the extent of it will be known
to you. Let all be done before the Lord, for in comparison with his
great majesty of love the trouble will seem to be as nothing.

PSALM 143

**Enter not into judgment with thy servant: for in thy sight shall
no man living be justified.** *Psalm 143:2.*

Enter not into judgment with thy servant. He had entreated for audience at the mercy-seat. But he has no wish to appear before the judgment-seat. Though clear before men, he could not claim innocence before God. Even though he knew himself to be the Lord's **servant,** yet he did not claim perfection, or plead merit. Even as a servant he was unprofitable. If such be the humble cry of a servant, what ought to be the pleading of a sinner?

For in thy sight shall no man living be justified. None can stand before God upon the footing of the law. God's sight is piercing and discriminating. The slightest flaw is seen and judged. Therefore pretence and profession cannot avail where that glance reads all the secrets of the soul. In this verse David told out the doctrine of universal condemnation by the law long before Paul had taken his pen to write the same truth. To this day it stands true even to the same extent as in David's day. **No man living** even at this moment may dare to present himself for trial before the throne of the Great King on the footing of the law.

I remember the days of old; I meditate on all thy works; I muse on the work of thy hands. *Psalm 143:5.*

I remember the days of old. When we see nothing new which can cheer us, let us think upon old things. We once had merry days, days of deliverance, and joy and thanksgiving. Why not again? Jehovah rescued his people in the ages which lie back, centuries ago. Why should he not do the like again? We ourselves have a rich past to look back upon. We have sunny memories, sacred memories, satisfactory memories. These are as flowers for the bees of faith to visit, from whence they may make honey for present use. **I meditate on all thy works.** When my own works reproach me, thy works refresh me. If at the first view the deeds of the Lord do not encourage us, let us think them over again, ruminating and considering the histories of divine providence. We ought to take a wide and large view of *all* God's works. As a whole they work together for good, and in each part they are worthy of reverent study.

I muse on the work of thy hands. This he had done in former days, even in his most trying hours. Creation had been the book in which he read of the wisdom and goodness of the Lord. He repeats his perusal of the page of nature, and counts it a balm for his wounds, a cordial for his cares, to see what the Lord has made by his skilful hands. When the work of our own hand grieves us, let us look to the work of God's hands. Memory, meditation, and musing are here set together as the three graces, ministering grace to a mind depressed and likely to be diseased. As David with his harp played away the evil spirit from Saul, so does he here chase away gloom from his own soul by holy communion with God.

Cause me to know the way wherein I should walk; for I lift up my soul unto thee. *Psalm 143:8.*

The Great First Cause must **cause** us **to know.** Spiritual senses are dependent upon God, and heavenly knowledge comes from him alone. To know the way we ought to take is exceedingly needful, for how can we be exact in obedience to a law with which we are not acquainted? Or how can there be an ignorant holiness? If we know not the way, how shall we keep in it? If we know not **wherein we should walk,** how shall we be likely to follow the right path? The Psalmist lifts up his **soul.** Faith is good at a dead lift. The soul that trusts will rise. We will not allow our hope to sink, but we will strive to get up and rise out of our daily griefs. This is wise.

When David was in any difficulty as to his way he lifted his soul towards God himself. Then he knew that he could not go very far wrong. If the soul will not rise of itself we must lift it, lift it up unto God. This is good argument in prayer. Surely the God to whom we endeavour to lift up our soul will condescend to show us what he would have us to do. Let us attend to David's example. When our heart is low, let us heartily endeavour to lift it up, not so much to comfort as to the Lord himself.

PSALM 144

Blessed be the Lord my strength, which teacheth my hands to war, and my fingers to fight. *Psalm 144:1.*

Blessed be the Lord my strength. With all his strength David blesses the God of his **strength.** We ought not to receive so great a boon as strength to resist evil, to defend truth, and to conquer error, without knowing who gave it to us, and rendering to him the glory of it.

Which teacheth my hands to war, and my fingers to fight. The Psalmist sets forth the Lord as teacher in the arts of war. If we have strength, we are not much the better unless we have skill also. Untrained force is often an injury to the man who possesses it. It even becomes a danger to those who are round about him. Therefore the Psalmist blesses the Lord as much for teaching as for strength. To a fighting man the education of the **hands** is of far more value than mere book-learning could ever be. He who has to use a sling or a bow needs suitable training, quite as much as a scientific man or a classical professor. Men are too apt to fancy that an artisan's efficiency is to be ascribed to himself. But this is a popular fallacy. A clergyman may be supposed to be taught of God. But people do not allow this to be true of weavers or workers in brass. Yet these callings are specially mentioned in the Bible as having been taught to holy women and earnest men when the tabernacle was set up at the first. All wisdom and skill are from the Lord, and for them he deserves to be gratefully extolled. This teaching extends to the smallest members of our frame. The Lord teaches **fingers** as well as hands. Indeed, it sometimes happens that if the finger is not well trained the whole hand is incapable.

I will sing a new song unto thee, O God: upon a psaltery and an instrument of ten strings will I sing praises unto thee. *Psalm 144:9.*

I will sing a new song unto thee, O God. Fired with fresh enthusiasm, my gratitude shall make a new channel for itself. **I will sing** as others have done. But it shall be a **new song,** such as no others have sung. That song shall be all and altogether for my **God,** from whom my deliverance has come. **Upon a psaltery and an instrument of ten strings will I sing praises unto thee.** His hand should aid his tongue, not as in the case of the wicked, co-operating in deceit. But his hand should unite with his mouth in truthful praise. David intended to tune his best instruments as well as to use his best vocal music. The best is all too poor for so great a God, and therefore we must not fall short of our utmost. He meant to use many instruments of music, that by all means he might express his great joy in God.

The Old Testament dispensation abounded in types, and figures, and outward ritual, and therefore music dropped naturally into its place in the worldly sanctuary. But, after all, it can do no more than represent praise, and assist our expression of it. The real praise is in the heart. The true music is that of the soul. When music drowns the voice, and artistic skill takes a higher place than hearty singing, it is time that instruments were banished from public worship. The private worshipper, singing his solo unto the Lord, has often found it helpful to accompany himself on some familiar instrument. David in the present Psalm is an instance, for he says, **I will sing praises unto thee**—that is, not so much in the company of others as by himself alone. He saith not *we,* but **I.**

PSALM 145

Every day will I bless thee; and I will praise thy name for ever and ever. *Psalm 145:2.*

Every day will I bless thee. Whatever the character of the day, or of my circumstances and conditions during that day, I will continue to glorify God. Were we well to consider the matter we should see abundant cause in **every day** for rendering special blessing unto the Lord. All before the day, all in the day, all following the day should constrain us to magnify our God every day, all the year round. Our love to God is not a matter of holy days. Every day is alike holy to holy men. David here comes closer to God than when he said, *I will bless thy name*. It is now, **I will bless** *thee*. This is the centre and kernel of true devotion. We do not only admire the Lord's words and works, but himself. Without realising the personality of God, praise is well-nigh impossible. You cannot extol an abstraction.

And I will praise thy name for ever and ever. He said he would bless that name, and now he vows to **praise** it. He will extol the Lord in every sense and way. Eternal worship shall not be without its variations. It will never become monotonous. Heavenly music is not harping upon one string, but all strings shall be tuned to one praise. Observe the personal pronoun here: *I* **will.** Praise is not to be discharged by proxy. There must be your very self in it, or there is nothing in it.

One generation shall praise thy works to another, and shall declare thy mighty acts. *Psalm 145:4.*

One generation shall praise thy works to another. There shall be a tradition of **praise.** Men shall hand on the service. They shall make it a point to instruct their descendants in this hallowed exercise. We look back upon the experience of our fathers, and sing of it. Even thus shall our sons learn praise from the Lord's works among ourselves. Let us see to it that we praise God before our children, and never make them think that his service is an unhappy one.

And shall declare thy mighty acts. The generations shall herein unite. Together they shall make up an extraordinary history. Each generation shall contribute its chapter, and all the generations together shall compose a volume of matchless character. David began with *I*, but he has in this verse soon reached to an inconceivable multitude, comprehending all the myriads of our race of every age. The praise of the Lord enlarges the heart, and as it grows upon us our minds grow with it. God's works of goodness and acts of power make up a subject which all the eras of human story can never exhaust. A praiseful heart seems to live in all the centuries in delightful companionship with all the good. We are not afraid that the incense will ever cease to burn upon the altars of Jehovah. The priests die, but the adoration lives on.

All glory be unto him who remains the same Lord throughout all generations.

The Lord is nigh unto all them that call upon him, to all that call upon him in truth. *Psalm 145:18.*

The Lord is nigh unto all them that call upon him. Not only near by his omnipresence, but to sympathise and favour. He does not leave praying men, and men who confess his name, to battle with the world alone. He is ever at their side. This favour is not for a few of those who invoke him, but for each one of the pious company. **All** who place themselves beneath the shield of his glorious name by calling themselves by it, and by calling upon it in supplication, shall find him to be a very present help in trouble.

To all that call upon him in truth. There are many whose formal prayers and false professions will never bring them into communion with the Lord. To pray **in truth,** we must have a true heart, and the truth in our heart. Then we must be humble, for pride is a falsehood; and be earnest, or else prayer is a lie. A God of truth cannot be nigh to the spirit of hypocrisy. This he knows and hates. Neither can he be far removed from a sincere spirit, since it is his work, and he forsakes not the work of his own hands.

PSALM 146

While I live will I praise the Lord: I will sing praises unto my God while I have any being. *Psalm 146:2.*

While I live will I praise the Lord. I shall not live here for ever. This mortal life will find a finis in death. But **while** it lasts I will laud the Lord my God. I cannot tell how long or short my life may be. But every hour of it shall be given to the praises of my God. While I live, I'll love. While I breathe, I'll bless. It is but for a while, and I will not while that time away in idleness, but consecrate it to that same service which shall occupy eternity. As our life is the gift of God's mercy, it should be used for his glory.

I will sing praises unto my God while I have any being. When I am no longer in being on earth, I hope to have a higher being in heaven. There I will not only praise, but *sing* **praises.** Here I have to sigh and praise, but there I shall only sing and praise. This **while I have any being** will be a great while. But the whole of it shall be filled up with adoration, for the glorious Jehovah is my God, my own God by covenant, and by blood relationship in Christ Jesus. I have no being apart from my God. Therefore, I will not attempt to enjoy my being otherwise than by singing to his honour. Twice the Psalmist says **I will**. Here first thoughts and second thoughts are alike good. We cannot be too firm in the holy resolve to praise God. It is the chief end of our living and being that we should glorify God and enjoy him for ever.

The Lord preserveth the strangers; he relieveth the fatherless and widow: but the way of the wicked he turneth upside down. *Psalm 146:9.*

The Lord preserveth the strangers. Many monarchs hunted aliens down, or transported them from place to place, or left them as outlaws unworthy of the rights of man. Jehovah made special laws for their shelter within his domain. In this country the stranger was, a little while ago, looked upon as a vagabond—a kind of wild beast to be avoided if not to be assaulted. Even to this day there are prejudices against foreigners which are contrary to our holy religion. Our God and King is never strange to any of his creatures. If any are left in a solitary and forlorn condition he has a special eye to their preservation.

He relieveth the fatherless and widow. These excite his compassion, and he shows it in a practical way by upraising them from their forlorn condition. The Mosaic law made provision for these destitute persons. When the secondary fatherhood is gone, the child falls back upon the primary fatherhood of the Creator. When the husband of earth is removed, the godly widow casts herself upon the care of her Maker. **But the way of the wicked he turneth upside down.** He fills it with crooked places. He reverses it, sets it down, or upsets it. That which the man aimed at he misses, and he secures that for himself which he would gladly have avoided. The wicked man's way is in itself a turning of things upside down morally, and the Lord makes it so to him providentially. Everything goes wrong with him who goes wrong.

PSALM 147

He healeth the broken in heart, and bindeth up all their wounds. *Psalm 147:3.*

This the Holy Spirit mentions as a part of the glory of God, and a reason for our declaring his praise: the Lord is not only a Builder, but a Healer. He restores broken hearts as well as broken walls. The kings of the earth think to be great through their loftiness. But Jehovah becomes really so by his condescension. Behold, the Most High has to do with the sick and the sorry, with the wretched and the wounded!

He walks the hospitals as the good Physician! His deep sympathy with mourners is a special mark of his goodness. Few will associate with the despondent. But Jehovah chooses their company, and abides with them till he has healed them by his comforts. He deigns to handle and heal broken hearts. He himself lays on the ointment of grace, and the soft bandages of love, and thus binds up the bleeding wounds of those convinced of sin.

This is compassion like a God. Well may those praise him to whom he has acted so gracious a part. The Lord is always healing and binding. This is no new work to him, he has done it of old. And it is not a thing of the past of which he is now weary, for he is still healing and still binding, as the original hath it. Come, broken hearts, come to the Physician who never fails to heal. Uncover your wounds to him who so tenderly binds them up!

The Lord taketh pleasure in them that fear him, in those that hope in his mercy. *Psalm 147:11.*

While the bodily powers give no content to God, spiritual qualities are his delight. He cares most for those emotions which centre in himself. The **fear** which he approves is fear of **him** and the **hope** which he accepts is hope **in his mercy.** It is a striking thought that God should not only be at peace with some kinds of men, but even find a solace and a joy in their company. Oh! the matchless condescension of the Lord, that his greatness **taketh pleasure** in the insignificant creatures of his hand.

Who are these favoured men in whom Jehovah takes pleasure? Some of them are the least in his family, who have never risen beyond hoping and fearing. Others of them are more fully developed, but still they exhibit a blended character composed of fear and hope. They **fear** God with holy awe and filial reverence, and they also **hope** for forgiveness and blessedness because of the divine **mercy.** As a father takes pleasure in his own children, so doth the Lord solace himself in his own beloved ones, whose marks of new birth are fear and hope. They fear, for they are sinners. They hope, for God is merciful. They fear him, for he is great. They hope in him, for he is good. Their fear sobers their hope. Their hope brightens their fear. God takes pleasure in them both in their trembling and in their rejoicing.

PSALM 148

Praise ye the Lord. Praise ye the Lord from the heavens: praise him in the heights. *Psalm 148:1.*

Praise ye the Lord. This exhortation can never be out of place, speak it where we may; and never out of time, speak it when we may. **Praise ye the Lord from the heavens.** Since ye are nearest to the High and lofty One, be ye sure to lead the song. Ye angels, ye cherubim and seraphim, and all others who dwell in the precincts of his courts, praise ye Jehovah. **Praise him in the heights.** This is no vain repetition. After the manner of attractive poesy the truth is emphasised by reiteration in other words. Moreover, God is not only to be praised *from* the heights, but *in* them. The adoration is to be perfected in the heavens from which it takes its rise. No place is too high for the praises of the most High. On the summit of creation the glory of the Lord is to be revealed, even as the tops of the highest Alps are tipped with the golden light of the same sun which glads the valleys. Heavens and heights become the higher and the more heavenly as they are made to resound with the praises of Jehovah.

See how the Psalmist trumpets out the word **Praise.** It sounds forth some nine times in the first five verses of this song. Like minute-guns, exultant exhortations are sounded forth in tremendous force—*Praise! Praise! Praise!* The drum of the great King beats round the world with this one note—*Praise! Praise! Praise!* Hallelujah! All this praise is distinctly and personally for Jehovah. Praise not his servants nor his works. But praise *him.* Is he not worthy of all possible praise? Pour it forth before *him* in full volume! Pour it only there!

Praise ye him, sun and moon: praise him, all ye stars of light. *Psalm 148:3.*

Praise ye him, sun and moon. The Psalmist enters into detail as to the heavenly hosts. As all, so each, must praise the God of each and all. The **sun and moon,** as joint rulers of day and night, are paired in praise. The one is the complement of the other, and so they are closely associated in the summons to worship. The sun has his peculiar mode of glorifying the Great Father of lights, and the moon has her own special method of reflecting his brightness. There is a perpetual adoration of the Lord in the skies. It varies with night and day, but it ever continues while sun and moon endure. There is ever a lamp burning before the high altar of the Lord.

Praise him, all ye stars of light. Nor are the greater luminaries allowed to drown with their floods of light the glory of the lesser brilliants, for all the **stars** are bidden to the banquet of praise. Stars are many, so many that no one can count the host included under the words **all ye stars.** Yet no one of them refuses to praise its Maker. From their extreme brilliance they are fitly named **stars of light.** This light is praise in a visible form twinkling to true music. Light is song glittering before the eye instead of resounding in the ear. Stars without light would render no praise. Christians without light rob the Lord of his glory. However small our beam, we must not hide it. If we cannot be **sun** or **moon**, we must aim to be one of the **stars of light**, and our every twinkling must be to the honour of our Lord.

PSALM 149

The Lord taketh pleasure in his people: he will beautify the meek with salvation. *Psalm 149:4.*

The Lord taketh pleasure in his people. Therefore they should take pleasure in him. If our joy be pleasing to him let us make it full. What condescension is this on Jehovah's part, to notice, to love, and to delight in his chosen! Surely there is nothing in our persons, or our actions, which could cause pleasure to the Ever-blessed One, were it not that he condescends to men of low estate. **He will beautify the meek with salvation.** They are humble, and feel their need of **salvation.** He is gracious, and bestows it upon them. They lament their deformity, and he puts a beauty upon them of the choicest sort. He saves them by sanctifying them, and thus they wear the beauty of holiness, and the beauty of a joy which springs out of full salvation. He makes his people **meek,** and then makes the meek beautiful. Herein is grand argument for worshipping the Lord with the utmost exultation. He who takes such a pleasure in us must be approached with every token of exceeding joy.

God taketh pleasure in all his children as Jacob loved all his sons. But the meek are his Josephs. Upon these he puts the coat of many colours, beautifying them with peace, content, joy, holiness, and influence. When God himself beautifies a man, he becomes beautiful indeed and beautiful for ever. The verse may be read *He shall beautify the meek with salvation* or *He shall beautify the afflicted with deliverance* or *He shall beautify the meek with victory.* Each of these readings gives a new shade of meaning, well worthy of quiet consideration. Each reading also suggests new cause for joyful adoration. *O come, let us sing unto the Lord.*

Let the saints be joyful in glory: let them sing aloud upon their beds. *Psalm 149:5.*

Let the saints be joyful in glory. God has honoured them, and put a rare **glory** upon them. Therefore let them exult therein. Shall those to whom God is their glory be cast down and troubled? Nay, let their joy proclaim their honourable estate. **Let them sing aloud upon their**

beds. Their exultation should express itself in shouts and songs, for it is not a feeling of which they have any need to be ashamed.

That which is so fully justified by fact, may well be loudly proclaimed. Even in their quietest retreats let them burst into song. When no one hears them, let them sing aloud unto God. If confined by sickness, let them joy in God. In the night watches let them not lie awake and weep, but like nightingales let them charm the midnight hours. Their shouts are not now for the battlefield, but for the places of their rest. They can peacefully lie down and yet enjoy the victory with which the Lord has beautified them. Without fighting, faith wins and sings the victory. What a blessing to have our beds made into thrones, and our retirements turned into triumphs!

PSALM 150

Praise ye the Lord. Praise God in his sanctuary: praise him in the firmament of his power. *Psalm 150:1.*

Praise ye the Lord. Hallelujah! The exhortation is to all things in earth or in heaven. Should they not all declare the glory of him for whose glory they are, and were created? To give the least particle of his honour to another is treason. To refuse to render it to him is robbery. **Praise God in his sanctuary.** Praise *El*, or *the strong one*, in his *holy place.* See how power is mentioned with holiness in this change of names. Praise begins at home. In God's own house pronounce his praise. In his church below and in his courts above hallelujahs should be continually presented. In the person of Jesus God finds a holy dwelling or sanctuary, and there he is greatly to be praised. He may also be said to dwell in holiness, for all his ways are right and good. For this we ought to extol him with heart and with voice. Whenever we assemble for holy purposes our main work should be to present praises unto the Lord our God.

Praise him in the firmament of his power. It is a blessed thing that in our God holiness and power are united. **Power** without righteousness would be oppression. Righteousness without power would be too weak for usefulness. Put the two together in an infinite degree and we have God. What an expanse we have in the boundless **firmament** of divine **power!** Let it all be filled with praise. Let the heavens, so great and strong, echo with the praise of the thrice holy Jehovah, while the sanctuaries of earth magnify the Almighty One.

Praise him with the sound of the trumpet: praise him with the psaltery and harp. *Psalm 150:3.*

266

Praise him with the sound of the trumpet. With the loudest, clearest note call the people together. Make all men to know that we are not ashamed to worship. Summon them with unmistakable sound to bow before their God. **The sound of the trumpet** is associated with the grandest and most solemn events, such as the giving of the law, the proclamation of jubilee, the coronation of Jewish kings, and the raging of war. It is to be thought of in reference to the coming of our Lord in his second advent and the raising of the dead. If we cannot give voice to this martial instrument, at least let our praise be as decided and bold as if we could give a blast upon the horn. Let us never sound a trumpet before us to our own honour, but reserve all our trumpeting for God's glory.

When the people have been gathered by blast of trumpet, then proceed to **praise him with the psaltery and harp.** Stringed instruments are to be used as well as those which are rendered vocal by wind. Dulcet notes are to be consecrated as well as more startling sounds. The gospel meaning is that all powers and faculties should praise the Lord —all sorts of persons, under all circumstances, and with differing constitutions, should do honour unto the Lord of all. If there be any virtue, if there be any talent, if there be any influence, let all be consecrated to the service of the universal Benefactor. Harp and lyre—the choicest, the sweetest, must be all our Lord's.